David Riccio, co-author of *Heart and Soul*, is an award-winning senior sports writer for *The Daily Telegraph* and *The Sunday Telegraph*. One of Australia's leading sports reporters, he has worked for News Limited over the past twenty years, winning several awards for his writing on swimming, rugby league and horse racing. He has served as sports editor of *The Sunday Telegraph* and is a contributor to 2GB's Continuous Call Team, Fox Sports and Channel Nine. He has also covered major sporting events including the Olympics, Melbourne Cup, Rugby League World Cup, State of Origin and NRL grand finals. This is David's second book as he also co-authored Alex McKinnon's autobiography *Unbroken*.

HEART AND SOUL

My Story

Paul Gallen
with David Riccio

ALLEN&UNWIN
SYDNEY·MELBOURNE·AUCKLAND·LONDON

First published in 2019

Allen & Unwin
83 Alexander Street
Crows Nest NSW 2065
Australia
Phone: (61 2) 8425 0100
Email: info@allenandunwin.com
Web: www.allenandunwin.com

 A catalogue record for this
book is available from the
National Library of Australia

ISBN 978 1 76029 358 1

Index by Puddingburn
Set in 12.5/17 pt Adobe Garamond Pro by Midland Typesetters, Australia
Printed and bound in Australia by Griffin Press, part of Ovato

10 9 8 7 6 5 4 3 2 1

CONTENTS

CONTENTS

1

Turn Your Porch Lights Off

I watch the old footage and don't remember the TV interviews. I need the replay of it to remind me of who I turned to first and the emotion that took complete control of my body.

One moment I'm crying, and then the next moment I'm embracing a teammate, who I have stood beside at training and in every game since the beginning of the season. I'm standing there, and it is the most chaotic, surreal, euphoric feeling of pandemonium of my entire career.

The images show me wrapping my arms around our hooker, Michael Ennis. In his final NRL match, he's won a grand final. I turn around and grab our little halfback, Chad Townsend. He's the only local junior in the entire Cronulla squad, and he's the first halfback to have ever won a premiership with the Sharks. I let Chad go and move on to the next person. Who else can I hug?

Of all the players, coaching staff and club administration standing in the middle of a manic ANZ Stadium, Cronulla club legend Andrew 'ET' Ettingshausen is someone I never expected to see. But without hesitation, I grabbed him. I hugged him so tight, tears burst from my eyes. ET was crying, too.

It felt like we were the only two people inside the stadium. 'Yes, yes, yes' is all I kept screaming into ET's ear. I had no sense that directly in front of me stood NRL photographer Grant Trouville. In an instant, he had snapped the now-famous photo of ET and me. It's a photo that encapsulates raw relief.

The embrace between ET and me also represented the unbridled emotion that needed to be released on behalf of every past Cronulla player who, for the last 49 years, had busted their backsides to achieve what we were now celebrating. I was thrilled that, amid the pandemonium, someone like ET was there with us.

At that moment, I finally felt complete. I believed that I had now achieved everything I had ever wanted to as a player. Few sportspeople are ever satisfied. But at that exact moment, that's how I felt.

Then, suddenly, every ounce of elation turned quickly into a stomach-churning feeling of queasy dizziness. I think I'm going to faint.

Physically, I was exhausted from the match and low on energy due to a bout of shingles (which I'll discuss later in the book). When you throw emotion on top of that, it's no wonder I was now feeling unsteady.

I began to worry that I was going to pass out up on stage as I accepted the NRL premiership trophy. Imagine that! The most defining moment in the Cronulla club's history, and as the captain holds up the trophy . . . he faints.

Our head trainer, Andrew Gray, could see that I wasn't doing so well. He hurried over to stand beside me before I was called up on stage to accept the Provan–Summons trophy. 'Don't pass out in front of millions of people' is all I kept telling myself. The fact that I was the last player to be called up on stage bought me time to calm down and gather myself.

The funny thing about my victory speech is that, because I didn't want to pre-empt the result, I didn't plan or write anything down before the game.

Earlier in the day, as I arrived at ANZ Stadium, my good mate Scotty Hogan sent me a text message: 'Don't forget, when you win it, to tell everyone they can turn their porch lights off now.' As soon as I read the text message, I was furious. Scotty knows how superstitious and paranoid I am—particularly two hours before the biggest game of my life—so he should not have messaged me.

I was angry that I had even looked down at my phone. Straightaway, I deleted the message. It was gone within one second. However, history now shows that the text message proved to be a winner.

Because of my refusal to plan a victory speech, you can actually see me looking down at our Cronulla jersey as I thank our major sponsors. I didn't want to miss anyone. I also wanted to make sure I thanked the Melbourne Storm, Cameron Smith, Craig Bellamy and ANZ Stadium, as well as Shane 'Flanno' Flanagan, his coaching staff and my teammates.

I needed to ensure that every past player who had ever pulled on the Sharks jersey felt like they had played a role in this victory, too. And I wanted our fans to know how much their support was cherished by the club and the players both now and for the past 49 years.

I couldn't name everyone individually, but I wanted to thank them all.

And then, as if the crowd sensed that I had one final word to say, the most magical momentary silence fell over the entire ANZ Stadium. I delivered the line that Scotty had texted to me: 'And to all you people back in the Shire, turn your porch lights off because we're coming home with the trophy!' I still smile when I hear or see a replay of it. It literally brings tears to my eyes every time I hear those words.

After my speech, the party began. The lap of honour around the stadium was pure joy. I grabbed my wife, Anne, and the kids, wanting them to enjoy the moment. The euphoria refused to subside. Everywhere you turned, there was an ecstatic blur of blue, black and white. Fans were stopped short of leaping the fence.

Such was the madness, I had no idea—until I was shown a photo three weeks later—that I had stopped to have a photo with my sister and her husband, who had been leaning over the fence.

After tracking down my closest family and friends, Flanno and I were the last two members of the squad to return to the dressing rooms. Spontaneously, in front of all our fans above the tunnel, I slapped a wet kiss on Flanno's cheek for the photographers.

I wanted to hold the trophy forever, but I placed it down in the middle of the room so that the squad members could take turns in having photos with it. We then moved into a separate room—a large space used as a warm-up area before matches—where our friends and family were waiting. As one, we sang the loudest ever rendition of 'Up, Up Cronulla' amid a shower of champagne and beer.

I have never seen that room so full. There were twice as many people inside that room than when New South Wales won the 2014 State of Origin series at the same stadium.

There was so much going on. I wanted ten minutes with the team, so I grabbed Flanno. He explained to the squad that, as a team, we would return to the field. But before that, I wanted to see Cam Smith.

I left our dressing rooms and walked across the tunnel and into the Storm dressing rooms. I found the Melbourne boys having a quiet beer together, with Cam among them.

As we shook hands, we spoke only briefly. Cam said, 'It's weird winning your first one, isn't it?' I nodded and thanked him for the season and the game.

It would've been after midnight when the Sharks playing group and coaching staff made their way out onto the ANZ Stadium turf. And, wow, what a special moment that was.

Standing together in a big circle out in the middle of the field, this was a moment just for those within the inner sanctum of the Cronulla Sharks. It was for those people who had been part of this group from day one of pre-season. This was for the players who had participated all year as well as those who had trained as part of our first-grade squad but weren't able to play a game. In their own way, they had all played their part in the 2016 season.

Staff members, too, were there—everyone from our gear steward and our GPS technicians to those who had never been paid for their help. It was awesome.

We had the trophy in the middle of our circle, and we sang our victory song again inside a now completely empty ANZ Stadium. To a man, we knew that we had a party to get to with the thousands of fans back in the Shire. We returned to the dressing rooms before climbing aboard our team bus.

I remember thinking as I left ANZ Stadium that, as a player, I'd never been one to keep my playing strip from any of the matches I had played in. But this time, I was going to save everything: my grand-final boots, socks, shorts and jersey.

On the team bus bound for the Shire, the mayhem was alive and well as we sang and danced. I checked my mobile phone and smiled at the several hundred text messages that I had received. I simply couldn't reply to everyone, but I made certain to reply to Mum and Dad.

The bus pulled into our home ground of Shark Park. We climbed the back stairs of the Andrew Ettingshausen grandstand and emerged with the trophy. It was close to 1 a.m., but standing below us on Shark Park were thousands of fans, who were cheering, crying and singing as one. It was yet another special moment to be able to thank our most loyal of supporters, who had dreamed of this win just as much as the players had.

We then moved to a private room, which the club had organised for close friends and family and past players inside the Cronulla Sutherland Leagues Club adjacent to Shark Park. I have to admit, I was hurting due to the shingles that I'd been diagnosed with prior to the grand final. Inside the club, I needed to sit down.

I told myself to harden up, as I'd just won the premiership. The smiles and elation of our friends, family and fans kept me charged, but once I finally did sit down, I couldn't get back up again. My legs and arms felt like jelly.

At about 3 a.m., our team doctor, Dr George Pitsis, looked at me and said, 'I'm driving you home.' I didn't even consider arguing with him.

At home, I lay down for 40 minutes. Feeling worse than before, I rang the Doc. 'You've got to go to hospital. I'll take you,' he said. By now, it was close to 4 a.m. on Monday morning.

Feeling weak and sick, I walked out of my front door. There on the steps were my closest mates, holding drinks and ready to celebrate long and hard—this was the very moment that we had all dreamed about as kids playing for Wentworthville. I had to ignore their demand for me to join them.

I climbed into the Doc's car. Upon arriving at Sutherland Hospital, I was given medication for the shingles and an intra-venous drip to increase my fluids. I was then able to close my eyes and rest. When I look back, it seems crazy that I was sleeping in hospital as the world around me was celebrating wildly.

At midday on Monday, a huge fan day with the players and the premiership trophy was scheduled to begin at Shark Park. At 11 a.m., I was still in hospital.

I told the medical staff that I had to get to Shark Park, as I couldn't miss the fan day. They explained explicitly that rest was what I required. So I signed myself out.

I made it to Shark Park with twenty minutes to spare. Our loyal fans were none the wiser that I had just arrived from hospital. Not surprisingly, the rest of the boys were nowhere near as fragile as me. The majority of the playing group had spent the night at Shark Park. Even our trainer, Mark Noakes, had slept under his desk.

As soon as I walked into the dressing room, where we were gathering before greeting the fans, Andrew Fifita had, let's just say, a stern word with me about going missing. Ricky Leutele, who wouldn't say boo any other day, was demanding that I explain myself and skol a drink. And our five-eighth, Jimmy Maloney, was relentless, refusing to listen to anything I was attempting to say about my absence.

But I didn't crack; I didn't have a drink because I just couldn't. I felt terrible. I was disappointed in myself. I wanted to go as hard as everyone else, but I couldn't.

I was committed to the fan day, but once we'd signed our last autograph, I returned home. It would've been around 6 p.m. that night when, sitting on the lounge, Anne turned to me and said, 'Are you serious? What are you doing—go out and enjoy it.'

The players had congregated at Northies, so I drove to the famous Cronulla establishment for a few hours. The entire pub was heaving. Players and staff were crowd-surfing; strangers were hugging each other and bragging about the photo they had just taken with a particular member of the grand-final team. I didn't have a drink—given the buzzing atmosphere, I didn't really need to.

The next morning, I woke and rang the doctor. 'Doc, I've just won a grand final—will I die if I have a few drinks?' He said no. And that was all I needed.

I organised a minibus into the city for the players who were eager to receive a 'Premiers' tattoo. In total, eighteen of the players climbed aboard the bus to get their tattoo before we then found the coaching staff celebrating at The Rocks in Sydney.

It was a great night—and I still think it was the best night of the grand-final celebrations, because we were all together again. Mick Ennis took over the microphone from a band that was playing at the pub we were at. He may even have performed a cheeky rendition of the 'Viking Clap'—a repeat of his efforts only a few weeks earlier following our epic win over Canberra in the nation's capital.

That night launched an entire week of celebrations. I had something organised—be it a lunch or drinks with teammates at various pubs—every day until the following Monday.

It was during the aftermath of our premiership win that my Test career came to an end. I wasn't sure if national team head coach Mal Meninga would select me as part of his 2016 Four Nations squad to go to England, but I was hopeful.

What gave me hope was what he had said to the entire ANZAC Test team earlier in the year in Newcastle. After I had received the man-of-the-match award in the ANZAC Test, Mal stated that if we did the right thing by him, he would do the right thing by us. The premiership victory, I felt, only aided my chances.

But as soon as Mal rang me on the Tuesday after the grand final, I knew I wasn't going to be selected. He said, 'You've been a great servant for us, but we're going to go in another direction.'

While I was disappointed, it didn't overly shock me. I accepted it and moved on. The premiership ring on my finger certainly helped soothe any dissatisfaction. Deep down, I knew that I'd given everything to Australia, and the premiership victory was now the icing on the cake as far as my club football career went.

After hanging up from Mal, I told Anne that I wouldn't be going on tour. I moved to the kitchen table and sat down. Despite the continuing hype and fanfare of the grand-final celebrations, I said to myself, 'Right, what's next?'

The answer came easily—I wanted to win another premiership.

2

Tough Love

We were known as 'Westies'. It was the stereotypical nickname for anyone who called the suburbs of Western Sydney home.

I would eventually move from the west to the Sutherland Shire, located in Sydney's south, which boasts great beaches and pristine waterways. But for the first eighteen years of my life, almost two decades of my upbringing, Western Sydney was my home. It was where my childhood began.

The oldest of five siblings, I was raised by Mum and Dad in a three-bedroom fibro house in the Western Sydney suburb of Guildford.

I was born on 14 August 1981. My mum, Kerry, still smiles when anyone asks how I was as a baby. She takes great delight in telling people that, even in those first three to six months, there was something a little different about me. It's somewhat difficult to believe, but Mum swears until she's blue in the face that I could walk when I was just five months old.

I wasn't the baby of the Gallen house for very long. Just fourteen months after I was born, Mum and Dad were celebrating the birth of their first baby girl and my first sister, Julie. Our family continued to grow quickly—just ten months after Julie, my second sister, Nikki, was born. Three kids under the age of two made for a busy home and a hectic schedule of feeding, sleeping, bottles and nappies for Mum to take care of.

My dad, Garry, was a plumber. He'd set his alarm early, leaving for work each morning before sunrise. Most days, he would return home twelve hours later. This meant that, until I was almost five, I was mostly surrounded by the love of my mum and two sisters.

However, the pro-female dominance of the Gallen house in those early days was altered by the arrival of my first brother, Stevie, who was born in 1986. Being the big brother, I enjoyed having two younger sisters to play with, to teach and to also protect. But I would be lying if I said that I didn't feel a strong sense of excitement when Stevie arrived.

When Stevie was a baby, I would climb into bed beside him and pull his blanket up over both of us, falling asleep right beside him. Mum would've enjoyed watching her eldest son show that type of love for her youngest boy—largely because I spent every other waking hour trying to tackle Stevie and rough him up.

The majority of the time, Stevie was a quiet boy. He was always softly spoken and well mannered. But every now and then, a switch flicked inside Stevie and a little craziness filled our home. Out would come a mini madman, who would run wildly around the house. Perhaps Stevie learned a bit of cheekiness from me, although I wasn't aware of my own developing character at the time.

The youngest member of the Gallen family, my baby brother Peter, arrived in 1990, providing the final piece of the family jigsaw puzzle. Stevie and I were both over the moon to have another boy in the house to muck around with.

My childhood growing up in Guildford was no different to that of the majority of other kids in this blue-collar area of

Western Sydney. My siblings and I were never spoiled, and our lives were far from extravagant. But we never felt like we missed out on anything, either. We played in our small street, rode our bikes, played with our neighbours at the local park and visited Nan at her house not too far away in Lidcombe. On the weekends, when Dad wasn't working, he would load us into the car and drive us to the local A-grade footy matches to watch our uncles and cousins play.

By the time I was five, Mum and Dad had saved enough money so that they could build a new home fifteen minutes west of Guildford, in a suburb called Greystanes. Not long after we moved into our new home, I played my first game of junior rugby league with the Greystanes Bulldogs.

It was early one morning when Dad walked into my bedroom and said, 'C'mon Paul, you're coming with me. We're going to sign you up for footy.' At the age of five, I didn't really know what Dad meant by 'signing me up'. But I jumped in the car with him anyway.

Dad was my first footy coach. In that season with the Bulldogs, our team was made up of kids who were all playing their first year of rugby league. They were fun days.

I remember Dad being surprised by how quickly we all seemed to handle our introduction to rugby league. Like a lot of things in life that you look back on, it's difficult to recall every single moment of your childhood. But it's funny how you can remember happy or sad snapshots with ease.

One of the clearest things I recall about that first year is how much I loved tackling the opposition. Other kids would be slightly cautious about colliding with a boy on the other team, someone who they'd never met or seen before. But not me—I couldn't get enough of it. I thought it was great fun to roll around, pulling and tackling the opposition to the ground.

Maybe even back then, I loved the sense of being challenged. That sensation stayed with me throughout my entire career.

Dad must have had a decent grasp on the footy coaching caper, because we remained undefeated during our entire first season. Winning every weekend left me instantly hooked on playing footy.

To Dad's credit, he could see how much I enjoyed playing footy, and he wanted me to be happy. Such was my love for pulling on footy boots, running around and tackling at training until I was overcome by exhaustion, I made Dad register me with a second club, the neighbouring Wentworthville Magpies. That enabled me to play for the Magpies on Saturdays and the Bulldogs on Sundays. For a little boy who loved his footy, life was complete.

By the time I was eight, I was playing twice a week for two different clubs in my local area. Could it be possible for our kids today to play for two separate rugby league clubs, training twice a week and then playing twice a week, while also maintaining a focus on schoolwork? Probably not. At 8 I had an appendix operation and only missed one week of footy—I strapped a nappy to my stomach for padding to play.

My entire week was a build-up to the weekend spent at footy grounds across Western Sydney. Winter felt like one long Christmas for me.

Believe it or not, I was a halfback during my days playing in the under 10s for Wentworthville, as my ability to pass the footy and kick wasn't too bad at that age. In that same year, the Magpies and Bulldogs both won their grand finals.

Here's another memory that I'll never forget. Our opposition, Girraween, was so confident they would beat us that year, they arrived at the oval on grand-final day with 'premiers' jackets and a cake with 'premiers' iced across the top. But they never received those shiny new jackets or that big creamy cake. We beat them.

They were great days, when life was all about having fun at the footy and with your friends. It wouldn't last forever.

When I was twelve, the environment within our home began to change. Being the oldest sibling, I was the first to notice the tension increasing between Mum and Dad. Arguments occurred more and more frequently. On some nights, Julie, Nikki, Stevie, Peter and I would sit in our bedrooms with the doors closed, trying not to listen to Mum and Dad argue.

Dad had been working for a kitchen company, but its unexpected closure had impacted on his ability to provide a weekly income for the family. The lack of financial stability placed great stress on Mum and Dad's relationship, to the point where it became unrepairable. Mum was exhausted and fed up with the arguments. Eventually, she told Dad she wanted to move out of our Greystanes home.

The collapse of Mum and Dad's marriage caused Mum immense emotional pain and anguish. She deteriorated terribly as a result. Being the oldest of my siblings, I was cognisant of the shocking state Mum was in. She wasn't her normal self. She suffered a nervous breakdown and, as a result, she developed a frightening twitch in her eye.

I felt scared, worried and confused. It impacted on me heavily. Watching Mum go through that emotional and physical upheaval affected my ability to concentrate and focus on high school, which I had just begun at Newman High in Greystanes.

At the end of Year 7, my first year of high school, the principal of Newman High sat me down and asked if I would be willing to leave the school to give myself a greater chance of committing to my classes and homework. It was a nice way of saying that I was being expelled after having a fight.

I was only thirteen, but here I was, already being kicked out of high school. And it wasn't like I didn't deserve the shake-up.

I was being increasingly seen as a troublemaker. That first year, I was forever falling foul of the rules and disobeying the teachers. I often ended up in fights and scuffles with other students in the playground.

On several occasions, I was sent out of class for being a distraction and then ordered to meet with the school counsellor. I managed to drag my feet into one or two meetings, but that was about it. Every other time, I offered any excuse possible to avoid attending the meetings. Why was I so rebellious? That's difficult to pinpoint.

I certainly wasn't proud of my behaviour. I knew what I was doing was wrong, but at that age of adolescence it was like I had dug this hole for myself by creating a persona as the tough, crazy kid who seemingly wasn't afraid of superiors or finding trouble.

Later in my life, I would attend proper counselling sessions (which I will document for you in this book). The country's best psychologists would conclude that the instability at home and the breakdown of Mum and Dad's marriage were contributing factors to my behaviour.

From the ages of thirteen to fourteen, my life shifted from one issue to another. Or, should I say, one house to another. In total, over an eighteen-month period, I lived in seven different houses. That's right, seven. It was a platform, if you could even call it that, for disharmony, imbalance and a constant feeling of instability at an age when stability is such a critical influence on who you are.

At the time of Mum and Dad's separation, it was Dad who eventually packed his bags and moved out of the house. I was worried about Mum and her health, so I said goodbye to Dad and stayed with her when we moved to our third home, not far away in Merrylands.

My time with Mum was short lived. It wasn't long before, just like with Dad, she'd had enough of me, too. Due to my poor behaviour and disregard for school, it got to the stage where Mum was no longer able to control me. In other words, I was out of control.

I walked around filled with constant anger and pent-up frustration. Despite Mum's own concerns and heartache, I often directed my angst towards her. Even though there were obvious reasons for the breakdown of Mum and Dad's marriage, my adolescent mind simply couldn't understand why she wouldn't let Dad come home. In my heart, I just wanted them to be normal, happily married parents, and that was the one thing that always stirred my emotions.

Perhaps to punish Mum for splitting up with Dad, I rebelled against everything she asked of me. I was highly emotional, and the smallest of disagreements with her would send my teenage mind into a rage.

During one particular night of rampage, I trashed our entire house. I punched and kicked holes in our lounge room walls. I had no respect for Mum's house and hard work whatsoever. The frightening ugliness inside me emerged, I believe, because I felt torn between Dad and Mum. Dad would talk to me and tell me one thing, and then Mum would say that what Dad had told me wasn't true. My only reaction was to become violent and angry.

On more than one occasion, Mum called the police. She would have the local command knock on the front door in an attempt to frighten me enough so that I would settle down.

I had become so difficult for Mum that she sat down with my high school principal to discuss in detail the benefits I would receive from being sent to an institution for troubled teenage boys. Of course, when Mum told me about that possibility, I despised the idea and refused to discuss it. I didn't see Mum's next course of action—her last resort—coming at all.

Exhausted and unable to instil any discipline into me, Mum told me to get out of the house. 'I have four other kids to look after,' she said, as she pointed towards the front door. I was only thirteen, but I'd left my mum no other choice—I was out of control and she rightfully felt this was the only way to rein me in, while also allowing her to raise my brothers and sisters with the attention they deserved.

Mum wanted me out of the house immediately. Everything up until I was twelve had felt so normal but suddenly everything had changed overnight.

Unfortunately, moving in with Dad to find stability and fix my behaviour wasn't a realistic option, as he was more than happy enjoying the life of a single man. The only other genuine choice I had was to turn to the friends from my local area who I played junior footy with.

I became a teenage gypsy and, as a result, footy—the one constant in my life since I was five—was no longer an interest or a priority. For the next few weeks, I found myself at a different friend's house, sleeping on their lounge-room floor or spare mattress.

Brian and Karen Smith from Wentworthville took me in for a few months. I'm forever grateful for their care and willingness to accommodate a lost fourteen-year-old boy who wasn't their son but required nurturing and feeding. The Smiths cooked me breakfast, lunch and dinner and housed me, but it soon became clear that they wanted to focus on raising their own three boys. So I was on the move again.

My Aunty Suey and Uncle Lance looked after me for the next six months. Like the Smiths, they were unbelievably good to me from the moment I walked through their front door. I'll never forget how much of a positive influence they were on me.

I was accepted into Parramatta Marist High School to commence Year 8. Aunty Suey and Uncle Lance did everything they could humanly do to instigate a level of normality back into my life. They both worked for Cadbury and would make certain that, before they started work each day, I was at school every morning on time for my first class.

Aunty Suey and Uncle Lance took me under their wing until Dad found his own level of stability and another house in Greystanes, which I then moved into at fourteen years of age. It was a small house, situated on the busy corner of Merrylands Road and the Cumberland Highway. Whether it was breakfast, lunch or dinner, the thundering sound of B-double semitrailers would shake the walls of our lounge room.

My four brothers and sisters remained living with Mum. Any contact with Mum or my siblings was almost non-existent. That was what Mum wanted. The phone number for her new house remained a mystery to me. Even if I wanted to have dinner once or twice a week with the rest of my family, I couldn't.

Dad was always trying to earn an extra dollar. He would chase work as a plumber, finishing his twelve- to fourteen-hour day before arriving home late. A lot of the time, I was a teenager fending for myself. It may sound lonely, and there were times that it was. But once I moved in with Dad, I didn't mind the freedom of doing things my way. What teenager doesn't like to think they're already an adult?

Being independent was something I always felt comfortable with. And maybe because I was thrust into this situation of looking after myself at a young age, it made me feel older than what I actually was. For example, I tried to get a job at the local Chili's—part of a Tex-Mex restaurant chain—when I was fourteen. Of course, the manager turned me away as I was considered too young for employment. But even at that age, I had a real sense of acceptance towards owning the situation and fending for myself.

Dad would work so hard to make sure there was food in the house, but some days the cupboards were plain empty. I would live off a diet of dried pasta and vegetables.

On most days, I would do almost everything for myself, including the cooking and cleaning. I say almost, because I never picked up an iron. I hated ironing. I would rather wear my clothes crumpled and crushed than stand ironing my school shirts and shorts.

It would take a few months of living with Dad before I began to find some form of stability. Mum could see the change in me, and after she had moved to a new house in Blacktown with my brothers and sisters, she invited me back into her life. Mum would collect me once a week from Dad's place so that I could have dinner with my brothers and sisters, before returning me to Greystanes.

It was just before my fifteenth birthday when I landed my first job cooking chicken and chips at Red Rooster in Merrylands. The store manager gave me two shifts a week to work. I earned $27 for each shift at Red Rooster. But because Dad was working or having a beer with his mates at the pub, there were times when I would end up spending half of my wage on the taxi fare home from work.

Dad was also rarely around on weekends. So, with a little extra cash in my pocket thanks to Red Rooster, it wasn't long before the other staples in my life became alcohol and parties.

Footy was the furthest thing from my mind.

3

The Riot

Where I grew up, trouble was both as far away and as close as you wanted it to be.

As teenagers, my circle of mates never began the day looking for a fight. But in the gritty, tough neighbourhoods of Western Sydney, that was the culture of the area. As 'Westies', we stood our ground. The result? A regular test of physicality and violence was never far away.

However, absolutely nothing came close to 'The Riot'. We'd had our share of fights before—too many to recall—but they were nothing compared to this night.

I knew our teenage bravado and readiness for a fight had gone too far when, on this night in the back streets of Greystanes, a group of revved-up teens from outside our neighbourhood stood opposite, armed with bottles and blocks of wood. The equation was fairly simple—we could run, or we could fight. We chose the latter.

'The Riot' was a bloodied mess of breaks and bruises. There were cuts and scores of stitches required. One close mate had his front teeth knocked out. There would've been 30 or 40 teenagers throwing punches. It was idiotic and mad. To this day, I have never seen anything else like it. I still wonder how no one was seriously injured, or even killed.

I was sixteen and still living with Dad. My mates and I had obtained fake identification, which acted as our ticket to a whole new world of underage drinking, pubs and nightclubs. With our fake IDs and all the pubescent confidence in the world, the Castle Hill Tavern and Parramatta's Argyle Street Hotel soon became the meeting places for my mates and me on almost every weekend until Year 12.

As you may be starting to realise, we were young and without a care in the world. And with more than a dash of alcohol added, our carefree attitude had the potential to become a lethal cocktail.

The scar from the six stitches I required above my left eye after being glassed at the Castle Hill Tavern remains visible to this day. But a separate incident at the Argyle Street Hotel was significantly more dangerous. Following an altercation earlier in the night, one of my friends was set upon. He was slashed in the head with a knife and required 30 staples.

It's so easy to see now—although I would never have admitted it at the time—that I was heading down a destructive path, which clearly could've changed my life forever. It was a terribly dark road that could've led to alcohol abuse and possibly recreational drug use. It was a frightening way of life that led some of my closest friends at the time into a world of courtrooms and prison cells. That could quite easily have been me.

Years later, following my social media outburst directed at the NRL hierarchy in 2014, I would be forced to confront my past via a leadership course. I also undertook counselling in order to better understand the errors of my ways and who I am—and was—as a person.

The warning signs of a troubled teenage life began flashing when I was fourteen. They continued to burn bright when I was fifteen, before reaching a crescendo of danger at sixteen.

Even though I had been expelled from Newman High in Greystanes, I had been lucky enough to obtain a second chance in Year 8 at Parramatta Marist High School—a highly regarded rugby league school. Thanks largely to Mark Perry—a teacher at Parramatta Marist and a friend of Dad's, who played touch football with him—I was able to continue my high school education. Incidentally, he is also the father of Ellyse Perry, an Australian cricketer and soccer player.

From Monday to Friday, life was normal. I was never an A-grade student, but I wasn't on the bottom rung, either. I would attend school each day before returning home to hang with my mates or with Dad. I saw Dad as one of my mates, largely because it was just us at home, cooking, cleaning or kicking the footy together in the backyard.

But once the weekend arrived, we'd both go our separate ways. Dad would head out, leaving me the keys to the house. On a Friday or Saturday night, my group of mates would look for a party or nightclub to go to. If we couldn't find one, we'd all end up back at Dad's house. The parties were always a split second away from getting out of control.

One night, a mate kickstarted my motorbike, which I kept inside the kitchen of our house. I had begun racing dirt bikes on Sundays, so my motorbike was my pride and joy. Having heard the roar of the engine from the kitchen, I charged through the house. But rather than being angry or upset that someone had just fired up my favourite bike, I boasted, 'That's not how you do it.' I then began performing a series of doughnuts and burnouts on

Dad's kitchen floor. As I said, the parties were always on the verge of going haywire.

At that age, I had no care or responsibility, so Dad's house became the party place to be. I would wake up in the morning and there would be empty bottles and food strewn across the floor. You would walk into one room and find a mate passed out from drinking; in the next room, someone else would be flat on their back.

Every Sunday morning after a big night of partying, we'd order a $2 hamburger and bag of hot chips from our favourite local fast-food shop, Johnny's Top Diner. This was our ritual. We were young and carefree, and we were having a bloody good time.

Fights, parties, girls and alcohol were the weekend staples. Footy didn't raise a mention on my pecking order. Having fun with my mates was all that mattered.

Despite the encouragement of Dad and the coaches from my local footy club, Wentworthville, there had been a steady decline in my interest in footy from about the age of fourteen. From a skill level point of view, I had never been far away from trialling for selection in the representative sides. And it wasn't as though I didn't understand what benefits could emerge from playing in the representative teams.

I was given a taste of what life looked like as a professional footballer when I was twelve. In the school holidays over the summer of 1993, I was selected for the Parramatta Eels' summer coaching school.

I was preparing to play in the under 14s—with boys one year older than me—for Fairfield Patrician Brothers that coming season. So Dad thought it would be beneficial for me to gain a head start on my teammates and opposition by attending the training camp. Little did I know that, at the completion of the training camp, three kids would be chosen to become the Parramatta Eels' first-grade ball boy for the upcoming 1994 season.

On the final day of the training camp, I was selected alongside two other boys for the job. Here I was, this wide-eyed youngster, tossing the footy and carrying the sand bucket for household names at the time, including Paul Dunn, Michael Buettner, Scott Mahon, Lee Oudenryn and even Shane Flanagan, my future Cronulla coach, who played hooker for the Eels in 1994.

I would attend every game at Parramatta Stadium that year and travel on the team bus to all the away matches that the Eels played in Sydney. I loved it—it was an unforgettable experience.

But after my under 14s Fairfield Patrician Brothers team made the 1994 grand final that year—I watched the entire game from the reserves bench after breaking my finger the week before—I lost my love and desire to keep playing footy, and training became a chore. I was playing merely because my mates were.

Nevertheless, I trialled for the Roosters' under 15s Harold Matthews team at Henson Park. The problem was my age. I was still thirteen, and you had to be fourteen. I played well. So well, in fact, that a Roosters official tapped me on the shoulder after the game and said, 'We want you to join the squad.' I couldn't continue with the lie, so I admitted that I was too young to play.

I look back on that period during early 1995, when I was thirteen, and think how my focus and dedication to training were virtually non-existent. The only reason I was turning up each weekend was to enjoy the company of my mates.

Not surprisingly, I was later overlooked for selection for Parramatta's under 15s Harold Matthews representative side. It was hardly a shock, given my attitude towards training. In that year, 1996, I suffered a serious shoulder injury in just the second game of the season while playing for Wentworthville. My season was over.

It would mean that, for the first time since the age of five, I would spend virtually an entire year without footy on my mind. For me and those close to me, there is an obvious parallel that can be drawn between my first year of sitting on the sidelines and being a fifteen year old with a penchant for partying. Without footy training and playing on the weekends, I had nothing but time on my hands.

Despite the backdrop of partying and late nights, my shoulder injury eventually healed and in 1997 I turned up to train with the Wentworthville Magpies under 16s side. But I wasn't wanted by the coach, who almost certainly had become aware of my previous lack of focus towards training.

Amid the fog of growing up fast while living alone with Dad, I had noticed how, over the past two years, many of my mates had gained selection into the SG Ball and Harold Matthews representative teams with Parramatta. Having played throughout my junior career with and against them, I wondered why I couldn't be as good, if not better, than them. However, I managed to survive just one training session with the Magpies.

Strangely, it wasn't my lack of effort or desire to play and perform for the team. The coach simply didn't want me in the team. After the training session, he said, 'Sorry mate, we don't need you.'

Gutted, I had nowhere else to play rugby league except for my school side at Parramatta Marist every Thursday in the Metropolitan Catholic Schools (MCS) competition. The standard of competition wasn't great, but looking back now I realise that this was the year I rediscovered my passion for the game.

Playing second row against Catholic schools from across Sydney, we won the entire competition that year. On the day of the grand final, I snuck two $8 bottles of Passion Pop into my bag so that we could spray the fizzy alcohol around the dressing rooms after we won the premiership.

I'll never forget the look on my coach's face—he was also our teacher—as a bunch of sixteen year olds, all well under the legal drinking age, sprayed alcohol all over each other during school hours. At the time, I couldn't understand why he was so upset. I now realise how incredibly naive I was. But for me, it was merely about having fun.

Having that fun back in my life meant that footy would soon replace the ugly distractions of late nights, fights and trouble. The lure of signing my very first contract was on the horizon.

4

Eel Deal

After a year of rediscovering the fun of playing football with my schoolmates every Thursday for Parramatta Marist, I decided to dedicate more time to determining if maybe, just maybe, I could be more than just a park footballer for the rest of my life.

With my Year 10 school footy commitments over in November 1997, Mum drove me to a one-off trial match for the North Sydney Bears. It was for boys aged seventeen and under who were hoping to be selected in the SG Ball squad for the Bears. I had heard about the trial opportunity from my high school friend, Brent Keegan, who had played in the Bears' Harold Matthews side the year before.

As Mum steered her car towards the car park, I was overcome by a rush of nervous energy. On the sideline, I began to pull my gear out of my bag. I scanned the faces of the other boys who were warming up. I didn't know a single person among them.

As we laced up our boots, the Bears' coaching staff divided almost 50 boys into four teams. We would be given roughly twenty minutes of playing time to show the selectors what we had to offer.

I had mentioned to one of the coaches that I had predominantly played as a back-rower, so I began the audition in my preferred position. During one of my first hit-ups, I split the defensive line. The nerves that had startled me prior to kick-off were now gone.

I spent the majority of my trial match in the back row, before finishing the last five minutes at hooker, stabbing a few handy kicks from dummy half, I must say. With my twenty-minute stint over, I walked from the field content that I had played well enough to be among the short list of players to make the final cut.

As I began pulling off my boots and jersey, North Sydney Bears coach Wayne Lambkin stood in front of me. He asked if I would like to begin pre-season training with the Bears' SG Ball squad. Despite the 70-kilometre round trip from Greystanes to training, I didn't hesitate before saying yes.

Over the next two weeks, as soon as the 3 p.m. bell sounded at school, Brent—who had also been selected in the squad—and I would catch the train from Westmead station to North Sydney. By the time I returned home from training, it was dark and I would walk through Dad's front door, hungry and absolutely exhausted. But I didn't care about the pain in the slightest. I was excited to be part of the rugby league system. For any sixteen year old who loved their footy, this meant a possible pathway to something bigger.

However, the Bears wouldn't be the only club I trialled with that year. Aware that the majority of my mates who I had played school footy with were planning to trial for Parramatta's SG Ball squad, I also decided to turn up to the Eels' trial matches, held the following weekend in Cabramatta.

Once again there were over 50 teenagers wanting to be chosen, this time to represent the blue and gold of Parramatta. The Eels boasted a rich nursery of talent and a long history of success within their junior representative ranks. Parramatta was the envy of every other NRL club, such was the plethora of junior talent playing in the district. Everyone trialling that day knew that if you were chosen to play for the Eels, you would be joining a rugby league pathway that would undoubtedly fast-track your development as a footballer, with the distinct possibility of one day playing first grade.

Like in the Bears trial, I played in the back-row position for the Eels. Without delivering anything particularly outstanding during the trial, I walked from the field confident that I had done all I could to warrant selection. However, I would be lying if I said my performance was free of any lowlights.

In possession of the football, I charged towards the opposition's tryline and planted it over the white stripe. Standing up, I pumped my fist and began walking back towards the halfway line. Suddenly, someone grabbed my jersey and began pulling me back down field. I had slammed the football down on the wrong line—a faded marking, possibly from a touch football game the night before, almost a metre before the actual tryline. Embarrassed, I tried desperately to block it out of my mind and play on.

The selectors were kind to me because, only a few days after the trial, a letter arrived in the mail from Eels officials, asking if I wanted to be part of their 1998 SG Ball squad. Suddenly, I was faced with a dilemma.

The two recruitment managers for the Eels at the time were Noel 'Crusher' Cleal and Kevin Wise, whose job focused on the Parramatta district junior development program. I happened to be friends at school with Crusher's son, Gareth, who was aware that I had already been asked to join the Bears' SG Ball squad. It didn't take long for Gareth to make both Crusher and Kevin aware of the decision I was required to make.

Undeterred, Crusher organised a meeting with Dad and me at the head office of the Parramatta Eels. It was there that Crusher and Kevin explained why they wanted me to join the Eels. They felt that I could develop under the club's tutelage and have an impact with the SG Ball side and then perhaps, depending on my ambition, progress up the chain to first grade.

In a gesture of intent to gain my signature, they offered me my first contract—a one-year deal worth $2000. You could've knocked me over with a feather. I was blown away. As a sixteen year old who had been working at Red Rooster to earn $27 a shift, the thought of receiving $2000 to play footy was almost too good to be true.

I was ready to agree to become a junior Eel there and then. However, Dad wasn't as eager as I was to put pen to paper. As we walked out of the meeting and drove home, Dad turned to me and said, 'I'm going straight back to Wayne Lambkin to see if Norths can give you the same money or better.'

It sounded like a good strategy from Dad, but during the phone call the Bears explained that they weren't in a position to offer me any money. So, in the end, it was a simple decision—I signed with Parramatta to be part of their SG Ball squad. I was buzzing.

I still wasn't convinced that I could make a career out of footy, but there was no doubt that making my first representative team flicked a switch inside me. The instability at home was beginning to level out, and while I still enjoyed going out with the boys on the weekend, I certainly wasn't as roguish as twelve months earlier. I began to train every day.

My shoulder weakness was a liability, so every night before bed I would curl a dumbbell to build up the muscle in my rotator cuff. Before closing my eyes each night, I would also perform 100 push-ups on my bedroom floor.

I quickly forged a strong mateship with Jason Cayless, the younger brother of former Parramatta Eels captain Nathan Cayless.

He was following a similar path to me, wanting to improve and develop as a footballer. Jason—who would go on to play first grade with Parramatta, the Sydney Roosters, St Helens and the Wests Tigers—was a year older than me and a member of the Eels' Jersey Flegg squad.

Like me, he lived in Greystanes, so we would often catch the bus home from school together. He also had his driver's licence and, once home, Jason would pick me up each afternoon from my house so we could train at the gym together. He was bigger and stronger than me, but he always pushed me hard to increase my level and volume of training. I learned a lot about training from Jason.

After a dedicated two months of pre-season training, I was named in the starting line-up for Round 1 by my 1998 SG Ball coach, former New Zealand captain Gary 'Wiz' Freeman. I was over the moon to be in the back row.

My teammates that first season of junior representative football included Luke Burt, Daniel Irvine and Brett Sargent. As I ran out for the first time in the blue and gold, I would never have believed that this season would be my first and only one with the Parramatta Eels. But that's exactly what happened.

After playing the first six games of the 1998 SG Ball season with the Eels, I began to struggle with my fitness due to illness. I was battling to get through matches and, after an appointment with my doctor, I was advised that my tonsils needed to be removed to prevent the continual onset of lethargy, high temperatures and lack of physical strength.

I accepted the diagnosis. But fearing how much footy I would miss as a result of the minor tonsil surgery, I did the wrong thing. I played for the Eels against St George at Kogarah Oval on the Saturday, and then I also played for my junior club, Wentworthville, on the Sunday of the same weekend.

Under the rules of the junior league, you weren't permitted to play for your junior club if you were one of the SG Ball Top 17 players. Naively, I really didn't think anyone would notice or care. But the problem was, I unwittingly ensured junior league officials were aware that I had played for Wentworthville.

After I had scored a try, an opposition player lunged their elbow into the back of my head as I lay stretched out over the tryline. Of course I reacted, standing up and throwing a bunch of manic punches, which led to a huge brawl that spilled into the crowd. As a result, I was sent from the field by Gavin Reynolds (future NRL referee).

Handed a one-match suspension, I then underwent tonsil surgery, watching the next three matches from the sideline. That was the beginning of the end for me at Parramatta. As soon as I was well enough, I returned to training at the Eels, hopeful of playing a role in the last few games of the season. But I was never picked to play again that season. I was disappointed.

However, I couldn't ignore the fact that I had gained plenty from the experience of playing representative football. It gave me a purpose each week, structure and a desire to become a better footballer. Unlike in past years, I was now playing and training as much as I could.

By the end of 1998, I had played for three different teams. There was the Eels' SG Ball side, which I was training and playing for—albeit for no game time by the end of the season—and I was also playing for my school team in Year 11 at Parramatta Marist in the MCS competition. In addition, I was playing for Wentworthville.

I was one of only a few players in the school side from Year 11, with the rest of the squad made up of students from Year 12. I was so happy to be selected in the school side, which was flush with rising NRL players including Jason Cayless, Chad Robinson, Daniel Irvine and Brett Sargent. We had a great season, progressing to the final of the national schoolboys competition, the Arrive Alive Cup. We lost the grand final to Canberra's Erindale College, 27–14.

In that year, I was one of the last-ever players permitted to play for their school side while also being contracted to a club. Under Parramatta first-grade coach Brian Smith, the directive was given that from 1999, any player contracted to the Eels would no longer be permitted to play for both the club and their school. We were told he was concerned about player burnout.

Once my SG Ball season was over, I began playing every Saturday in the local league for Wentworthville, in the under 17s competition. The Hills Bulls beat us that year in the grand final.

As I said, it was a huge year for me both mentally and physically. I can identify that year as a major turning point in my life. I thank Mum for driving me to the trial with the Bears, and I thank Dad for his advice to sign with the Eels.

For me, still navigating my way through my late teens, it was by far my most enjoyable year of footy, as it provided me with true self-belief and confidence in my ability as a footy player. By the end of the year, following a positive and rewarding twelve months, I decided to treat myself by spending my $2000 SG Ball contract money.

I purchased an old Mitsubishi Colt hatchback from a priest, who Dad had helped with some plumbing work. Dad said it was a steal because it had only clocked 17,000 kilometres, so I handed over my contract money.

The freedom of having a car was important for the twelve months that would follow. It was the year I would join a club that I would call home for the rest of my life.

5

Welcome to the Shire

In January 1999, ahead of my final year of high school at Parramatta Marist, I had no clue where my life was heading, or in what direction it was about to go. By December of that year, I would sign a contract with the Cronulla-Sutherland Sharks, and my days of living in Sydney's west were numbered.

It was Year 12, but studying and focusing on securing a top score in my Higher School Certificate (HSC) weren't exactly top priorities. They should've been. Because if I had never been fortunate enough to have forged a professional football career, I honestly don't know what I would've done to earn a living.

In Year 10, when it was part of the curriculum to undergo work experience, I chose to understand the world of painting. Let me just say that my respect for painters is forever unwavering. Because I hated it.

There's every chance, had rugby league never taken me to places beyond my dreams, I would've followed in Dad's footsteps and chosen to work as a plumber. I actually began a plumbing apprenticeship the year after finishing school, but I never completed it. As much as I now encourage every aspiring footballer to focus on their studies or an alternative career path outside the game, training hard to become a professional footballer was all I cared about back then.

In the summer of my final year of high school, I spent the entire month of January training with Jason Cayless. Despite this, I remained uncertain if, still being only seventeen, I would be chosen for Parramatta's Jersey Flegg (under 19s) squad that year.

I decided to continue playing for Wentworthville on the weekend and with my school team at Parramatta Marist every Thursday in the schoolboys competition. Year 12 is the most important year for a schoolboy footballer. It is the year when, if you're good enough, you can be selected in the Australian Schoolboys squad at the end of the year. It's a squad of twenty of the best schoolboy players from around the country. And so, instead of stressing about being chosen in the Eels' Jersey Flegg squad, making the Australian Schoolboys team by playing consistently well for Parramatta Marist became my obsession.

Our Parramatta Marist team that year boasted a string of seriously gifted footballers. Jamie Lyon, who would emerge as Manly's premicrship-winning captain, had arrived at Marist from Narrabri, in country New South Wales. Steve Witt (who went on to make his NRL debut with Newcastle), Daniel Irvine and Brett Sargent (who also played first grade) were members of our school side.

Too strong for our opposition, we won the state knockout competition and were crowned the best rugby league school in New South Wales. We then won the Metropolitan Catholic Schools (MCS) title—beating Terra Sancta College convincingly in the grand final. I was enjoying my football.

I was playing in the back row, and every game was a challenge that I looked forward to. Little did I know at the time, but people were watching me. I was soon to be exposed to the world of player agents.

I was aware of their presence only due to the fact that the majority of my teammates had already aligned themselves with an agent. Having an agent, or manager, was something that was always considered 'cool' among my mates. Naively, the perception among us teenage boys was that having a manager was an indication that you were on your way to the big time.

After a match for Parramatta Marist, David Riolo—a former first-grade player and teacher—approached me about becoming my agent. He asked if I had used a manager to negotiate a new contract with Parramatta, as my first contract, worth $2000, was set to expire.

I'd only ever turned to Dad for advice when it was time to discuss my contract, so naturally I was all ears when Dave said that he wanted me to be one of his first-ever rugby league clients. But Dave wasn't the only agent who was interested. I also had letters of interest from several other player agents. One of the proposals in particular stood out above the rest. It was from an experienced player agent called Darryl Mather—who at the time was the agent for a host of NRL stars.

I narrowed the decision down to Dave and Darryl. But because Dave only had two other clients—Ben Galea and Jason Cayless—Dad and I thought it would be wiser to go with Darryl, who boasted a much more experienced stable of rising and current stars.

I phoned Dave to inform him that I was going to align myself with Darryl. However, on the day we were due to meet with Darryl, he phoned Dad to explain that because a meeting organised with another player, Daniel Irvine—who lived close to my house—had been postponed, he was no longer heading west and so he would have to cancel his planned meeting with me. In Dad's eyes, that was a deal-breaker. 'If he can't drive out just to see you, then we're wasting our time with him,' Dad said.

Sheepishly, I quickly dialled Dave's number again. 'Will you still manage me?' I asked.

To his credit, Dave said, 'No problem.' It's funny when I look back and consider how close our relationship came to never getting off the ground.

At the time of retiring from the NRL, I did so as Dave's longest-serving client. With the percentage earnings he has received from contracts and sponsorship deals over almost two decades as my manager, I've probably paid for Dave's house, car and tennis court! All jokes aside, I'm grateful that Dave chose to manage me. His guidance and advice throughout my career have been invaluable.

Not long after signing with Dave, my footy went to another level. I was chosen in the MCS representative side to compete in a carnival against the best Catholic college teams in New South Wales, and, as a result of that match, I was selected in my first NSW state side—the NSW Combined Catholic Colleges (CCC) squad. The goal to make the Australian Schoolboys squad was now just one step away.

I travelled to the Gold Coast to represent NSW CCC, taking on the best schoolboys from Queensland and the Australian Capital Territory. We were strong through our pool matches before advancing to the final, which we won by beating Queensland. After the final, I swapped my jersey with my future Australian Kangaroos teammate, Corey Parker, who had played for Queensland.

I sat inside the dressing rooms feeling like I'd done enough to be chosen for the Aussie team. I was named man of the match in one of our pool matches and, looking back, every player who won a man of the match award through the pool matches went on to be chosen in the Australian Schoolboys side. Except me.

I'm not sure why I missed out. It was disappointing, but as I reflect on that time, I see now how the rejection was good for me. If I had made it, maybe I would've thought I was good enough and that I was ready, when possibly I wasn't.

With my personal ambition put aside momentarily, my focus returned to Parramatta Marist, which was competing in the Aussie Home Loans Cup (formerly the Commonwealth Bank Cup). Because Parramatta Marist was a feeder school for the Eels, we had the opportunity to mix and train with the Parramatta first-grade squad.

As schoolboys, it provided us with unrivalled exposure to the dedication required to become first-grade footballers. Here I was, still in Year 12, and I would be lining up opposite the likes of Dean Pay, Jason Smith, Jarrod McCracken and Jimmy Dymock during school training sessions.

I recall the Eels' head of recruitment, Noel 'Crusher' Cleal, chatting to me after one training session. Out of the blue, he said, 'Mate, you don't know how close you are to first grade.' I didn't believe him. I was still at school, and these guys were like gods.

I'm not sure if Crusher was even telling the truth, but if his intention was to give me a shot of belief and focus to work hard, he achieved his goal. I left nothing in the tank in my few remaining matches for Parramatta Marist.

We were the team to beat, and sure enough we made it to the semifinal against Palm Beach Currumbin at the Brisbane Broncos' former home ground, ANZ Stadium. It was a game we should've easily won. But in a tight contest, largely because we underestimated our opposition, the match finished as a 10-all draw. There was no such thing as golden-point extra time. And because Palm Beach had scored the first try of the match, they were declared the winners—advancing to the final. I was devastated.

It was the end of our schoolboy season, and the last game that I would ever play with those bunch of boys. My final year of school was over. Not really knowing what I should do with myself now that school was finished, I accepted a job making kitchens in a factory in Wetherill Park. I lasted a month.

I didn't know what to do with my life, where to turn next or how to support myself financially. For most teenagers, such uncertainty would be layered with stress and confusion. But life can sometimes find a way of taking you in a new direction, because not long after I finished up at the kitchen factory, Dave fielded interest for me to commence training with the Melbourne Storm, St George Illawarra Dragons and Wests Tigers. I also had the words of Crusher, who had told Dad that I should 'always come back to us [Parramatta]' if I ever considered leaving the Eels for another club.

In the meantime, I reached out to Brian Rule, my head trainer when I played for the NSW CCC side earlier that year. Brian was the Cronulla Sharks' Jersey Flegg trainer. Of all the clubs that had contacted me or that I could reach out to, the opportunity to join the Sharks excited me the most.

The Sharks were a force in 1999, having made the Super League grand final only two years earlier. They were flush with some of the game's best players, including Jason Stevens, David Peachey, Andrew Ettingshausen, Mat Rogers and Adam Dykes. And I just loved how they were virtually unbeatable at their home ground, Shark Park. I had to wait a few days for Brian to return my call.

While waiting for Brian's call, I met Melbourne's recruitment manager, Theo Burgess, at the Novotel Brighton Le Sands. I arrived at the meeting with a serious interest in playing for the Storm, who had just beaten the Dragons in the 1999 grand final. That was, until Theo explained that if I signed with the Storm, I would be based in

Queensland, playing for Melbourne's feeder club, Brisbane Norths. That didn't appeal to me at all.

I ruled a line through the Storm and also the Dragons pretty quickly, and instead I took up an offer to train with the Tigers at Leichhardt Oval. I was there for almost a month, but even when I applied myself, I just felt there was something missing in return. I felt a real sense that the coaching staff could take me or leave me as part of their squad. There was a distance, almost an unspoken divide, between the coaching staff and me. I just couldn't garner any feedback or purpose for remaining at the Tigers.

So it left the Sharks and potentially the Eels as my options going forward. Dave tracked down Brian, who by then had passed on my interest in joining the Sharks to Kurt Wrigley, who was a member of the Cronulla recruitment team. Kurt asked me to bring my boots to an open trial for juniors in the Sutherland Shire. However, I had just undergone minor shoulder surgery, so I was unable to play in the trial match.

Kurt suggested that Dave speak with former Sharks football manager Greg Pierce. Greg told Dave that the Sharks would give me a shot. Knowing that the Sharks were willing to give me a chance, I did as Crusher asked and called Parramatta.

I had always shared a good relationship with Crusher, and I knew he was being honest with me when he said that, even though he believed I could play a role in the Eels' Jersey Flegg squad (which would change its age restriction to under 20s in 2000), he didn't think there would be a clear pathway for me to first grade due to their stock of back-rowers at the club. Crusher basically made the decision for me. I was heading to the Sutherland Shire to take up the offer with the Sharks.

I signed a one-year contract worth $2000, which was actually $1200, once my living away from home allowance was deducted to pay my rent. The contract also included a reserve-grade bonus of $300 for a win and $100 for a loss, while the first-grade bonus, if I was ever to play, was worth $2000 per win.

With my next twelve months locked in at Cronulla, I began training with the Sharks prior to Christmas 1999—commuting each day from Greystanes in my Mitsubishi Colt—before finally farewelling Sydney's Western Suburbs, for a permanent move to Sydney's southern suburbs, in February 2000.

Without any finance behind me or any family or friends based in the Shire, I moved into Shark House—a home where players who had been signed to Cronulla from outlying areas or overseas were cared for. We were fed, our washing was done and we had a roof over our heads. Each week, we were required to pay $100 to Michelle Taylor and her husband, Colin, the owners of Shark House.

The other boys I lived with were Michelle's son Jared Taylor, who was signed from Port Macquarie, and former Australian Schoolboy Daniel Ninness. Brett Firman, who played first grade with the St George Illawarra Dragons, Sydney Roosters and North Queensland, also spent time at the house.

We all got on well and, because we barely knew anyone else in the Shire, we quickly formed a bond by spending time with each other. It made the adjustment easier to share a home with a couple of like-minded boys. And we all appreciated coming home to find dinner was cooked and ready on the table.

Financially, it was a struggle, and physically it was also taxing. I was waking at 5 a.m. to work as an apprentice plumber. I was lucky enough that Craig Pinn, who ran a plumbing business, took me on after former Sharks chief executive Steve Rogers had called him on my behalf.

I was on a first-year apprentice wage, but I took the job because my contract with the Sharks was only just enough to cover my rent, leaving me with little in my pocket once that was paid for. I'd finish work with Craig at 4 p.m. and be required at training with the Sharks' Jersey Flegg squad by 4.30 p.m. We'd train for two hours, which included a weights session and a ball-work session on the field. I would walk back in the front door of Shark House around 7.30 p.m.

Despite my new environment and a host of new challenges, I made a strong initial impression in my first season as a Shark in the 2000 Jersey Flegg squad. Such were the promising signs I had shown in the opening rounds of the Jersey Flegg season, it wasn't long before I was promoted to reserve grade—and I was still just eighteen years old.

For me, this was a huge moment in my career. One, it was recognition that my hard work and sacrifice were paying off. And two, it was such a major step up from Jersey Flegg to reserve grade.

It was such a great test of my ability as a footballer. Suddenly, I was playing with and against players—some of them ten years older than me—who had already experienced the rigours of the NRL. Either starting or coming off the bench in the back row for the majority of the reserve grade season, I returned to Jersey Flegg once they had confirmed their position in the semifinals.

Despite my football career beginning to take shape, off the field I was a worried mess. I found myself as anxious and stressed as I had ever been. What happens now if this is as good as it gets for me? What will I do with my life, if I never play first grade? What will I do to earn money?

As a teenager, I had cruised through life hardly giving my future a second thought. But now the penny had well and truly dropped. I was paying bills—how would I do this as an adult if my footy career finished tomorrow? Plumbing wasn't something I wanted to do for the rest of my life. It was simply a way to help pay the bills.

I was so lucky to have a boss like Craig, because he knew I didn't want to be there. That was a point I was reminded of sadly after Craig's funeral in 2015 when his wife, Janine, commented to me about how Craig would always say, 'Gal is a shit plumber, but he was good at carrying everything for us.'

Such was the anxiety I was carrying in my mind over what my future would look like without football in it, I would drive the 80-kilometre round trip from Cronulla to Greystanes each week to seek counsel from Mum. I would cry to her, asking, 'What am I going to do? What if I don't make it?'

Everything was new to me in Cronulla—and in life. It felt so difficult to juggle work with Craig, training, playing and living in the real world. I had endured what Mum and Dad had been through as a couple, their struggles to work hard and also raise a family. And because that was my only insight into life as an adult, I was petrified that I would also face the same struggles in my adult life.

Those major self-doubt issues are something that I never really overcame. Over time I have managed to find the tools to help ease the anxiety that I feel about the future and the unknown. But it remains a constant battle every day.

6

A Shark is Born

One of the most significant changes to the way footy clubs culti-vate the development of their lower-grade players now, compared to when I made my NRL debut in 2001, is just how closely the club's younger players interact with the first-grade squad and coaching staff.

In the pre-season of 2001, I had trained the entire summer with the Jersey Flegg squad. I was nineteen, and I had no sense or inkling that just four months later I would make my NRL debut. Unlike in the final years of my NRL career, when players as young as fifteen would train with the Sharks' first-grade squad, there was nothing like that level of close collaboration and opportunity to train with the stars and leaders of the club on a regular basis in the year that I made my first-grade debut.

John 'Langy' Lang was the head coach of the Sharks' NRL team in 2001, and the only communication I ever had with him in that pre-season was when he walked past me and said, 'Hello mate.' But in the last pre-season trial match for Jersey Flegg, in February 2001, I was taken from the field at half-time by the coaching staff. It would be the last time I ever played Jersey Flegg. The coaching staff explained to me that I needed to save my energy and my body for a first-division trial (also known as a reserve-grade trial), which was set to be played immediately after the Jersey Flegg trial. From that trial, I began the 2001 season with the Sharks' first-division squad.

I had signed a new two-year deal with the Sharks for the 2001 and 2002 seasons, which was worth a total of $13,000. Again, I had chosen to have bonuses written into the contract, including a first-division winning bonus and a further $5000 if I ever played an NRL match. The last incentive, while attractive, seemed well out of my reach.

As I said, I was nineteen in the summer of 2001, and I was still working each morning as a plumber with Craig Pinn. The balance between training and working continued to be a daily battle. Adding to the strain was the fact that I had moved out of Shark House to make way for the next crop of young players. I now lived in a unit at Cronulla with Daniel Ninness. The responsibility and pressure of fending for myself on a small income were a whole new challenge.

Weighing 100 kilograms, I was named in the first-division starting line-up each week through the early rounds of the 2001 season. With each match, I was growing in confidence.

It's funny how you remember the things that people say to you. Approaching the halfway point of the season, in about Round 10, Noel 'Crusher' Cleal's words to me two years earlier, while I was training with Parramatta Marist, rolled through my mind. He was right—I was closer than I had thought to playing first grade.

Each week, I would sit in the grandstand and watch the Sharks' NRL side perform against the Broncos, Sea Eagles, Cowboys and other teams. I would compare the performances of players out on the field—especially those in the back row—to how I was playing in first division. For the first time in my life, I felt that I was ready to take the step up to NRL.

One of John Lang's greatest attributes was that he was an extremely loyal coach. He had faith in the players who he consistently selected week in, week out, largely because they had delivered for him on so many occasions. And despite my increasing belief that I was ready for a call-up, I also knew that I would have to wait until an injury or suspension forced Langy's hand. That chance finally came in Round 15 of the 2001 NRL season.

It was a Monday morning when Langy called me into the office that he used inside the Andrew Ettingshausen grandstand, at our home ground of Shark Park. Langy had never called me into his office before, so there was a spring in my step as I tapped on his door.

Having watched like a hawk the first-grade players' every move, I was aware that a couple of key players were struggling with injury. So I was trying not to smile as I walked in and said, 'You wanted to see me, Langy?'

'Gal, you've been going well—you're going to play first grade this week,' Langy said. 'I'll see you at training tomorrow.' Langy had just said more to me in the last few seconds than he had over the past six months. But it didn't matter—it was all I had ever wanted to hear from him.

Smiling, I stood there and said, 'Thank you.' However, there was a slight concern that I needed to tell Langy about. 'I've got a sore calf. I don't think I can train tomorrow,' I admitted.

I felt certain he would instantly change his mind and pick someone else to play instead of me, right there and then. But to his credit, Langy pointed me straight towards the physiotherapy room. 'Get yourself right. Don't let them [the physios] tell you it's anything else, and I'll see you the day after tomorrow,' Langy said.

I left his office and rang Dad straightaway. 'Great news mate, well done,' Dad said down the phone line.

I then rang my mum and the close mates I had grown up with. 'This is it, I'm making my first-grade debut.'

With my calf responding to the treatment by the Sharks' physio-therapist, much to my relief I was ready to go once game day arrived. The week itself had flown by so quickly that there wasn't too much time to analyse and think about the match until the day of the game was upon me.

It was a Sunday afternoon at Shark Park and, coincidentally, our Round 15 opponents just happened to be Parramatta. You may think that I was salivating at the prospect of making my NRL debut against the Eels. That because I had slipped their net after being part of their junior system, I felt animosity towards the decision-makers at Parramatta. But that wasn't the case at all.

When I was at the Eels, the prospect of playing first grade wasn't something I had ever considered as a possibility. It seemed so far away. So it would be incorrect to suggest they didn't have faith in me—truth be told, I didn't have faith in myself.

Perhaps the one aspect of playing against Parramatta that did excite me was coming up against my ex-Parramatta Marist High School teammate, Jamie 'Killer' Lyon. He and I had always shared a good mateship, and it was great to see that he had established himself not only as a starting centre for the Eels, but also as one of the most damaging ball-runners in the game.

On game day, my family were obviously anxious and excited for me. Before the match, they visited me at my unit in Cronulla. It was nice to have them there, showing their support, but without wanting to be rude, I kindly asked them to leave not long after they had arrived. I was nervous, and I just wanted to be alone in a quiet space.

I drove myself to Shark Park and headed straight for the first-grade dressing rooms in order to commence my routine. Langy had named me on the interchange bench, so I wasn't sure when my time would come to enter the action. Eventually, the call came down from the coaches' box midway through the first half. 'You're on, Gal.'

I finished the match with a total of 53 minutes on the field, making eighteen tackles and producing twelve runs for 83 metres. However, it was far from the fairytale debut that I was hoping for. Parramatta smashed us 36–6.

While memories of my debut are now a blur of excitement and the feeling of how quickly that match came and went, there are a couple of things I'll never forget. First, the speed and intensity were like nothing I had ever experienced. Every tackle rattled your bones, and every run was faster than the one before. It was nothing like first division.

Second, I came up with a shocker, a brain fade that my former teammates still rib me about when we see each other to this day. During my stint on the field, I must have thought I was Allan Langer, because for some bizarre reason I attempted a chip and chase. Who does that during their NRL debut?

During an attacking set, I had the football in my hands 5 metres out from the Parramatta tryline. All I could see were opposition forwards Michael Vella and Andrew Ryan in front of me, with Eels fullback Brett Hodgson nowhere to be seen. Or so I thought. I chipped a little kick through the Eels' defensive line, thinking I was about to score an unforgettable debut try . . . when Hodgson swooped. He picked up the bouncing footy and raced 15 metres down field. I can only imagine what Langy was thinking. 'What does this kid think he's doing?'

The other lasting memory I have is quite funny. I'm not sure if it was naivety or my desire to leave an impression, but I have never heard a nineteen-year-old debutant tell an Australian Test prop to 'piss off, it's my run.' But, yes, I did that, too.

Wanting to cart the footy forward during the match, I called for my run at the very moment my Sharks teammate—and one of the most respected players at the club—Jason 'Stevo' Stevens was also calling for the ball. 'It's my run,' Stevo yelled.

'No, it's not. I'm taking it,' I fired back.

'Move out of the way,' Stevo said.

'Piss off, it's my run,' I shouted as I charged forward, tucking the footy under my arm, and into the Eels' defensive line.

Six months later, Stevo reminded me of our on-field 'discussion'. Much to my surprise, he smiled and explained that he had faith in me and knew that my first-grade career would prosper because 'nobody had ever told a Test forward to move out of the way' before. It would be the beginning of a lasting friendship.

Stevo has remained a huge influence on my life. His support and advice throughout my career always left an impression on me. He is a close mate and someone I turn to when I'm in need of a quiet word or gentle nudge. It's a pretty special thing to say that our relationship began on the day I made my first-grade debut.

After the match, I sat down in the dressing room happy with the way I had played, despite the result. I was chuffed, too, when our five-eighth, Adam Dykes, said, 'Well done, Gal. You were probably one of our better forwards today . . . but as a team we need to get back to work.' That said, I found myself back with the first-division team for the next nine weeks.

It's incredible to think how much confidence that one first-grade game gave me. Because unlike during the years prior to that game, when I felt I was so far away from playing NRL, I was actually disappointed and constantly dejected that I was being chosen to play first division. I would be named Cronulla's first-division player of the year in 2001, and I think that was largely due to the experience I gained from playing that one first-grade game.

Those 53 minutes in the NRL taught me how to play smarter and tougher.

I was prepared for my second shot at the first grade in the weeks following, when Langy called to say that I would be travelling to Auckland, where the Sharks were due to face the New Zealand Warriors in Round 23. I flew over to Auckland, hoping that I would play, but 24 hours before the match I was told that I wouldn't be required. I was to warm up as the eighteenth man.

Still, the trip was memorable, as my roommate was our brilliantly gifted half and fullback, Preston Campbell. He was in such red-hot form that he won the Dally M Player of the Year medal in that 2001 season.

My second NRL appearance finally occurred the week after travelling back from New Zealand, in Round 24 against the 2000 premiers, the Brisbane Broncos. Again, it was a home game at Shark Park. But unlike my debut, I didn't find out about my call-up until the day of the game.

I was busy preparing to play first division. I was fully dressed in my playing kit— jersey, shorts, boots, socks—and I only had to pop in my mouthguard, when a Sharks official came screaming through the dressing room, telling me not to bother about running out with the rest of the first-division team.

Unbeknown to me, Sharks winger and club great Mat Rogers had injured his back and was out of the match against the Broncos. It meant that rangy Sharks back-rower Chris McKenna had to be shuffled from the forwards to the back line, leaving a hole for me to fill. I had just enough time to make a quick phone call to Mum and Dad to let them know I was playing. They drove straight to the game from Greystanes.

This was a 'pinch yourself moment', as I was about to play against the Broncos. This team boasted the biggest names in the game, including Petero Civoniceva, Lote Tuqiri, Darren Lockyer, Gorden Tallis, Shane Webcke and Wendell Sailor. But once I got out there on the field, I just tried to do my job, ignoring who I was running towards or about to tackle.

From the interchange bench, I was handed 29 minutes of game time, making eleven tackles and nine runs for 54 metres. We won the game 24–16. It was my first win as a Cronulla Sharks NRL player.

Under Langy, the Sharks had a terrific season in 2001, finishing fifth on the NRL ladder—advancing all the way to the preliminary final. Amid huge excitement and hope within the Shire that this could be the Year of the Shark, the first-grade team lost the grand-final qualifier 18–10 to the eventual 2001 premiers, Newcastle. I had a front-row seat to the disappointment.

It was just before the Sharks' first-grade squad began to prepare for the 2001 finals series that Langy tapped me on the shoulder to explain that I would need to continue training with the first-grade side. Should there be injuries, I would have a chance of playing in the finals. I never played a role in the Sharks' finals campaign, but that month of September was an awesome experience for a rookie like me. It was invaluable.

The year 2001 was a pivotal one in my life. The opportunity that Langy had afforded me by allowing me to play in two first-grade matches had ratified what I had begun to believe halfway through the year and for the first time in my life—that I could forge an NRL career.

At the end of that year, I decided to direct my entire focus towards football. In doing so, I quit my job working as an apprentice plumber. My toughest work was about to begin.

7

Survival of the Fittest

At the conclusion of the 2001 season, I was planning to take an end-of-year holiday with a few of my Cronulla teammates. It would be a chance to relax and unwind before knuckling down for the new season. But the arrival of a new head coach at the Sharks, Chris 'Opes' Anderson—replacing the departed John Lang—prompted an urgent phone call to our travel agent. The cocktails and suntan would have to wait.

From the day he walked through the front gates at Cronulla, Opes made it clear to every single squad member that we were about to embark on one of the toughest pre-seasons we'd ever endure. We may not have been the most skilful side in the competition in 2002, but we were going be the toughest.

The arrival of Opes was something I embraced. Often, the arrival of a new coach at a footy club can prove daunting for the playing group. Any ties or trust that you shared with your previous coach are gone, and suddenly everyone is on the same rung in the eyes of the new coach.

Depending on where you are in your career, the arrival of a new coach can mean different things to different people. I had only played two first-grade games under Langy, and I was honoured to have done so. But Opes had no loyalty towards anyone, and he would therefore pick the team based on the actions displayed at training or in the gym. This, for me, was why the pre-season of 2002 was so important for my push to become a regular starting NRL player.

For the first three months of pre-season training, we hardly touched a football. Under Opes and his coaching staff, that entire summer became a survival of the fittest. If there was a location in the Sutherland Shire that we didn't run, ride or climb, I haven't seen it. We would spend early mornings running through the thick bushland of the Royal National Park. We would spend afternoons trudging through the soft sand of Cronulla Beach. A day rarely went by when we weren't churning through countless kilometres.

Opes—who had arrived from the Melbourne Storm, where he had won the 1999 premiership—was seen as somewhat of a saviour by the Sharks' board and our loyal band of supporters. If he could deliver the holy grail to a start-up club like the Storm in 1999, in just their third season of existence, why couldn't he deliver the same pot of gold to Cronulla, who were still chasing their first-ever premiership?

Opes was also the Australian Test coach in 2002, which meant he arrived at Cronulla with a certain lustre. And he brought premiership-winning halfback Brett Kimmorley with him to the club. So, as players, who were we to challenge his résumé?

His pre-season training instructions were old-school, but we did as we were told. He wanted us fit first, and the footy would come second. Having just turned twenty, this was an incredible shock to my system. My attitude towards training had improved dramatically since the age of seventeen, when I would do anything to train with Jason Cayless after school each day. But under Opes, I never trained so hard in my life.

Providing an incentive for me to go the extra mile was the fact that my $6500 contract with the Sharks was set to end at the close of the 2002 season. It would be July—considered late in a season for a player in the top 25 first-grade squad to determine their future—before I would be able to lock in a contract extension with the Sharks. So ahead of the 2002 season, my financial situation—despite a $10,000 bonus for playing first grade twice in 2001—remained a week-to-week proposition.

I knew that I couldn't rely on my football wage alone. I was in a bind, so I decided that I would use the entire 2002 pre-season to earn some extra money, and then I would quit working once the NRL season began.

Not for the first time, I picked up the phone to Brian Rule, the Sharks' Jersey Flegg trainer, who had originally prised open the door to the Sharks for me and who also owned a martial arts store in Tempe, 15 kilometres from the Sutherland Shire. 'Can I do some work for you?' I asked Brian. By the following week, Brian had given me a job—filling punching bags with stuffing. He paid me $10 for every punching bag I could fill.

The commute to Tempe each day was manageable during the early block of pre-season training, but as the intensity increased ahead of the 2002 trial matches in February, I was so physically drained and exhausted that driving to Brian's store became an added burden. Being the quality man that he is, Brian would make life easier for me by dropping a cardboard box full of punching bags to my unit, where I'd spend every night stuffing them on my lounge-room floor.

Once the trial matches began and the countdown to the 2002 NRL season was well and truly on, I thanked Brian for the work that he had given me, but reiterated that I couldn't keep juggling the workload as footy had to be my only focus.

In February 2002, I was included among Opes's first-grade squad that travelled to Christchurch for a series of pre-season trial matches against local clubs from the South Island area. We would also tackle the New Zealand Warriors in Christchurch. With a rock-hard fitness base as a result of our gruelling pre-season under Opes, the confidence and belief I carried with me as we arrived in Christchurch were nothing like my energy levels of twelve months earlier.

One year earlier, I was rising early each morning to begin work as a plumber before arriving at training every afternoon with either the Jersey Flegg or first-division squad. Now, I was training at a high level of intensity with the first-grade squad and being physically tested every morning and afternoon.

I put my best foot forward in Christchurch, earning a man of the match award in one of our trial matches. It provided me with the belief that I could cement a permanent position in the Sharks first seventeen in 2002. Just four weeks later, I was named in our Round 1 side to face St George Illawarra at Aussie Stadium in Sydney.

It was a satisfying feeling to know that the belief in myself had also developed into something real and impactful through the eyes of the Sharks' coaching staff. In a match that would see me run for over 100 metres for the first time in my career, we beat our neighbouring rivals, the Dragons, 24–18.

Our 2002 season, which would culminate with us finishing the regular season in fifth position on the competition table—after Canterbury had been stripped of 37 competition points for salary cap breaches—was underway. I would play 21 matches in first grade in 2002, and throughout the year I began to learn more about myself as a footballer and as a person, largely due to the challenges Opes continually threw my way.

There is one day in particular that year that I recall vividly. I was battling a shoulder injury prior to our Round 8 match against the Canberra Raiders, when Opes called me. 'Are you going to play?' he asked in a short and abrupt tone.

'I want to, but I don't know if I can,' I said.

'Just get it right,' Opes said before hanging up. But I couldn't get my shoulder right. I missed our 36–10 loss against the Raiders, and I felt like I had let the team and Opes down.

With my shoulder on the mend, I approached Opes a few days after the Raiders loss to see if I was going to be selected for our next match against Parramatta. 'No mate, you're in first division,' he said. I was shattered. Opes left me playing first division for the next fortnight. At the time, I was filthy. But I know now that Opes wanted to teach me a lesson, by challenging my resolve and ability to play on with pain and injury.

Our loss to Canberra was during a period in which the first-grade side lost seven straight matches. Opes searched high and low for answers, trying every coaching tool in the manual in a bid to snap our losing run and restore a few 'Ws' next to our name. At his wits' end as the losses continued to mount, Opes introduced Australia's most respected boxing trainer, Johnny Lewis, to our training sessions.

On alternate afternoons, Johnny would arrive at Shark Park, leaving us sweating, spitting and cursing. After a month of intense conditioning under Johnny, he called for a sparring session to be organised among the players. We were paired up with an opponent before we faced off in the ring.

Opes declared that I was to take on former Queensland State of Origin prop and Cronulla hard man Chris 'Beats' Beattie. This was no coincidence. Opes was aware that there was a 'young' versus 'old' divide that had begun to develop within the playing ranks, and he was using me to break down the wall between the 'boys' and the 'men'. Beats was a big man who had hands like kettle bells. I was shitting myself.

As I climbed through the ropes and into the ring, I turned to devout Christian and Sharkies teammate Jason Stevens and said, 'Say a prayer for me.' The entire team was gathered around the ring, and I knew that, as frightened as I was, I couldn't back away. I don't know how, but I ended up pummelling Beats with some heavy punches. Johnny gave me the victory. But more importantly, in those two minutes I had gained the respect of the senior players. Opes didn't say a word—he just walked out of the gym with a grin on his face.

Whether it was a turning point, I'm not sure. But from that sparring session onwards, there was a unity within the playing group that we hadn't experienced before. And to Opes's delight, it translated into results on the football field.

Amid the backdrop of drama and controversy following Opes's decision to play Dally M winner Preston Campbell in first division—which would result in Presto's departure from the club in August—we strung together eleven wins in a row, equalling the club's record run at the time of most consecutive wins. And as a result of our winning ways, I was rewarded with a new two-year deal for the 2003 and 2004 seasons.

One week before the finals, we ended the regular season with our first loss in almost three months, against the Sydney Roosters. The following week, in the opening round of the finals series, we took another beating from the Roosters, 32–20. We then took care of St George Illawarra in a do-or-die match in week two of the finals, elevating us to just one win away from the grand final. We only had to beat the New Zealand Warriors in the 2002 grand-final qualifier at Telstra Stadium to deliver the club a rare grand-final berth.

My personal development on the footy field had enabled me to progress to the starting side for the club's biggest game of the year. For the Sharks and the entire community of faithful supporters, this was our best shot in years at a first-ever premiership. But as was the case on so many occasions during my career at the Sharks, the football gods weren't on our side. We lost to the Warriors 16–10, in a game that we could've won quite easily.

After saving a try in the first half, Sharks winger Paul Mellor had the chance to level the scores at 16–all with only a few minutes left on the clock. But with the footy in hand, he collapsed just metres out from the tryline with a rib injury. So bad was the injury, he was taken to hospital after the game.

I have no doubt that we had the side to win the 2002 premiership. It would've been a dream to reach the grand final against the Roosters. I have been asked many times if that Sharks side was the best I ever played with during my career. It's such a difficult question to answer. I find it almost impossible to compare teams from different eras. But with the likes of Brett Kimmorley, David Peachey, Jason Stevens, Dean Treister, Nick Graham, myself and a young Greg Bird, there's no reason why we shouldn't have gone all the way.

At the end of the day, it was one of the many ifs and maybes every footballer experiences throughout their career. Being a rugby league player is like that. It can knock you down, just when you feel like you're getting on top. It's how you navigate through the low points that can mean the difference between success and failure.

I discovered this for the first time during the eighteen months of the 2002–2003 season. When the 2003 pre-season began, I felt that I was finally where I wanted to be in my life. I had secured a contract with the Sharks for the 2003–2004 seasons, and after playing 21 out of 24 NRL matches in 2002, mentally I had proven to myself that I could sustain the physical test of playing an entire season in first grade. But there was a curve ball I wasn't prepared for in 2003. Losing.

Winning was all I had ever known. From my days as a junior playing grand finals each year with Wentworthville, to schoolboy titles with Parramatta Marist and my first three years at Cronulla in Jersey Flegg, first division and first grade, September had always meant finals football.

Despite the Sharks' positive season in 2002, narrowly missing out on featuring in the club's first grand final since the 1997 Super League grand final, Opes swept a hugely controversial broom through the Cronulla playing ranks at the beginning of the 2003 pre-season. Gone were Matthew Johns, Chris McKenna, Paul Mellor and Preston Campbell. By midway through the 2003 season, more players would follow.

The 2003 season began in shocking fashion, with us losing our first seven games, with our non-existent defence leaking on average 26 points a game. For the first two months of the season, we sat at the bottom of the ladder with South Sydney. Something had to change. So once again, Opes went searching for the trigger.

Hoping that an old-fashioned bonding session would ignite some passion, resolve and spirit within the squad, Opes locked us downstairs inside the Cronulla Sutherland Leagues Club one afternoon in April, with more alcohol than a Tasmanian brewery. The bonding session began slowly, but with avid Sharks fan and lead singer of the Hoodoo Gurus Dave Faulkner singing songs on his guitar, the afternoon soon transformed into the love-in that Opes had been hoping for. But, unfortunately, the high fives and hugs didn't last too long.

Before we knew it, a few home truths began to spill free from the mouths of certain individuals. At one point, Greg Bird and Chris Beattie threatened to trade punches during a drinking game. Then fingers began to be pointed at each other during a debate over how poorly we were playing as a team.

The night culminated in our experienced hooker Dean Treister and classy back-rower Nick Graham—two of the club's most experienced players and fan favourites—deciding that they would leave the club for England within days. If the season wasn't already degenerating into a lost cause, then the departure of Treister and Graham was a significant hammer blow.

Largely inexperienced, with just over 30 first-grade games from my past two and a half seasons, the frustration of trying to fill the void left by so many experienced players resulted in trouble. I displayed my inexperience in handling adversity when, in Round 11 of the 2003 season, I was sent from the field for collecting Newcastle's Sean Rudder with a high tackle. It was the first and last time I was sent off during my career. I was suspended for six weeks.

Having begun the season with the aspiration of improving on what was such a successful 2002 season, I was now useless on the sidelines as my teammates lost four of their six matches while I was suspended. Over the next two months we would win just two matches, with the low point of the entire season in Round 24—it is forever etched into the record books.

Playing against us at their home ground of Parramatta Stadium, the Eels scored a club record 70-point victory over what would end up being an eleven-man Sharks outfit. My old Parramatta Marist buddy, Jamie Lyon, scored a club record of five tries as the Eels ran in fourteen tries to one, hammering us with a 74–4 annihilation.

We had two players sent off—captain David Peachey and forward Dale Newton—and at one point we were reduced to ten men, with the sin-binning of Danny Nutley. Such was the ridiculous ease with which the Eels were scoring tries against us, Opes screamed message after message from the coaches' box to his staff on the sideline, telling us to purposely stand offside for the majority of the second half. 'Tell them to do it—the ref is too scared to keep blowing penalties,' Opes barked.

Incredibly, we had led the Eels 4–0 after I was able to drag a few of their defenders over the line to score our only try of the game. That night was one of the few occasions that I felt embarrassed to be a first-grade rugby league player. It remains one of the worst performances by a Cronulla side and a night our loyal fans will never forget, for all the wrong reasons.

We had to move on from the defeat as quickly as possible, turning our immediate focus towards trying to restore some level of pride back into the black, white and blue jumper just six days later against South Sydney. In a positive turnaround of fortunes, we bounced back against the Rabbitohs, winning 54–34.

As I look back, I realise now what this period taught me as a footballer. It's how you deal with adversity that matters most to your teammates and supporters. And just as importantly, be sure to enjoy success when it does come your way, because it will only aid your ability to work harder through the down times.

For the first time in my football career, there would be no September footy for me in 2003. As much as I hated it, I needed to know what that felt like, so I could use it as motivation going forward.

Like life, footy is about riding the roller-coaster, and at the end of the 2003 season I was at the bottom of the big dipper. I played seventeen games that season and scored five tries. But it's difficult to be positive about your own game when your team is losing.

What began nine months earlier as a year full of hope and promise, ended with us finishing twelfth. As a result, there would be blood on the floor.

In December, Opes was sacked as head coach. The Cronulla board was reacting to the poor season and the angst from sponsors and members, who were demanding that a change of leadership be made. Opes had become aware that support from the Sharks' board was in rapid decline more than a month out from the end of the season. When the Cronulla directors invited local junior Stuart Raper back from coaching Wigan in England to become an assistant coach, Opes knew that it wouldn't be long before he would be bidding us farewell.

A new era was set to begin for the Sharks.

8

Everywhere Man

I've played on the wing. I've played in the centres, at hooker, in the front row, back row, lock and even at five-eighth. I'm not making this up—it's true. Of all the positions that form a rugby league team, there are only two that I was never asked to play: fullback and halfback.

On separate occasions during both the 2002 and 2003 seasons, as a result of a shocking injury toll during those two years at the Sharks, I was handed a cameo appearance on the wing in first grade. And I'll avoid providing any further details about that match. Not many people will remember it—and that's just the way I like it.

In 2004, I played in every position in the forward pack. I also spent eight games at five-eighth for the Sharks, under new head coach Stuart Raper. Stu had been appointed to the position after the disappointing 2003 season led to the departure of Chris 'Opes' Anderson.

Stu made it clear to me soon after he arrived that he believed I could play in any position on the field. I may not have thought the same, but it was refreshing to hear that from a head coach.

So when Stu asked me to play five-eighth, as a result of our first-choice options in the halves being injured, I could hardly say no to him.

I knew that I was only ever a stopgap solution at pivot. My role in steering the team was minimal given that one of the best halfbacks I've ever played with, Brett Kimmorley, was in charge of pointing our team around the park in 2004. I felt sorry for our star recruit, New Zealand Test centre Nigel Vagana, who struggled to receive any quality service of the footy, or space and time to move, while I was playing at five-eighth. However, I did enjoy the challenge.

I made sure I studied the unfamiliar role of five-eighth and what was required to achieve success for the team. I only ever scored four two-try doubles during my career and, ironically, one of those was when I played five-eighth in a match against Manly in 2004. Despite this minor success, 2004—Stu's first season as head coach—would be an indifferent year for the club.

In my fourth NRL season, I now felt like I belonged in first grade. As a club, we were determined to improve as a group, following the failure of 2003. But the confidence within the team ahead of Round 1 was soon shattered by injuries.

As part of the NRL's season-opening double-header against the Wests Tigers at Stadium Australia at Sydney Olympic Park, I lined up to tackle hard-running forward John Skandalis. As I drove my shoulder in for the tackle, the collision was heavy. We wrestled each other to the ground, and John jabbed a cheeky elbow into the back of my head.

Too experienced for me, he knew exactly how I would react and, in turn, the advantage his team would gain from my retaliation. Not for the first time—or the last time—in my career, I reacted to the niggle by throwing punches, not one of which made any contact. A scuffle ensued. When my teammate, Jason Stevens, rushed to my side, he grabbed Skandalis's jersey and threw him to the ground, also shoving me off balance in the process.

As I turned awkwardly, the impact of hitting the ground resulted in the dislocation of my right elbow. The pain was instant. Lying there with my elbow at a right angle, I wrenched it back into its socket as the referee called out my name. He delivered a final warning: behave or I would be watching the rest of the game from the grandstand.

Retreating to defend the next set following the Tigers' penalty, I put on a brave face, but I was merely masking the agony. I quickly signalled to the sideline. Former Canterbury Bulldogs forward and then Sharks trainer Simon Gillies, a renowned hard nut with an old-school approach to playing on through pain and injury, told me to get my elbow strapped and get back out on the field.

I did what I was told, strapping the elbow up in the dressing rooms before returning to the sideline. But as I warmed up in front of the interchange bench, I was in so much pain that I felt certain I was going to be physically sick. My game was over.

Scans the next day revealed significant damage: a medial and lateral ligament tear in my elbow, and a small fracture, with a section of my tricep torn. During a subsequent appointment, a specialist advised that I had two options: season-ending reconstructive surgery or round-the-clock physiotherapy in the hope that the injury would respond to treatment. Not wanting to surrender my spot in first grade and also wanting to impress Stu in his first season, I chose the latter.

After three weeks of intense rehabilitation, during which I desperately wanted to get back on the field to help the team (we'd won just one game in the first month), the Cronulla medical staff ordered me to wear a child's knee brace, which would be fixed to my elbow during every game I played for the remainder of the season. I would also require painkilling injections before every game. It may have been a slightly dramatic plan, but I don't know any player who wouldn't have said, 'Let's do it.'

I returned to the field after missing a total of four matches. Despite the early-season setback, I became comfortable enough with the brace on my elbow. I actually managed to find a rhythm and a level of consistency with my footy. My ability to wear the collisions with opposition players was also different from seasons past. Feeling stronger and perhaps better conditioned for first grade, I could tell that I was becoming a handful for the opposition.

In seventeen of my nineteen appearances in 2004, I ran for over 100 metres. I was able to run for over 200 metres on two separate occasions that year. The Sharks were impressed with my form, offering me a three-year deal—the longest-term contract that I had ever been given. But for the first time, other clubs were also showing more than just a rudimentary interest in me.

My manager, David Riolo, found that his phone was ringing frequently in the couple of weeks prior to the Sharks' offer. The one phone call that had interested me the most was from Parramatta. The head coach of the Eels at the time was Brian Smith.

My interaction with Brian up until that phone call in 2004 had been minimal. Any previous interaction with him was only when I was in the Eels' junior system, and even then it was when I was in a group scenario. I'd never met or spoken to Brian one on one before, so I didn't have a great rapport with him—although, it must be said, I didn't have a poor relationship, either.

I agreed to meet Brian and the Eels' football manager, Tony 'Zap' Zappia, who ironically would take up the role of Sharks chief executive in 2007. I felt that the meeting was held in a positive fashion. Brian sat opposite me, explaining in detail how he had been closely watching my game and my development as a player. He rattled off key statistics from my matches over the past two seasons, but he added, 'I reckon we could add a little bit of spit and polish to your game.'

Dave was honest with both Brian and Zap. He explained that I already had an offer from the Sharks on the table for three years, worth just over $100,000 a season.

I had a relationship with Zap, having met him through my extended family when I was twelve. So he didn't hesitate to call me immediately after Dave and I had walked out of the meeting. He explained that it was a pretty simple equation—Brian was torn between signing me and another player. I didn't know who that other player was, but Zap said that he wanted a lot more money than my asking price to join the Eels.

Another phone call, only a couple of weeks later, ended any possibility of me heading back to Parramatta. Dave called to say that the Eels were close to signing Glenn Morrison, from the North Queensland Cowboys. He was 'the player'. Despite the significant dent that Morrison's signing would make in the Eels' salary cap, they went with him. So I made my decision to stay at the Sharks, putting pen to paper in July of the 2004 season.

The security of a new three-year deal was the only high point of the season. The Sharks missed the finals for a second consecutive year, finishing eleventh—just one position higher than in 2003. With another disappointing season over, I reflected on my year and recalled a conversation I had had with Stu halfway through the season. 'If you continue the way you're playing, you won't be far away from representative footy,' he had said. So that became my goal moving forward.

I grabbed a pen and paper and wrote down what I wanted to achieve in 2005. Playing representative football was one of the first things I wrote down on my list. Focused on achieving my goals, I resorted to the one key ingredient that was truly the backbone to my entire career: training hard and often. What had begun in my youth, with after-school training sessions with Jason Cayless, had escalated under Chris Anderson, whose old-school methods built a resilience that allowed me to push through fatigue under adversity.

Someone who drove me during 2004 was our trainer, Simon Gillies, who had arrived at the Sharks with Chris Anderson. Simon didn't like me at first—I knew that. But through repeated sessions and effort, he slowly warmed to me.

Simon's ruthlessness and approach to training served me well ahead of the 2005 pre-season, where I strived to ensure that I was the fittest I had ever been. I introduced my own private sand-dune sessions once a week to my training—on top of the Sharks' busy schedule.

My goal to be at peak fitness for the 2005 season was supported by the arrival of a new trainer at the Sharks, Trent 'Elk' Elkin. He had a hardened exterior, but he brought a modern approach to training with his no-nonsense attitude towards ensuring that the fitness of the entire squad was his number-one priority. By the time Round 1 of the 2005 season arrived, I was rock-hard fit and ready to go. I had all the confidence of a big season ahead of me thanks to a positive off-season, under the guidance of Elk and Stu.

As a team, we flew out of the blocks, winning four out of our first five matches. We lost only two matches in our first ten games, and by Round 11—approaching the representative block of the NRL season—we sat equal first on the premiership ladder.

Playing 80 minutes and averaging over 100 metres a match, I felt—if I was ever to have a chance to achieve my goals and be selected for City in the annual City–Country Origin fixture—I couldn't have done anything more. But clearly somebody thought I could've, because when the City Origin team was announced, I wasn't chosen. I was 23, and I was gutted.

I couldn't understand why I was overlooked. It took me a few days to shake off the disappointment. What other choice did I have, but to get back on the horse? Instead of aiming for a City jumper, I switched my focus towards a sky-blue one with New South Wales for the upcoming State of Origin series.

I knew I was coming from a long way back. I had been left out of the City Origin team and what had been billed as an Origin 'selection trial', but more importantly my greatest hurdle was just how difficult it was to break into the 2005 Blues side, which was chock-full of stars. The players who made up the NSW squad had no reason to be dropped after dominating Queensland in the 2004 series.

Sometimes, it doesn't matter how much you want something. It's how you handle that rejection and learn that if you keep working hard enough, one day you will reap the rewards.

The disappointment of failing to achieve my representative goals was compounded by the flatlining of our season at the Sharks midway through 2005. After such an impressive start, we only won four of our remaining fourteen games of the season and limped into the semifinals in seventh position. But what mattered most was that we had made the finals. We were back where I wanted us to be, playing footy in September.

If there was a lack of belief in our ability to come together and succeed as a squad during the 2005 finals series, I certainly couldn't feel it. At 24, I had experienced semifinal football for the majority of my playing career. I was pumped and absolutely confident that we could turn our previous month of scratchy performances into something much more tangible.

We also had the motivation of sending off two of the club's greatest players, David Peachey and Jason Stevens, with the fondest of memories in their final season. Providing us with even further energy for the opening match of the finals series was the fact that we drew our arch rivals, St George Illawarra, at a wet and windy WIN Stadium in Wollongong.

We grabbed an early advantage by scoring first, but through too many Sharks errors the Dragons took control of the match late in the first half. With a late surge in the second half, we bridged the gap to 28–22. I scored the final try of the night with only a couple of minutes remaining, but in our last attacking raid we turned over the footy. Our season was over. We were unable to send off Peach and Stevo in the way they deserved.

The disappointment was countered by a year that, only now, I can look back on and be proud of. I was nominated for the first time for a Dally M award—Lock of the Year—which was won by Manly's Ben Kennedy. At the Sharks' annual end-of-season club presentation night, I was the recipient of the Chairman's Award after playing 25 games, averaging 80.1 minutes a game and running more than any other player that year in the entire NRL, with 3920 metres. I accepted the recognition with a smile.

But as I stood there, holding the award on stage inside the auditorium of Cronulla Sutherland Leagues Club, deep down I was far from satisfied. I wanted to still be playing. And I desperately wanted a representative jumper hanging in my wardrobe.

9
City Slicker

I'll never forget the X-ray. A disc in my lower back was not where it should be. Once out of line, it had now shifted and was stabbing on the nerve column of my spinal cord.

I had put up with back pain for as long as I could remember. Even in my teenage years, I always carried back soreness. And it would again be my back that threatened to crush my premiership dream years later, in 2016.

In January 2006, following a flight to Mount Isa for an NRL club community visit, such was the crippling pain that I virtually had to be prised from my plane seat after landing. The sharp, throbbing pain that was travelling down my legs was excruciating. Sitting still for any longer than three minutes had become impossible. Simply putting up with the pain was no longer an option.

I returned to Sydney a few days later and urgently booked an appointment with a specialist. The news wasn't good. 'You're going to need surgery if you want to play again this year,' the specialist said.

As I sat there listening, all I could think about were the goals I had scribbled down on a blank piece of paper at home. Any ambition and motivation to improve as a player and to extend myself after such a promising 2005 season were shattered inside that small doctor's surgery. But the pain was too much—I had no other choice but to go under the knife.

I was immediately booked in for surgery, six weeks before the opening round of the 2006 season. If the surgery was deemed a success, with no additional complications during recovery and rehabilitation, the specialist believed that I could be back playing by Round 6. I made it my mission to be back for the Sharks well before then.

The relief that I experienced just two days after surgery was unexplainable. My back pain was completely gone. I could walk without a rush of pins and needles running down my spine, and I was able to move unrestrictedly.

The doctor's instructions were that I wasn't allowed to perform any physical activities or place any strain on my back for six weeks after the surgery. While my comfort level had improved dramatically, the flip side was that, physically, all the conditioning I had built up over the two previous pre-seasons was evaporating. As a result of the surgery, my impressive core strength was now weakening.

The effects of the surgery would also be long-lasting. Due to the delicate procedure of removing the dislodged disc from my spinal cord, I was unable to squat or dead lift during weights training for the next two years of my career. Instead, I turned to Pilates.

Committing to almost daily classes with men and women of all ages, I attended each Pilates session intent on rebuilding the muscles that were required to support my back. I found that the Pilates classes were hugely beneficial.

As I battled my own torment off the field, on the field my teammates were also struggling. Despite the arrival of key signing Lance Thompson from St George Illawarra during the 2006 off-season, we managed just one win from our first four matches, losing to Brisbane, Manly and the Sydney Roosters.

While the specialist had said a return in Round 6 was possible, it wasn't long after the operation that I circled Round 5, against the Wests Tigers, on my calendar. This was my target round to return from back surgery. I achieved my goal, playing 26 minutes from the interchange bench against the Tigers at Campbelltown Stadium. We were soundly beaten 42–16. But the team's fortunes were about to change and, as a by-product, I also began to make major personal gains.

Winning our next four matches, the performance of my Sharks teammates aided my late bid for City–Country Origin selection. Finally, the goal I had set two seasons earlier—to play representative football—was achieved when I was selected on the interchange bench for the City Origin side by coach Tim Sheens. It was my first major representative jumper.

Even when I was in my hospital bed, recovering from back surgery four months earlier, I always believed that if I did everything possible in my rehabilitation, I would retain a chance to reach my goal. And when my name was called, I knew that all the hard work had paid off.

Back then, the City–Country Origin fixture was something special. Before the annual contest was scrapped by the NRL (it was played for the final time in 2017), we'd seen some players pull on the City or Country Origin jersey despite having appeared in only a handful of first-grade games. It took me six years of playing NRL to gain representative selection. I can never be sure, but I'd like to think the way I performed in that game played a vital role in my selection for New South Wales just two months later.

The City–Country Origin match was played in the NSW town of Dubbo. I finished the game extremely proud and quite stunned, after I was voted City Origin team Player's Player—an award that was presented after the votes of my City teammates were collated. But there was no time to lap up the applause, because the next morning I had a 5 a.m. wake-up call. I needed to hit the highway for the Sharks' match against Canberra on a Sunday afternoon in the nation's capital.

During the representative period, I was never one to take too much notice of the hype and predictions made by journalists and experts in the newspapers. One day a report can be spot-on, and the next day it can be so far off the mark it isn't funny.

Following my City–Country Origin performance, I was part of our 38–28 win over the Raiders—scoring a try and playing the full 80 minutes. The next day, the headlines suggested that after two timely performances of consistent football, I would be right in the frame for NSW State of Origin selection.

I tried to ignore the hype, knowing that any Origin selection was out my control. As I had told myself time and again previously, there was nothing more I could've done on the field to gain the selectors' attention. It's a good thing that I knew what it felt like to be overlooked by the selectors. Just like when I missed out on the Australian Schoolboys side as a teenager, and how I was forced to keep knocking on the door before earning a City Origin jumper, I chose to again use the fact that I was overlooked for Origin I and II of the 2006 State of Origin series as motivation. There was no use sulking about it—I had no other choice but to put my head down for the Sharks.

As a team, we were gaining real momentum, winning four out of five games at the midway point of the season. We were bursting with confidence and, even though we trailed Newcastle 10–0 at their home ground in Round 16, we clawed our way back into the game before finishing over the top of the Andrew Johns-led Knights.

I feel that this match was one of my best performances of the 2006 season—I even managed to set up a try for Adam Dykes in our 26–16 win. Little did I know, it was the match that would lead to one of the proudest moments of my career.

10
Baby Blue

I never liked Queensland. Even when I was eight years old, playing for Wentworthville, I would race home from Wednesday night footy training just so I wouldn't miss a minute of State of Origin and New South Wales giving it to those Queenslanders.

As a little fella, I would tell the commentators to hurry up with the pre-game chitchat, so that I could see which brave Blue would take the first run of the match. Later, as if I were still that little boy in his lounge room watching the TV, I would go hunting instinctively for that first run during every State of Origin I played in.

At our house, I'd jump on Mum's lounge as if I were riding on the back of NSW hard men—such as forward Paul 'The Chief' Harragon or fearless front-rower Mark 'Spud' Carroll—who would catapult their bodies into the Maroons' defensive line. The odd part about this was that I wasn't the most avid rugby league fan growing up.

I absolutely loved playing footy with my mates, but as far as any deep passion for a particular club or player went, I can't say I was ever like that as a boy. If anything, the only reason I declared my support for the Canberra Raiders, when other kids asked who

I barracked for, was because the Green Machine and Balmain were two of the most successful teams of the late 1980s and early 1990s—around the time I was nine and ten years old. But State of Origin . . . well, that was different.

Unlike other kids, who felt that Origin was nothing more than an obstacle in the way of their teams playing each weekend, I was mad for the whole state versus state concept. I loved the 'us' against 'them' theme that both sides thrived on, and even though my mates cheered for a different team in the regular NRL competition, everyone from my neighbourhood was united in loving New South Wales and hating Queensland. You'd struggle to find any young boy or girl living in Western Sydney who felt differently.

Fast-forward twenty years and, quite ironically, it was a Queenslander who delivered the news of my call-up and the proudest moment of my entire career. Following a midweek training session at Shark Park in 2006, former Maroons halfback Adrian 'Lammy' Lam approached me in the Cronulla Sharks' dressing rooms to break the news that I had been chosen to make my State of Origin debut for New South Wales in the deciding match of the 2006 series in Melbourne.

At the age of 24, in my sixth season of NRL, I stood there staring back at Lammy as I realised that I had achieved what I would love to say was my boyhood dream. But truth be told, this was a moment that I had probably only begun to entertain as a possibility in my mind a few years prior. As a little fella, I would cheer on Spud and The Chief, but never once did I ever consider that I would wear the same colour jersey as them.

In 2006, Lammy was working as an assistant coach at Cronulla alongside Stu Raper, and I'll never forget how excited Lammy was when he and Stu walked across the dressing room to reveal the good news. He was genuinely thrilled for me, and I guess that as a former Queensland representative himself, he was acutely aware of what being chosen for your state meant to every young player, even if I was from New South Wales.

The late Graham 'Muzza' Murray coached the Blues for the 2006 and 2007 State of Origin series. Before Muzza made the brave call to pick an Origin debutant in the third and deciding match of the series—the biggest game of the year—I would like to think he recalled my performance during my City Origin debut only a few weeks earlier.

Perhaps it was my shaven head, hair cropped short in a bid to raise money for charity, that assisted my ambition to stand out for the City side that day. Or maybe Muzza saw how determined I was to keep working hard for the Sharks, despite being rejected for Origin I and II, and he didn't want the disappointment of being overlooked to derail my footy.

With Lammy's good news, I packed a bag and caught a taxi straight to the NSW Origin team's hotel. Although I was 24, I felt like I was twelve years old when I arrived at Coogee. We then flew to Melbourne to commence our ten-day preparation for Origin III. I gained an early insight into how significant Origin was when, for the first time in my life, I flew business class to Melbourne.

Once we touched down at Tullamarine, we were handed our room numbers and told whom we would be sharing our hotel room with. I was roomed with former Australian back-rower and Manly legend Steve 'Beaver' Menzies. It was the first time I had ever met him in my life.

To this day, I've got no doubt that Beaver offered me wonderful advice that enabled me to settle in to camp as an Origin player, and that he supported me in every way possible to ensure I took a positive mindset into the decider. However, the main piece of advice I took away from Beaver—and I'm sorry for this, Steve—is how to create the most perfectly shaped Windsor knot, as I would be required to wear a tie to formal occasions during camp.

Had I got my own way, I would have avoided attending those functions every chance I had—because I mostly kept to myself that entire camp. It's safe to say, I got to know that hotel room well, largely because the only time I left my room was when I was told to. Shy and not sure how to fit in ahead of my Origin debut, I decided that I couldn't say the wrong thing or upset anyone if I kept to myself.

Having enjoyed a rich run of form with the Sharks, I knew my footy was good enough to be selected. But let's be honest, the 2006 Blues was an all-star side. It was a team that boasted incredible footballers who had been playing together at Origin and Test level for many years. Guys like NSW captain Danny Buderus, Nathan Hindmarsh, Willie Mason, Mark O'Meley, Mark Gasnier and Steve Menzies would walk into camp and pick up a conversation that they had shared during the previous camp. Or they would all stand there, cracking up at a joke they had shared during a Test match the year before.

I would just smile and go along with the joke, having no clue what they were talking about. So ahead of my debut for New South Wales, my Sony PlayStation became my best friend. I adopted a low profile, worked hard at training and, quite boringly, went to bed early. By the end of each day, I was absolutely exhausted.

As each day passed in the countdown to my debut, I found myself mentally drained by the many promotions and media commitments that came with being a NSW Origin player. Being asked to sit with sponsors, talk to media, sign autographs, conduct kids' coaching clinics and pose for photographs with fans and for the press was something that I—as a young NRL player in my sixth season with the Sharks—just wasn't used to or prepared for.

At Cronulla we had the likes of David Peachey, Jason Stevens, Brett Kimmorley and Adam Dykes to cater for the majority of media requests, sponsor lunches and dinners and the extra meetings with staff. The Origin build-up of shaking hands with strangers and smiling for TV cameras was all new to me. And, as the week progressed, I was becoming increasingly stressed that all these 'extra' commitments would impact on my preparation for the biggest game of my career.

In the latter stages of my Origin career, how I handled all those unfamiliar commitments during my first Origin camp was a story I often shared with the next rookie or group of young Blues members. It's the build-up during the week leading into a State of Origin match that can cause so many talented and gifted players to falter when the time finally arrives for them to deliver on the field. They're simply not used to being pushed and pulled everywhere for ten days before a game of football, let alone one of such enormous significance on the rugby league calendar as an Origin decider.

The media scrutiny can be over the top, with the major newspapers and TV networks from both states taking turns in sledging or targeting a particular player—or the entire team. I suppose that's what makes Origin so appealing and popular. The media coverage at that time of year is like nothing else in the game, and that can prove incredibly taxing if the subject on the front and back pages is you.

As the years passed during my own Origin career, I learned to embrace and enjoy all the fanfare that goes with the build-up to an Origin match. I felt that was a crucial ingredient to arriving for kick-off with the right level of energy and focus.

I'll give you an example of how the game, media and supporters thrive on the hatred between the two states—and this is a story

I've never told anyone before. In 2014, with the entire Sydney sporting media seated inside a Sydney hotel at a gala luncheon where the NSW Blues team for Origin I was set to be announced, I stood on stage and was asked what I thought of heading to Brisbane to take on the Queenslanders. 'We're going into a very hostile environment, and I suppose the most hostile part is during the week,' I said into the microphone. 'We don't often go to the mall too much or, if we do, we go with four or five of us because they absolutely spray us and tell us what they think of us.

'So I think if you let that part of the week affect you, it can affect your game. But if you just take it as it comes and enjoy it, enjoy that part of it, and enjoy getting up there and listening to the two-heads give it to you . . . we've got to get the job done on the field and that's where it counts.'

And with that, the media had their headline. Every news bulletin from both states ran with: 'Gallen calls Maroons fans Two-Heads'. Predictably, I became public enemy number one north of the border. But I had a fan in former NRL chief executive Dave Smith.

The next morning, NSWRL chief executive David Trodden received a phone call from Smith. 'Thank Gal for me,' Smith said. Apparently, within 24 hours of my comments, a further 7500 tickets had been sold for Origin I at Suncorp Stadium.

Smith must have remembered the impact my comments had on ticket sales, because just over twelve months later, after I had missed Origin I, he phoned me ahead of Origin II, which was to be played in Melbourne. 'I'll give you $20,000 to spark up Origin II by getting stuck into Queensland at the next press conference,' Smith said.

I didn't know how to take it. But Smith assured me that it would be for the good of the game. And besides, given I had assumed the role of State of Origin villain for almost a decade, it was hardly a stretch for me to throw a few shots across the border. So when the media gathered in Melbourne, I called out the Queensland players as 'grubby' and 'disrespectful'. I made the comments with absolutely no harm intended, but merely to ensure that, even in Victoria, State of Origin was on the front and back pages.

But in 2006, my rookie nerves had worsened ahead of my Origin debut largely because of a startling statement from Muzza. When the NSW squad was originally announced for the deciding third game to be played at the Telstra Dome in Melbourne, I was chosen on the interchange bench. But on the very first day that I arrived at the team hotel, Muzza told me that I would be starting the match.

Playing in his customary centre position in Origin I and II, Mark 'Gaz' Gasnier was surprisingly named at five-eighth along-side Craig Gower as a brand-new set of halves for New South Wales in the decider. Gaz and Gower were picked ahead of the previously chosen halves pairing from Origin I and II, Braith Anasta and Brett Finch.

In Origin I, Finch's 35-metre field goal with less than two minutes remaining proved the difference in the Blues' 17–16 victory. But a 30–6 hammering from the Maroons in Origin II in Brisbane resulted in calls for a change in the halves for the all-important Origin III decider.

Selecting Gaz at five-eighth felt like an odd move to me, as the greatest games I'd ever seen him play were at centre. But who was I to judge? And besides, I still harboured the belief that Gaz and Gower were a halves combination that could guide us to the 2006 State of Origin series win.

With nine minutes to go and New South Wales leading 14–4 in the decider, it was a bold but winning strategy from the NSW selection panel. Then the nightmare began that would devastate Blues fans on the night and provide a recurring nightmare for the next seven years. Queensland halves Johnathan 'JT' Thurston and Darren Lockyer showed everyone just why they're two of the classiest players to have ever played rugby league.

I was catching my breath from the bench when the Maroons began their comeback with just under ten minutes remaining in the decider. It all started in typical fashion, with a JT show-and-go. He needed only a millisecond to dummy his way past NSW back-rower Luke O'Donnell, glide through a small gap and find Queensland centre Brent Tate unmarked and in support. Tate raced away down the Telstra Dome sideline to whittle back our lead to 14–10 after the conversion.

We were merely marking time. With fresh legs, I was immediately recalled into the match. Unfortunately, I had a front-row seat to Queensland scoring their final try, which clinched the decider and, as fate would have it, the next seven series that would follow.

With the game clock showing four minutes remaining, Queensland kicked long to the right-hand corner of NSW winger Eric Grothe Jr. During the ensuing play the ball, NSW fullback Brett Hodgson threw a lofted pass from dummy half that appeared to float forever. Hurrying back into position for the next hit-up, I was in the perfect place to see the pass emerge from Hodgson's hands—it would be the pass that decided the series.

At first, the ball didn't seem to leave his grip too badly. Perhaps it was a gust of wind, or possibly even fate, but the ball failed to find its intended Blues receiver. Enter Darren Lockyer. The Queensland skipper swooped on the loose ball, and all we could do was watch in shock as he ran 15 metres to score the match-winning try beneath the goal posts in front of 54,833 fans. And that was it. Queensland won, 16–14, and the series was over.

It was the first series win for Queensland since 2001, and would be the first in their record run of eight straight series wins.

The gut-wrenching loss resulted in one of the quietest dressing rooms I have ever been in. Great players with much more experience than me were speechless. We all just sat there, stunned. Across the room, players were staring through the wall opposite them. Willie Mason was the first to speak. He asked the entire room, 'Is this what losing a grand final feels like?' No one answered.

I didn't know what to do. I didn't say anything, that's for sure. Perhaps it was because I was young and on debut, but I was just so happy to have made the team. Sure, I was gutted, but my disappointment with the loss was tempered by a feeling of pride—not only had I been chosen to play Origin for New South Wales, but I had also held my own during the intense match environment. That was how I felt as I sat there in silence.

It would be a week later before I would pause to think about those feelings. And wow—I had the shits with myself. I thought: 'what a poor attitude'. How could I just be happy to be in this team? You should never be content with only being 'happy' to be selected in any team, I told myself. That was when I changed my attitude and approach towards every game and every team I ever played for again.

I told myself that never again would I just be happy to part of a team, or content to just be a player on the field—I wanted to make a difference in every game, in every action. From that Origin debut forward, in every game I played, I chose to put myself out on the ledge a little.

I knew it would mean taking risks on the footy field—taking a chance down the short side or slipping in an off-load when it did not seem suitable. But for me, it was about pushing the parameters and challenging myself to go harder and further. Sometimes that attitude reaped rewards, and sometimes it also rendered me open to heavy ridicule and criticism.

It might have been my first Origin match and also my first bitter taste of defeat. But I left that series for New South Wales with an attitude that stayed with me for the remainder of my career.

11

Almost an Eagle

If it weren't for Ricky Stuart, I would have signed with the Manly Warringah Sea Eagles in 2007 and most likely finished my career on the peninsula. I was as good as gone.

My days as a Cronulla Shark met a crossroad when, one afternoon in September 2006, my manager received a phone call. It was a call that I never saw coming. But timing is everything in rugby league.

While the Brisbane Broncos and the Melbourne Storm were preparing to meet in the 2006 grand final, instability had once again engulfed the Sharks. The hunt was on for someone to replace Stuart Raper, who had been sacked a fortnight earlier by the Cronulla board, despite having one year remaining on his contract.

The end of the 2006 season had been a disaster. Failing to win a single game after Round 16, we lost ten consecutive matches—a new record for the club at the time. We finished third last on the competition ladder, in thirteenth position.

I genuinely felt sorry for Stu and the way his coaching career came to an end. A local junior and popular figure within the Sutherland Shire community, Stu was extremely passionate about achieving success at the Sharks. He desperately wanted to be the coach who delivered the club its first NRL premiership.

And he could coach, too. In fact, he was one of my all-time favourite coaches. Stu was the first coach to instil true confidence within me, while helping me to understand and realise how far I could stretch my potential as a player. Stu never coached again after being let go by the Sharks, and it was a sorry end to his coaching career. In that period of ten losses, he deserved better from us as a playing group.

The Sharks' board made the call to sever ties with Stu, well aware that given Ricky Stuart's own sacking from the Sydney Roosters that same season, the club could now make a serious play for the Australian Test coach. Having taken the Sydney Roosters to three straight grand finals in 2002–2004, the eventual signing of Ricky was considered a huge coup for the Cronulla club, which was desperate to secure their first NRL title.

Like Ricky, who took his time before agreeing to join the Sharks on a two-year deal, I was also faced with a career-defining decision. As I said, I didn't see the offer from Manly coming at all. Until that phone call from an influential member of the Sea Eagles' hierarchy, I had no intention of leaving the Sharks.

I still had the entire 2007 season left on my contract, so any thought of staying or going was not something I needed to occupy my time with. However, when the Sea Eagles made their approach, they were serious about making sure that my life going forward was with Manly. The offer was worth double what I stood to earn in 2007 at Cronulla.

Manly's rich history of premiership wins and their strong culture of success was something I couldn't ignore. I had always had a huge amount of respect for the tough brand of footy the Sea Eagles played and the ruthless attitude they always exuded.

I simply couldn't disregard the approach. So, wanting to be up-front and honest, I knocked on the office door of Sharks chief executive Greg Pierce, ready to discuss the Sea Eagles' bid to lure me away from the Shire.

Nervously, I explained to Greg that if I were to join Manly for the 2007 season, which was set to commence in just six months, I would need the Sharks' board to release me from the final year of my contract. To Greg's credit, he listened intently as I explained why I was treating Manly's approach with serious consideration. Greg said he would need a few days to discuss my situation with the board, before coming back to me with a definitive answer.

One contributing factor that I had failed to consider was the power of the fans. If you—the supporter or member—fear that your opinion carries little weight with your football club, think again. Only a few weeks earlier, I had been voted the Cronulla 'Supporters' Player of the Year' at the Sharks' 2006 presentation dinner. So when the same loyal fans caught wind of Manly's bid to steal me away from the Shire, they made their thoughts known, penning letters to Greg and posting a backlash of comments directed at the club on fan forums and on the club's website.

Reacting to the protests of Sharks fans, Greg called me straight back into his office. This time he was far less accepting or accommodating towards my predicament. 'There's no bloody way you're leaving,' he said. 'That's the end of this discussion.'

Despite what Greg had said, I could've made the Manly deal happen if I had wanted to. But if my chances of joining the Sea Eagles weren't thwarted by Greg, they most definitely were when Ricky learned of their bid to poach me.

I hadn't spoken to Ricky, even prior to being included in his Australian team train-on squad in mid-September 2006. At that time, Ricky was still in the throes of deciding if he would take over as coach of the Sharks. However, within league circles, Manly's attempts to sign me were now public knowledge.

I had just completed a training session at the Sydney Football Stadium with the Australian train-on squad and was about to head home, when Ricky walked over and asked me for my mobile number. Only a short distance into my drive home, my phone rang. It was Ricky. He avoided any small talk and got straight to the point. 'I'm not coming to Cronulla if you leave,' he said.

I laughed, not taking his threat seriously for one second. He assured me that he was serious. We then began chatting about the decision I was about to make. I spoke about my ambition and shared my goals and beliefs. We talked freely for the next 25 minutes. The more we swapped stories, the more I began to realise that Ricky had a very similar character to me. Heavily devoted to winning, we shared many common goals, none more important than wanting to win Cronulla's first-ever premiership.

As I've explained, I had had nothing to do with Ricky until meeting him as part of the Australian team train-on squad. But I was immediately drawn to his intensity and focus on winning. With the Sharks not willing to budge on me leaving, I told Ricky I would knock back the Manly offer and work under him as our coach, fulfilling my contract with the club in 2007. But beyond 2007, I gave him no guarantees.

Manly accepted my decision to stay with the Sharks in 2007, but they made it abundantly clear that they weren't done chasing me yet. The offer remained on the table to join them in 2008, once my contract had expired with Cronulla at the end of the 2007 season.

After playing in my first Prime Minister's XIII team against Papua New Guinea in October 2006, I returned to Cronulla to commence my first full pre-season under Ricky, who was intent on overhauling the Sharks. In the back of my mind throughout the 2007 pre-season was the fact that I still hadn't secured my future beyond the end of the upcoming season. And when I suffered a serious ankle injury during a trial match against South Sydney in Gosford, my stress levels were at an all-time high.

Scans confirmed that I had suffered a syndesmosis ankle ligament injury. The original medical advice was that I could miss up to three months of football. But subsequent scans revealed that I wouldn't require an operation, and with a positive recovery I would be able to return in Round 4, against St George Illawarra.

However, my focus on recovering from the injury was overcome by the process of considering one of the biggest decisions of my career—whether to stay a Shark or become a Sea Eagle in 2008. 'It's definitely weighing on my mind,' I said during an interview with *The Sydney Morning Herald* on 27 February. 'I'd like to think I'll have made a decision by the time I come back [from injury], so [going forward] I've only got to worry about footy. I'd really like to be a one-club man and stay ten years [at Cronulla], but in saying that, I do want to see what interest is out there.'

Unable to train as I recovered from my ankle injury, I spent my weekends looking at properties on the Northern Beaches. I even stayed at a mate's house in Collaroy, just so I could get a feel for the area. To be brutally honest, I really didn't enjoy the small taste of the area that I received, and the traffic on Pittwater Road was a nightmare. But Manly's offer was too good to bin on account of traffic congestion. Their three-year deal, for 2008, 2009 and 2010, was worth $300,000 more than the Sharks' offer.

I was in regular contact with Manly's recruitment manager, Noel 'Crusher' Cleal, who had moved over from Parramatta. I had always shared a solid relationship with him. On every occasion that I spoke to Crusher, he made it clear that the Sea Eagles had a

Above: Five months old and already on the move at my family's first home in Guildford.

Below: Cutie, wasn't I? My first birthday.

Right: Getting up to mischief as a three year old.

Top left: Four years of age, and my first taste of footy as ball boy for the Western Suburbs Magpies' reserve-grade team, where Dad was the trainer.

Top right: Where it all began. Playing my first season of footy as a five year old with the Greystanes Bulldogs.

Left: Under 8s with the Wentworthville Magpies. I played with the Magpies on Saturdays and the Bulldogs on Sundays.

I've always loved my bikes. Here I am as a fourteen year old on the back of a trail bike in my neighbour's backyard in Greystanes.

Road hog in Caringbah, 2013. I've owned three Harley-Davidsons, and this one was my second— a Softail Blackline.

Taking a hit-up for the Magpies against the Hills Bulls in the under 16s in 1997.

My first junior representative team. I played back row for Parramatta's SG Ball side in 1998 against the Newcastle Knights.

The new wave. My first newspaper photo in Sharks gear during the pre-season of 2002. Left to right are rookies Pat Gibson, Danny Nutley, Dean Bosnich, myself and Matt Bickerstaff. *Newspix*

What a Knight! A game to remember for Sharks fans—and one of the biggest wins of my entire career—beating Newcastle 64–14 in 2002. *NRL Photos*

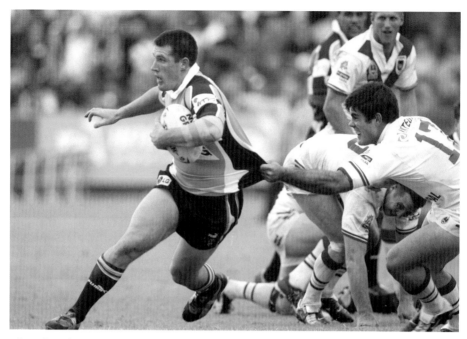

I loved nothing more than playing in the local derby against St George Illawarra. The year 2003 was a tough one for us, finishing twelfth under Chris Anderson. *NRL Photos*

I can't recall if I got the ball away here for an off-load against the Roosters in 2004. But I do recall that this was one of our best wins of the season against one of the premiership heavyweights. *NRL Photos*

A try I'll never forget, running 30 to 40 metres and fending off champion Cowboys fullback Matt Bowen to score in 2005. *NRL Photos*

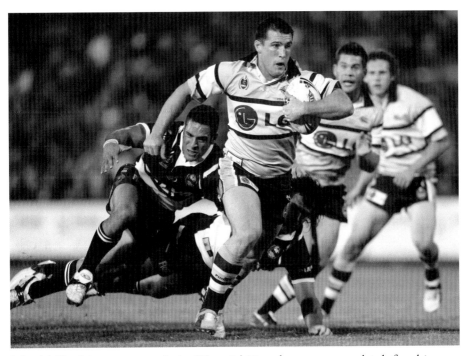

My old Sharkies teammate Luke 'Dougie' Douglas owes me a drink for this. From this tackle bust against the Panthers in 2006, I was able to put Dougie over for a try. *NRL Photos*

Looking to off-load against the Warriors in 2007.
NRL Photos

The year 2008 was a great one for the Sharks under Ricky Stuart, as we finished equal first at the end of the regular season. *NRL Photos*

The expression on our faces says it all after another loss. The 2009–11 period was tough. *NRL Photos*

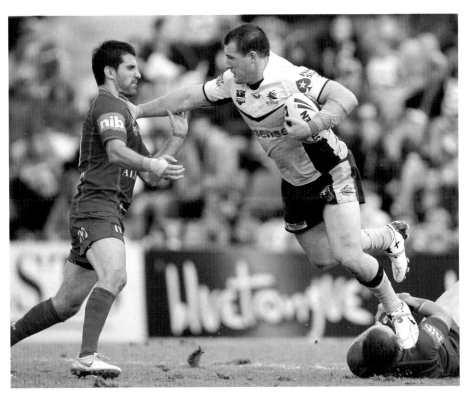

Having beaten one Knights defender in this 2010 clash, I'd like to think that I powered past my old mate, Isaac De Gois, as well. *NRL Photos*

This is a photo I love. Because it's one of my best mates in footy unable to drag me back to stop me from scoring against the Gold Coast in 2011. I bagged two tries that night. *NRL Photos*

A proud moment. Holding the Steve Rogers Memorial Trophy after beating arch rivals the Sea Eagles in 2012. *NRL Photos*

Leading the boys out during the ASADA scandal was mentally exhausting. The loyalty from our supporters before our Round 1 win against the Gold Coast in 2013 was incredible.
NRL Photos

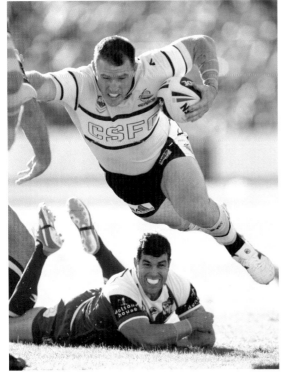

Got ya, Mick! My premiership-winning teammate Michael Ennis will hate this 2013 photo, but he was one of the best competitors I ever played with.
NRL Photos

What a horrible time this was for everyone at the club in 2014. Thrust into the role of head coach, Peter Sharp shows the strain during a post-match press conference after another loss. *NRL Photos*

A face only a mother could love. I was left with a few stitches after this heavy cut in 2014. *NRL Photos*

True story: I've known referee Ashley Klein since we were kids in Greystanes. I was best mates with his brother, Lindsay, and I would have sleepovers at his house. *NRL Photos.*

We did it. The moment I collapsed as the full-time siren sounded in the 2016 grand final, knowing that my career was complete with a premiership ring. *NRL Photos*

The best moment of my rugby league career, after winning the 2016 NRL premiership . . . and just one second before one of the most iconic photos in Australian sport. That embrace with Cronulla club legend Andrew Ettingshausen still gives me chills. *NRL Photos*

One of the most loyal men I know, Sharks trainer Mark Noakes. He was a mainstay and confidant through every up and down of my footy career. I'm so glad we were able to share this moment. *NRL Photos*

The only captain to lead Cronulla to a premiership . . . this incredible moment was for every past Sharks player and every one of our loyal supporters. *NRL Photos*

Probably my most favourite photo of all time. Just me and my little man, Kody, in the dressing room at ANZ Stadium with the premiership trophy in 2016. To be able to share that with him—and my entire family—was special. *NRL Photos*

My old mate Flanno. I shared a great bond with this special coach. We were the last to leave the ANZ Stadium pitch with the premiership trophy. *NRL Photos*

My family. Nothing in my career would be possible without them. *NRL Photos*

squad that was ready to win a premiership in the next few years. Sure enough, they won the title the following year, in 2008.

My conversations with Crusher were always positive. On numerous occasions, I would hang up the phone ready and willing to sign on the dotted line. But I wanted to respect Cronulla by giving them the last right of reply.

It may sound odd, but I was overcome by anxiety and stress every time I thought that I was ready to make a call one way or the other. I felt an attachment to the Sharks, the players, the fans and the community. My relationship with Ricky was developing, and the lure of trying to win the club's first premiership was the greatest carrot of all.

But for a couple of seasons prior to 2007, I felt that I had been well underpaid at the Sharks. The fact that Manly's offer was $300,000 more than Cronulla's only reaffirmed that belief. Having made my State of Origin debut in 2006 and been chosen in the Australian team train-on squad, I saw my next contract as my chance to finally start earning the salary of a representative player.

I had great respect for Manly as a club. Their belief that I could be their replacement for Test forward Ben Kennedy, who had retired from the Sea Eagles in 2006, was a huge sign of their faith in me, and it was a challenge I was prepared to welcome.

One way or another, I wanted my future sorted prior to my return from injury, so my manager, David Riolo, met with me at a cafe in Cronulla. Dave and I sat down with pen and paper. We ruled two columns, listing the pros and cons of staying or leaving the Sharks. I had a list of the playing rosters from both clubs for the next few years. On paper, I felt that, as far as potential was concerned, there wasn't much difference in the playing stock. It would be a few more weeks before I could make a final call.

By April, Ricky had had enough of not knowing whether I was staying or going. I, too, was tired of the mind games I was playing in my own head. Ricky could sense that I just wanted a decision made. He grabbed me in the gym after training and said, 'C'mon Gal, what's going on? I need to know. What else do you want?'

I didn't know what to say, so off the top of my head, I replied, 'Help me buy a car, a Lexus.' I knew that Ricky drove a Lexus and that they were worth about $80,000—effectively the monetary difference between Manly's bid and Cronulla's latest offer. 'If you can help get me a Lexus, I'll stay.'

A couple of days later, Ricky came back to me and said that he was sorry, but he couldn't assist with getting me the car. Ricky then asked me, Dave and Sharks assistant coach Shane Flanagan to sit down over coffee for a final meeting, to put an end to the uncertainty.

Once again, Ricky spoke of his determination for success over the next few years at the Sharks. He spoke about his confidence in the current roster and how, over the next few years, we would become a consistent force during the semifinals. However, Ricky had one final ace up his sleeve.

When Dave turned to Ricky and asked what it would mean for my representative career if I signed with Manly, Ricky replied without batting an eyelid, 'There wouldn't be a representative career.' I could tell he wasn't joking. That, along with Ricky's mission to make Cronulla a finals force, was almost enough to sway me. I just wanted one more thing.

Knowing Ricky had a close contact at Oakley Sunglasses, I said, 'If you get me a pair of sunnies, I'll sign.' Ricky quickly agreed. 'Okay, I'll stay,' I said. We shook hands and, a few days later, I signed a new four-year deal with the Sharks that secured my future until the end of 2011. To this day, I've never seen those sunglasses.

12

The Spotlight

Success and higher honours in this sport-loving nation of ours can provide accolades, recognition and flattery. It can also provide notoriety.

In 2007, for the first time in my career, I became deeply acquainted with the delicate balance between adulation and disparagement. Over the next three seasons in particular, but ultimately until the final days of my career, I would learn—on most occasions, in the hardest way—the difference between being a professional athlete with almost no profile and being an athlete with an increasing one.

As I've previously mentioned in this book, I was never a diehard rugby league fan as a kid. I didn't have idols or posters on my walls of Peter Sterling, Laurie Daley or Ricky Stuart, like other kids my age. I loved State of Origin, but I never grew up trying to be someone else, or wanting to be anyone else. I just wanted to be 'me'. And where life would take 'me', I was never sure.

Over the closing stages of my professional football career, I was acutely aware that 'me' being 'me' wasn't always what the fans, the media or the public wanted. Perhaps it was my character—raw, just like my upbringing—that some people didn't like. Perhaps it was my emotions—which, at times, spilled onto the surface, just like during my teenage years—that some people didn't like. Maybe I was just too honest.

Even though the media and the public want our sportspeople to speak freely and say what they're thinking during an interview, giving more of themselves than just the standard response of 'we're just taking it one week at a time', plenty of people tried to change 'me' during my career. And sure, I'll admit that there were times when I needed to change.

Sometimes I needed to take a step back and stay out of the spotlight. But I have always wondered—if I wasn't 'me', would I have been able to be the player I was? And, in turn, would I have ever been able to achieve the many memorable moments in my career if I had tried to be someone else?

Having recovered from the setback of an ankle injury suffered during the 2007 trials, I returned in Round 4 on a Monday night to play 43 minutes in our 40–4 thrashing of St George Illawarra at Shark Park. It was our second win of the season, and the seven-try romp repositioned us inside the top eight.

Over the next six weeks, we thrived under Ricky's tough brand of footy. While our captain, Brett Kimmorley, was in charge of steering us around the park each week, our regular starting seventeen included Isaac De Gois, Reece Williams, Ben Pomeroy, Luke Douglas and Kevin Kingston, who were all beginning to establish themselves as regular first-graders.

We had a youthful exuberance to our side. But that inexperience under adversity also provided us with challenges once injuries began to set in. As a result, the victories began to dry up. And our losses that year were the hardest type of defeats that a team can take.

Under Ricky in 2007, we lost nine games by four points or less. It was one of the most challenging and frustrating seasons of football I have ever been a part of. Our fans at Cronulla were incredibly loyal that year as they walked out of Shark Park after each narrow loss, their next week at work or school ruined by our three-, two- or even one-point deficit.

Amid the gloom, we had a handful of wins in 2007. These indicated to me that, despite our young side, there was a tough underbelly that was developing within the squad—one that we would be able to call upon in the future.

After back-to-back losses, we travelled to Kogarah in Round 13. Our gutsy 20–16 win over the Dragons was not only one of our most promising victories, but it would also be the starting point of the drama, headlines and controversy that would fill my next three seasons. Following the spiteful local derby against our arch rivals, the issue of players taking a 'dive' to gain an advantage or penalty became the lead news story of the day.

During the game, Dragons forward Adam Peek had been sent off for hitting our half, Adam 'Dyksey' Dykes, above the shoulders with his elbow. During the after-match press conference, questions from the throng of journalists to Ricky and Dragons coach Nathan Brown focused on whether Peek should've been sent off—and whether Dyksey had purposely stayed down to gain a penalty. 'Even though Dykesy would have got an Oscar, I can't condone what [Peek] did,' Brown told the reporters.

Asked about the possibility that Dykes had lain down, Ricky said, 'Look at his [bloodied] ear. He didn't lie down. It is something that is creeping into the game. I don't agree with it and it's disappointing, but eradicating it is difficult. If there's 30 seconds to go and you're down by one point in the grand final, what would you do?'

The incident ensured debate would continue for days to come. But it would be a photo of me, after being hit in the jaw by St George Illawarra's Richie Williams, that would end up on the pages of the Sydney newspapers the following day.

The photo showed me winking after I had climbed to my feet. The wink was cheeky, I'll admit. However, it was directed solely at Dragons hooker Simon Woolford, who had been at his brilliant niggling self throughout the entire match.

The photo suggested that I had conned the referee—by staying down after the hit—into awarding us a crucial penalty. But, as I said, the wink was for Woolford. Wink or no wink, Williams's hit on me was high. 'I was hit in the head and it hurt,' I told *The Daily Telegraph*. 'It didn't miss my jaw. The referee saw it, and we got the penalty.'

The incident dominated talkback radio the next day. Call me naive, but I truly didn't know what all the fuss was about. Being at the centre of that furore wasn't something I was comfortable with. I had always played the game hard. I was competitive in everything I did as a footballer.

Our frustrating season of narrow losses under Ricky resulted in us missing the top eight, finishing eleventh. Amid the disappointment was a highlight, under seriously difficult circumstances. After missing out on selection in the opening two State of Origin games, I gained my second NSW Blues jumper in Origin III—a dead rubber in Queensland—alongside my close mate from Cronulla, Greg 'Birdy' Bird.

The challenging aspect of this honour was that, in just our second Origin appearance, we were being asked to be part of a Blues side that was attempting to avoid the first Queensland whitewash in twelve years. With a nothing-to-lose attitude, we gave it everything we had.

We played physically, we pushed and shoved, and we tried to bend the Maroons backwards in every tackle. Perhaps it was our youthful exuberance and our 'no fear' approach towards restoring pride back into the sky-blue jumper that allowed us to prevail 18–4 at Suncorp Stadium.

Playing in the position of five-eighth, Birdy was named man of the match. Our aggression and determination to challenge the likes of Queensland's experienced forwards, including Steve Price, Petero Civoniceva and Tonie Carroll, resulted in high praise from the Sydney media. We woke to the headline 'Blues Bash Brothers restore pride for New South Wales'.

A month earlier, I had been the focus of negative headlines after the match against the Dragons, and now Birdy and I were receiving praise and positive press for merely doing our jobs. It was my first lesson in how the media can be a supportive tool, but it can also weigh you down at times.

Such was the performance that Birdy and I delivered in Origin III, we both earned our first call-up to make our Australian Test debut in the Trans-Tasman Test against New Zealand in October. Because we had failed to reach the finals with Cronulla, finishing just one win away from a finals berth, Birdy and I were sent to Papua New Guinea to play for the Prime Minister's XIII.

During the match, I injured my shoulder. I knew it wasn't great from the moment I reeled out of the tackle. The minute I walked from the field, I had ice strapped to my right shoulder. If there was something more I could've done to rehabilitate my rotator cuff tear, I would've. I desperately wanted to be part of Ricky's upcoming Trans-Tasman Test team.

I tried hyperbaric-chamber sessions and intense physiotherapy, and I even wore a necklace made of magnets, which I flippantly purchased after someone swore to me that it would lead to a miracle recovery. 'I just want to do everything I can—I wake up at seven in the morning, go straight to the gym, then to Caringbah Pool. I hope I'm not doing too much, actually. I'm just trying to get it right,' I told *The Sydney Morning Herald* upon my return from Port Moresby.

In between rehab sessions, I spoke to Ricky and, to his credit, he gave me until the day that the Test team was due to fly out to New Zealand—Saturday, 6 October—to prove my fitness. In the end, it wouldn't matter. The shoulder required surgery and, after the team's final session at Wentworth Park in Sydney, Australian team doctor Hugh Hazard officially ruled me out. Melbourne's Dallas Johnson, originally named as eighteenth man, was drafted straight into the starting side.

I was gutted, and that dejection was made worse when the Kangaroos smashed the Kiwis 58–0 at Westpac Stadium in Wellington. The match is also memorable because Israel Folau, at 18 years and 194 days, became the youngest Kangaroos Test player in history. My withdrawal from the Australian team capped a roller-coaster year—but the real drama was just about to begin.

If ever there was an episode during my career that epitomised the pitfalls of an increasing profile, it was the one that occurred a few days after missing out on selection for the Test match in October. After presenting trophies at a Wentworthville junior rugby league presentation day, I returned to the Shire with my younger brother, Stevie, and my close friend, Brett Sargent. We decided to head out for a few drinks at a bar in Cronulla.

Later on, Stevie emerged from the men's toilets with an anxious look on his face. 'I've just had an argument with a couple of massive blokes in the toilets—they're coming out to get me,' Stevie said. Sure enough, the men came rolling towards us.

I purposely positioned myself between Stevie and one of the guys who had been arguing with my little brother in the toilets. After a few choice words, the big fella grabbed me. I reacted by pushing him back before we then wrestled each other to the ground. Within seconds, four or five people were on top of us, including several security guards.

Once we were back on our feet, we traded a few more words before we cooled down and called a truce. We shook hands, and he said, 'Let's leave it at that.' We both agreed to move on and forget about it. While I was fine with leaving it there, I had a sixth sense that something wasn't right.

The next morning, I received a phone call from the owner of the bar. 'This guy is going to cause you trouble—you should consider giving him some money to shut him up,' he said. I wondered if he was serious. I hadn't thrown a punch and, the way I saw it, I was simply looking out for my younger brother.

Wanting to avoid any controversy or scandalous headlines, I pondered how much money I would have to pay him. Maybe $1000 or $2000? But why should I? It was nothing more than two blokes arguing after a few drinks. There was pushing and shoving, and that was it. Why do I need to pay him?

So I told the owner of the bar, 'No, I'm not paying him.' A few hours later, Cronulla Sharks chief executive Tony 'Zap' Zappia called. Zap said that he'd received an 'off-the-record' phone call from a lawyer claiming to be a representative of the guy who I had wrestled with. The lawyer was asking for $50,000 to make the drama go away.

I was gobsmacked. I couldn't believe what I was hearing. The last thing I recall doing at the bar was shaking hands with the guy as we agreed to forget what was nothing more than a push and shove that night. But now this? 'No way, Zap—that's ridiculous,' I said. 'I'm not giving him $50,000. I'm not giving him anything.'

By 6 p.m., the guy had appeared on the national news, claiming that I had beaten him up. Within an hour of the news bulletin airing, a police officer had called and asked me to attend Sutherland Police Station to answer some questions.

I still couldn't believe how far this had gone, but, wanting to cooperate, I drove myself to the police station as requested. It was the best thing I could've done because, during the inquiry at the police station, I was shown the CCTV footage of the incident. It wasn't the grainy footage you usually see on the latest episode of *COPS*. It was crystal-clear imagery of the entire incident.

The pictures clearly showed the guy grabbing me first and then our wrestle to the ground. The police were satisfied with my version of events. I was never interviewed by the police again, nor did I ever hear of the big guy again. Had I been another player, fearing what the news of a wrestle inside a bar could do to my career, I could've easily been bribed into parting ways with $50,000. It was a valuable lesson.

I would like to say that this is where my dramas ended. But, unfortunately, there would be darker days to come.

13

Captaincy Meets Controversy

When I arrived at Cronulla at the end of 2000, I had no way of knowing that I would retire from professional rugby league as the longest-serving captain in the Sharks' proud history. To be frank, I would've thought that the notion of being named as a captain of any NRL team was absolute madness. But to finish my career having shared the same responsibilities as so many great former Cronulla captains—including Mitch Healey, Andrew Ettingshausen, Brett 'Noddy' Kimmorley, Gavin Miller, David Hatch, Dan Stains and Steve Rogers, to name only a few—is one of my proudest achievements.

Becoming captain of the Sharks was never something I actively campaigned for. Rather, it was a role I inherited. It began on a part-time basis at the end of the 2007 season, before Ricky Stuart appointed me as the full-time Cronulla captain ahead of the 2008 season.

Noddy, our halfback and captain, was sidelined due to a knee injury that had occurred in the 2007 State of Origin series. During his absence, I was able to experience what it meant to lead my Cronulla teammates out onto Shark Park for the first time.

Noddy was a special player. After playing halfback his whole life, he had naturally developed into a vocal leader and a person of authority as he marshalled his teammates around the park on a weekly basis. His ability to communicate and his knowledge of the game were unrivalled at our club. He could pick apart the opposition with a pinpoint pass or kick, or by steering us towards a particular part of the field. All we had to do was follow his lead and do our job.

I was a very different character to Noddy. In the majority of the matches where I captained the Sharks or New South Wales, I can count on one hand the Churchillian speeches I attempted. When I spoke, I preferred to speak calmly and straight to the point. On the field, I always wanted to lead by example and trust that my teammates would follow. It definitely took time for me to learn the responsibilities of being a captain.

In my final few years as Cronulla captain, I purposely took a step back from the role in a bid to encourage the development of the club's next crop of young leaders, in particular Wade Graham. In the pre-season of 2016, I vividly recall huddling together Wade and our halfback, Chad Townsend, after training one day at Shark Park. 'Don't think you're treading on my toes by speaking up and taking the team in a certain direction,' I told them. 'I don't need to be the only voice in this team. You should feel comfortable that I'll take your lead if you want to go in a certain direction.'

I was 26 when Ricky appointed me Cronulla captain in 2008. 'To have the job on a permanent basis is a great honour,' I said during a press gathering after being given the title. 'Getting the news today is a big thrill. Noddy will be a hard act to follow, but I realise I still have a lot to learn as far as the captaincy goes, and he's one guy I'll be looking for to provide advice and guidance.'

The thing is, if it weren't for Noddy's sacrifice, I probably wouldn't have assumed the role of captain at the time that I did. 'While I know I've still got plenty to offer the team, I thought it best that I worry about myself and my own footy rather than also dealing with the responsibility of the captaincy,' Noddy told journalists at the time. 'Gal did a great job while I was on the sideline last year. I'm sure he'll do well in the role again next season, and I'll be giving him my 100 per cent support.'

As captain, one of my first duties was to represent the club at the 2008 NRL season launch. I wanted to keep a low profile. But as I was sipping a glass of water at the back of the room, a handful of reporters walked over and asked me to predict the level of success the Sharks would have during the upcoming season. 'First things first, we'll beat Manly in Round 1,' I said confidently. And we did. Despite being outsiders with the bookies, we won 16–10 at Brookvale Oval, one of the toughest road trips in the NRL and especially for our club.

We had formed a strong roster heading into the 2008 season under Ricky, with two quality halves in Noddy and five-eighth Brett Seymour. We boasted a hardworking pack that included Adam Peek, Bryan Norrie, Kade Snowden, Luke Douglas, Greg Bird and myself, with a sprinkling of spark in attack from the ever-elusive Brett Kearney at fullback. And our frustrating 2007 season of narrow losses had enabled our group to develop a certain resolve, leading to a sense of optimism that we might just be able to return to the finals in 2008.

In Round 2, we travelled south to Melbourne. At the full-time whistle, we had clinched a one-point win, 17–16, at Olympic

Park Stadium. In our first two matches, we had managed victories at the two toughest away venues in the entire competition. March was not yet over, but already the media and the bookies were talking up our chances, saying that this could be the year of the Shark. How quickly a week can change your fortunes in football.

We travelled to the Gold Coast in Round 3 of the season. We lost the game, but that's not what made this match the focus of mass media coverage. It all began when I lined up to tackle Gold Coast Titans forward Anthony Laffranchi. He ran straight at me and, as I bent my back to make the tackle, our heads clashed heavily. When I stood up out of the tackle, I could see blood beginning to spill from Laffranchi's head. I touched my own forehead. I was okay—no blood.

Wanting to gain any advantage over my opponents, I looked back at Laffranchi—who was one of the Titans' best players—and thought, 'Beauty, he'll have to leave the field now because he's bleeding.' There was nothing untoward or illegal about the tackle, but I immediately felt that with him being unable to stay on the field, it would only aid our chances of victory.

Laffranchi spent a good period of the first half off the field before returning with the cut on his head now covered in strapping tape. As soon as he grabbed the footy, I prepared myself to again meet him in the defensive line. I thought that if I could rattle him a second time, it might leave him questioning if he really wanted to keep bringing the footy back to us each time.

I played my footy like every hit-up was a battle. I took every tackle personally, and I never wanted to let my opposition get over the top of me. So as I rose to my feet after tackling Laffranchi,

I placed my hand on the tape strapped over his cut before lever-aging off his head to get to my feet. Not once did I 'rip' or 'rake' at Laffranchi's head, as Titans chief executive Michael Searle tried ever so hard to suggest to the local media on the Gold Coast at the time.

The on-field referee saw nothing illegal in the tackle. I was penalised simply for holding down Laffranchi for too long. Our winning start to the season would come to an end that night, going down to the Titans 18–4. After the game, Ricky directed a heavy verbal barrage my way because I had given away that penalty to Laffranchi.

As a group, we decided to move on quickly from the loss and prepare for our next clash with St George Illawarra. If only I could've been so lucky. By the time we arrived back from the Gold Coast, it was like rugby league's version of Armageddon had occurred. Switching my phone on upon landing in Sydney, it began humming. As we waited for our bags, I turned to Ricky and said, 'There's talk that the match-review committee could suspend me for that tackle on Laffranchi.'

Ricky thought I was crazy. 'Please! What, you'll get suspended for getting up with your hand on his head?' he snapped. 'That happens in every game.'

By the time I had driven home to Cronulla, the media was going into overdrive. It only got worse when I woke up the next morning. The back-page headline read: 'Gallen's a grub'. And so it went on . . . for the next four days.

One Fairfax reporter didn't hold back, for some reason suggesting that I should go to gaol for what I had done. That's right, prison. It was a bizarre rant that also included a dare to file a defamation case against him.

Amid the firestorm, Ricky was also being pressured by sections of the media to strip me of the Cronulla captaincy. 'Certainly, I wouldn't take the captaincy off Paul for this, no,' Stuart told Sydney radio station 2KY. 'I've got a bloke who is very passionate and emotional about the job, and there's no way that I would take it off him. It's just something he has to learn from. I'm disappointed, but disappointed for the players.'

As was often the response of the administration at the time, the NRL ultimately bowed down to media pressure. I was hit with a grade-two contrary conduct charge and given a three-week suspension. It wasn't Long Bay, like some were asking for, but it was still a heavy price to pay.

It was in the same game that I was accused of grabbing Gold Coast forward Josh Graham on the testicles. I can't deny that it happened, but it was certainly not in the context that Graham or others were claiming. In a bid to achieve a quick play-the-ball, as I was tackled I pushed my hand up, hoping to remove the Titans' defender who was on top of me.

In the process of shoving my hand, bang—the palm of my hand smashed upwards, right in between Graham's legs. It just happened. I never thought of intentionally grabbing Graham on the 'wheels', as some reports claimed. The match-review committee also agreed that it was merely an accident and that I had no case to answer.

What frustrated me about this incident was that Graham felt the need to use a reporter to complain publicly. I can't tell you how many times I was grabbed on the testicles during my career—it was at least twenty times. But not once did I run to a reporter to complain about being grabbed on the 'wheels'.

I have also been eye-gouged by one of the biggest names to ever play the game. The outing of his name would have made front-page news for a week. But did I want to drag his name through the mud? No, never.

As I said, I was never penalised for the testicles incident or charged by the judiciary.

14

Roo Beauty

My three-game suspension following the Anthony Laffranchi incident left me shattered. For Rounds 4, 5 and 6 of the 2008 season, I was of little use to my teammates. I was their captain, but how was I leading by example? By watching from the sidelines. It was a poor way to commence my term with the 'C' next to my name.

I was fortunate that the boys, in my absence, began the season with purpose and vigour, dropping just one match during the length of my suspension. By Round 6, the boys had conjured a 4–2 winning ratio.

As content as I was with how the team was travelling, a tight knot remained in my stomach. I was certain that my three-week ban would ultimately cost me the chance to achieve my longstanding goal of representing Australia. The suspension would leave me with just one game to play before the Kangaroos squad was chosen for the celebratory Centenary Test match against New Zealand at the Sydney Cricket Ground in May.

In my return match from suspension, against the Wests Tigers in Round 7, I had just 80 minutes to show Ricky and the selectors that I was worthy of being chosen to make my Test debut. Dallas Johnson had replaced me in the Australian team following my withdrawal from the Trans-Tasman Test six months earlier, so I was well aware that I would need a strong performance to prove that my fitness levels hadn't suffered after three weeks on the sidelines.

Disappointingly, we lost a tight match to the Tigers, 20–16. Despite the loss, I enjoyed one of my better games, playing the entire match to finish with 203 metres, eleven tackle busts, nine off-loads and two line breaks. It was enough to satisfy Ricky and the selectors.

A few days later, I was chosen to make my Test debut, playing in the back row. I had achieved my goal. And what an experience that entire week was! I headed into camp with my good mate, Greg Bird, who was chosen at lock, and I was playing with the likes of Billy Slater, Darren Lockyer, Johnathan Thurston and Cameron Smith for the first time in my career.

I was roomed with champion Queensland front-row forward Petero Civoniceva. I would quickly learn that Petero is an even better human being than he is a footballer—and he was a damn good footballer. Petero is one of the nicest people I have ever met in rugby league. I was just a rookie, but Petero couldn't have been more accommodating and helpful in making sure my preparation was spot-on if he tried. Of a morning, if I was asleep and the room was still dark, he would resist switching on the light to get ready for the day, just so he wouldn't disturb me.

Prior to kick-off in my Test debut, we—both the Australian and New Zealand players—stood as one, facing the packed SCG members' pavilion. The crowd quietened down as a minute's silence was held for the sad passing of legendary coach Jack Gibson, who had lost his long battle with illness that afternoon. The moment of respect only added to the occasion.

I made an effort to keep my emotions in check in readiness for my first hit-up for my country at the revered Sydney Cricket Ground. It was the first time I had ever played at the famous old ground. From start to finish, it was a night loaded with what are now lifelong memories.

Images that are forever etched on my mind include wearing the Kangaroos' traditional maroon-and-blue hooped jersey, and Mark Gasnier's memorable try as a result of Greg Inglis's freakish over-the-shoulder flick pass. And, yes, so is scoring my first Test try for Australia. It might have been a simple barge-over try from short range, but I can still hear the noise and feel the incredible rush of excitement that raced down my spine as I planted the footy down for my country.

We led the Kiwis 22–0 after 22 minutes. Although we took the foot off the gas before closing out eventual winners, 28–12, it was a special victory cloaked in tradition and occasion.

The intensity of an NRL season doesn't allow you to soak up your own personal success for too long. The rugby league machine simply doesn't work like that. If it's a weekend between March and October, your club demands that you suit up for them—it's as simple as that. It doesn't matter whether you've won a Test match for your country or represented your state the night before, your club wants you to focus on them once that full-time whistle blows.

So, with little time to celebrate at the Sydney Cricket Ground, I woke early the next morning to catch a taxi straight to the airport with Ricky and Birdy. We were flying direct to Townsville for Cronulla's Round 9 match against the North Queensland Cowboys.

Playing off the interchange bench, I was given 46 minutes of game time by Ricky. A first-half scoring blitz, which saw Fraser

Anderson, Brett Kearney, Luke Douglas and me score tries, enabled us to hold off the fast-finishing Cowboys and record our fifth win of the season.

Having been chosen for only one State of Origin appearance for New South Wales in 2007—in Origin III—I was determined to be named for the opening game of the 2008 series. Because I had been chosen for Australia in the Centenary Test, I would've felt hugely embarrassed had I not been able to secure a spot in the Blues side under newly appointed NSW coach Craig Bellamy.

However, I had quickly learned throughout my career to never take anything for granted. And until my name was read out as starting lock for Origin I in Sydney on 21 May, I refused to listen to anyone who stated that I was a certainty to make the team.

Craig's appointment as NSW coach, after Graham Murray had stepped down following two series losses, was considered a major shift for the Blues. He had been rewarded with the NSW post following his success at the Melbourne Storm. Craig had also gained a wealth of experience as Country Origin coach and assistant coach with the Kangaroos. Craig's mission was to return the State of Origin shield back to New South Wales, and he felt the best way to do that was to use the same winning tactics he had implemented at the Storm.

In front of a parochial home crowd of 67,620 at ANZ Stadium, Craig and the entire state of New South Wales enjoyed a winning start to the 2008 series. Dictating terms thanks to the astute early kicking game of Blues halfback Peter Wallace—whose raking kicks down field forced Queensland fullback Billy Slater to repeatedly return the football from his own tryline—we were able to create a winning platform. This allowed us to sap the energy of the Maroons and slowly, over 80 minutes, break down their well-oiled machine.

My mate, Birdy, enjoyed a night he'll never forget. So dominant was Birdy that he was heralded as the Blues' version of Queensland's very own King Wally Lewis by rugby league Immortal Bob 'Bozo' Fulton. Birdy had a superb game, with his in-your-face defence rattling the Queenslanders, and his control at five-eighth alongside Wallace overshadowed the great Johnathan Thurston.

After we had held on to an 18–10 Origin I victory, Birdy was named man of the match, providing him with an avalanche of much-deserved praise. 'What Greg Bird did tonight shows he can handle pressure on a consistent basis. It shows he is made for this type of football,' Bozo told *The Daily Telegraph*. 'He is Wally-Lewis-like in the way he plays the game. He takes pressure off his halfback with his defence, and he's got a better passing game than anyone gives him credit for. Like Wally, he is very intimidating. He has that air about him. I'm not saying he is a carbon copy— but he has that consistency at this level.'

When the press asked me how I felt about Birdy being compared to Lewis, I disagreed slightly with Bozo. Not because I wanted to be disrespectful to Bozo or Birdy, but because I thought that we should liken him to one of our great NSW players of the past, instead of a great Queenslander. 'Wally was a Queenslander, so I don't want to put Greg alongside him,' I told the reporters. 'We'll have to think of someone from New South Wales.'

Queensland was panned by the critics for its Origin I performance. The public was led to believe that the series was ours—all we had to do was turn up. But as anyone who knows anything about Origin realises, it's how you perform in all three games, not just one match, that counts. The Maroons would have one more chance to save the series, at none other than their home ground of Suncorp Stadium, in front of 52,000 screaming Queenslanders.

Looking back, their response was predictable. We were completely dominated from start to finish, thrashed 30–0 by the time the final siren sounded. Greg Inglis, who had produced the worst performance of his career in Origin I according to the critics, delivered a man-of-the-match performance in Origin II. Our attempts to target half Scott Prince were nullified by his Queensland 'bodyguard', Brent Tate, who finished with over 30 tackles for the match. It was one of those games where the more we tried, the bigger the hole we dug for ourselves.

In the dressing rooms after the match, Craig spoke to us about learning from our mistakes. Amid the doom and gloom, he reminded us that only two weeks earlier we had been successful.

NSW teammate Craig Fitzgibbon was asked by the Sydney media if, given the drubbing, we could still win the decider in Sydney. 'Course we can,' he said. 'It's going to be hard. Sometimes you're not good enough on the night and we weren't, but we'll go back home for game three and give it a good lick. This is a good kick in the arse for all of us, I think.' Fitzy was spot-on.

We arrived for Origin III in Sydney with a feeling of confidence within the group, despite seven positional changes. Queensland retained the identical seventeen from Origin II.

A knee injury to Birdy, which he had suffered while scoring a try for the Sharks during our Round 15 win over Parramatta, robbed him of the chance to play in the decider. For game three, NSW selectors chose Braith Anasta and Mitchell Pearce, in his Origin debut, as a brand-new halves combination. As a group we shared the added motivation of sending captain and champion NSW hooker Danny Buderus out with the shield in his final Origin appearance.

The intense first half was everything you would expect of an Origin decider, and only two points—it was 10–8 in our favour—separated the sides at half-time. The second half wasn't much different. Even when Nate Myles survived being sent off for a lifting tackle on Blues prop Ben Cross—a tackle that later led to Nate being suspended for six weeks—I felt like the momentum was behind us.

But with thirteen minutes remaining in the decider, Johnathan 'JT' Thurston pulled our pants down. He did so with the one play we had focused on in the lead up to the decider—his famous show-and-go. Without fail, we had trained for that play during every single training session under Craig. But sure enough, that's what beat us.

NSW teammate Brett White couldn't slide across in defence in time, and halfback Mitchell Pearce was a millisecond too slow, as JT sliced through our defensive line positioned on the halfway line. He then found the ever-dependable Billy Slater in support, who put the ball down underneath the posts.

There was still enough time for us to level the match, but we were unable to find what was required. We lost 16–10, and Queensland recorded their third straight series win. At that point, it was the worst defeat I had ever experienced in my career. I had never felt a greater emptiness after a loss than that night.

Having led the series 1–0, we had been thrashed in Queensland and then beaten on our home turf. It would take me days, if not weeks, to get over it. The emotional and physical exhaustion that I felt after those three games was the equivalent of the toll that a whole NRL season took out of me. I would have to wait until 2011 before I was able play all three matches of an Origin series again. That's an indication of how many variables are at play before each game of every series, and how nothing can be taken for granted as a footballer.

I felt numb as Queensland paraded the shield around a half-empty ANZ Stadium. The pain would quickly turn to paranoia, as I was about to become the focus of the loss after giving away three crucial penalties during the match. The most significant of the three came when I dropped my shoulder into JT as he ran to chase his own kick. I put my hand up—it was a definite penalty, and a costly one. When isn't a penalty in Origin costly?

Devastated, and rightfully so, the emotional NSW fans needed a punching bag. Having played the role of villain earlier in the NRL season thanks to my run-in with Laffranchi, I bore a large proportion of the blame for the Blues' series-deciding defeat. That hurt.

So powerful is the beast that is the State of Origin, the level of disappointment from Blues fans led to further calls for me to be stripped of the Cronulla captaincy. My aggressive playing style—which had been applauded and underlined by the creation of the media-driven 'Blues Bash Brothers' only twelve months earlier—was now under scrutiny for being too contentious. The way I played had begun to polarise the league community. Once again, Ricky was under pressure to hand the captaincy to someone else at the Sharks who would be 'more fitting for the role'.

Amid the backlash, I received a phone call from Birdy, which at the time was telling. 'We're in this position [leading the NRL competition] because you play with your heart and soul,' Birdy said. 'The whole team loves who you are, the way you play and what you're about.' It was huge for Birdy to lift my spirits at that time. He was telling me to stay strong and continue to lead the Sharks.

As I said, giving away the JT penalty is something I happily put my hand up to. It was a poor decision. But there was no way in this world that anyone could say that the way I played in that decider cost us the result. I was out there, along with my sixteen NSW teammates, busting my backside for that victory.

In the end, we were beaten by a slice of individual brilliance from JT. We had more than ten minutes left on the clock to score after Slater's try. But Queensland was too good. The side would remain that way for a few more years to come.

15

Strike Action

The competitive footballer I strived to be each time I ran out onto the football field was far removed from the man I was once I walked back into the dressing room. On the field, I wanted to run where other players would think twice about running. I wanted to be that player who my teammates could count on to be stretching to make a tackle, whether the tackle needed to be made in the first minute or the last minute. However, this didn't mean that, once I walked back through the front door of my home, I was unable to press pause on my competitive juices and resume the role of loving father, son or mate.

It was in the latter stages of my career that I began to understand how important the balance between family and footy is. They were my two loves, and so during my career I worked as hard as possible on making both a success.

There were many layers to my love affair with rugby league: the years of sacrifice, the training, the pursuit of something that may not be achieved. And on the good days, that unexplainable sweet smell of a winning dressing room.

Unlike in everyday life, where we can choose who we forge relationships and friendships with, in professional sport—particularly a team sport such as the NRL—you are largely unable to pick who your mates are. Rugby league forces you to befriend people, personalities and individuals that you probably would never have otherwise associated with in your life had you never pulled on a pair of footy boots.

I suppose it is like that in most office blocks, worksites and industries. It's not a bad thing; it assists your own personal growth as an individual. And sometimes, on the odd occasion, those teammates or workmates become genuine lifelong friends.

Greg Bird was one of my closest mates throughout my footy career, on and off the football field, and he continues to be a lifelong friend. The platform for our mateship is that, overwhelmingly, we share very similar traits and characteristics. We are both extremely competitive—almost obsessed—and we both despise being beaten.

It's that competitive streak which led Sharks head coach Ricky Stuart to pull us both aside one day after training in 2007. 'You two better be careful. I've seen competitive mates like you two finish up punching the lights out of each other,' Ricky warned. We both laughed it off. But Ricky couldn't have been more serious. And sure enough, he was right.

It was during a night out with Birdy and half a dozen sponsors of the Sharks in 2007 that we clashed. Having had a few too many drinks, Birdy took offence at something I had said to him as we were playing a game of pool at a pub in Cronulla.

We traded cheap banter and as a joke, I told him to meet me outside, where we would settle our differences. As Birdy put down his drink and made his way directly towards the exit, he had no idea that I had absolutely no intention of going outside. I just wanted to sell Birdy a dummy, hoping that he would grow tired of waiting outside and head home.

What felt like a few hours later, I decided it was time to call it a night. As I peeled open the door to leave the pub, the first face I saw staring at me from across the road was Birdy's. He had been sitting there waiting the entire time. He called out, and I headed over to him.

Sure enough, we picked up arguing where we left off, over what I would never be able to recall. Safe to say, it was nothing of any significance. Walking towards Birdy in the dark of night, I was just about to stand face to face with him when, without warning, I collapsed heavily and fell flat on my face at his feet. I had walked directly into a landscaped rockery that happened to be hidden by the shadows.

Instead of laughing, Birdy reacted by jumping straight onto my back. Pinning me down, he had every chance to teach me a lesson right there and then. But he didn't. He let me up, said a few more words, and then we went our separate ways.

The next morning, as was typically the case, Ricky's 'spies' had told him about Birdy and me and the events of the night before. Ricky rang Birdy and me, telling us to meet him before training at the Greenhills Beach car park in Cronulla. Once there, Ricky stood in front of us and said, 'You two can either shake hands or you can fight each other right here and now.' He then went to sit in his car while Birdy and I contemplated his proposal. Sure enough, we shook hands. Birdy later told Ricky, 'I might be tough, but I'm not stupid.'

It was the mateship between Birdy and me that, while severely tested, allowed us to pull through the turmoil of the 2008 season. Amid my own ups and downs with the Anthony Laffranchi suspension, my Test debut for Australia and the pain of losing the State of Origin series with New South Wales, 2008 was also the year when I watched Birdy struggle through extreme pressures, uncertainty and frightening lows. It was the year that altered Birdy's life and career forever.

On a Sunday morning in late August, my phone rang. The night before, we had beaten the Sydney Roosters 22–0. It was a convincing victory and one that would give us huge momentum going into the next month of finals football.

I was watching a mate compete in a jujitsu competition in Sydney when Birdy's name appeared on my mobile phone. As soon as he said, 'Hi mate', I knew something wasn't right. His voice sounded low and almost scared.

He was distraught and, because he was rushing through whatever it was he was trying to tell me, I could hardly understand him. I told him to calm down, stop talking and that I would meet him in person. By the time I began driving towards Birdy's house in Cronulla, I had learned the significance and serious nature of what was about to transpire.

Birdy's name was all over talkback radio and news bulletins, with allegations of an altercation between him and his girlfriend. It was to be day one of a media frenzy that would continue unabated for the next 72 hours.

It was much sooner, however, that Birdy was cut off from any involvement with the Cronulla club. The Sharks moved quickly to distance themselves from the allegations surrounding Greg. With pressure from the NRL and threats from major sponsor Harvey Norman that they would pull their sponsorship if Greg were allowed to continue playing, there was little wiggle room for the then financially strapped Sharks to support Birdy. He was immediately banished from all club duties, including playing or training, and he was cut off from everything he had ever known as a professional rugby league player.

As difficult as the allegations were for Birdy and everyone involved at the club, I was a mate and, without knowing the intricate details surrounding the allegations—which were being played out every day in the media—I chose to do what any friend would do. I kept a close eye on my mate.

In his column for *The Sunday Telegraph* that diarised the week following Birdy's suspension, Ricky wrote: 'I have been having consistent dialogue with Gal, who is my biggest ally and greatest fear. He is Greg's best mate, and you can't tell a person how to handle tough times. I am keeping my eye on him.'

To this day, I have never once asked Greg what happened that night. I doubt I ever will. My only priority at the time was to throw an arm around my mate.

As captain of the club, I realised quickly what the loss of Greg from our team would mean to our chances of trying to win the club's first premiership. We were firing on all cylinders under Ricky— we had begun the 2008 season strongly, and from Rounds 12 to 16 we had won five straight matches. The loss of Birdy from our squad and the impact of his omission frightened me.

Almost every morning before training, I would talk to Ricky and our chief executive, Tony 'Zap' Zappia. 'What would other clubs do in this situation?' I kept asking.

Ricky, who was even more competitive than me, didn't disagree with the point I was trying to make. He was of the same opinion— that we needed Greg if we truly wanted to progress deep into the finals. But Ricky also knew that he was bound by the decision that the Sharks' board of directors had made.

Realising that neither Ricky nor I were going to sway the firm hand of the board, we—as a team—knuckled down, intent on driving the club towards the 2008 NRL finals series. Our first match without Birdy would be Round 25 against the Wests Tigers at Leichhardt Oval. It would be Friday night football, just five days after Birdy had phoned me, worried and distressed.

Our week began with news crews and reporters surrounding Shark Park. It was then, inside the four walls of our dressing room, that Ricky pulled the team together and handed each player a piece of paper. We were asked to write three areas where we felt we could improve as individuals and as a team. He then put every slip of paper into a box. They would remain secret until they were read out at a team meeting the following Monday.

Wanting to further galvanise the team, Ricky also decided that we would spend the night before our clash with the Tigers together as a group at a North Sydney hotel. For a Sydney match, it was an unprecedented move. By 9.30 p.m. the following night, we had thrashed the Tigers 32–6.

'Not many football teams could get through the kind of questions we've been asked outside of football this week,' Ricky said inside our winning dressing room. 'You don't win games like that if you don't stick together. I'd like to thank the senior players, Gal, Noddy [Brett Kimmorley], Rossy [Ben Ross], Nuts [Danny Nutley] and Cov [Luke Covell].'

After a Sunday team barbecue, we travelled to Townsville for the final round of the regular season. We beat North Queensland 28–22 to finish equal first with Melbourne and Manly on the competition ladder. It was only due to our inability to post big scores—with our attack inferior to both the Storm and Sea Eagles that year—that we would be relegated to third spot on the ladder. Our for-and-against stats were terrible.

Finishing third meant we would face Canberra at Shark Park in the first week of the finals. With Birdy watching on from the grandstand, we trounced the Raiders 36–10—and suddenly, all the hysteria and fear that we would struggle without our star player had been silenced. 'Everybody is trying to win a grand final,' our halfback, Brett Kimmorley, told the reporters at the after-match press conference. 'We've got a good bunch of blokes who are enjoying the ride.'

Not only were we winning without Birdy, but we were also just 80 minutes away from the club's first grand-final appearance since the Super League decider against Brisbane in 1997.

The damaging headlines had been replaced by talk that, through all the adversity and setbacks, this Cronulla team had galvanised and could win the club's first grand final without their suspended star, Greg Bird. Not surprisingly, Birdy had a much different view. And so my phone kept ringing.

Birdy would call, day in and day out, adamant that we couldn't make the grand final, let alone win our first premiership, without him. I found myself trying to console him, while also thinking to myself . . . 'well, hang on a second Birdy, we ARE winning'.

At training, all conversation with Ricky and Zap about Birdy's chances of coming back to play had virtually broken down. Instead of discussing Birdy's situation every day, it would become, at best, a once-a-week conversation. I guess that's how football clubs operate. Success can smooth over the debris sitting just under the surface.

Living in exile and desperate to resume his football career, Birdy wanted so badly to get back on the field that he asked me to gather the team and take strike action. He was losing hope, and if I were in his shoes I probably would have asked for the same thing. My immediate response was 'no way, I'm not going to ask the team to do that'.

Hindsight is a wonderful thing. I look back now and wish we could've done something more, even if it was just a veiled threat of a player strike. Because, like it or not, Birdy was right: we needed him. The Raiders victory would be our last of 2008.

Our grand-final dreams were gone when our season ended with an embarrassing 28–0 thrashing at the hands of the Melbourne Storm—who would be accused of breaking the salary cap that year—in the preliminary final at the Sydney Football Stadium. Even without Melbourne Storm captain Cameron Smith, who had been suspended for the match, we never looked like competing. What didn't help our chances was the loss of Brett Seymour, our influential five-eighth, four days before the game.

During training before the game, we wanted to keep the mood upbeat. With such an important match so close, we made it a light session with no heavy contact. We were playing soccer at Shark Park when teammate Danny Nutley accidentally clipped Brett, who fell hard enough to tear the anterior cruciate ligament in his knee. The entire playing group fell silent as Brett lay writhing on the grass.

Blake Green was chosen to replace Brett. Greeny was more than capable of filling the void, but it wouldn't have mattered if Brett was there because, as a team, we were terrible. I was ordinary; we all were. Without Birdy, who was in the best form of his career, we came within one game of reaching the grand final and a rare shot at creating history at the Sharks. But we couldn't finish the job.

We were footballers, paid to get results on the footy field. As a footballer, you may only get one chance to win a premiership. We had an undeniably big chance in 2008. It's my belief that Birdy could've helped get us there. Some would argue that our chance was shattered by the allegations against Greg at the time. Others would argue that it was shattered by a nervous board of directors who wouldn't stick by their player.

Me? I found myself thinking of how the Sydney Roosters or Manly Sea Eagles would've responded in a similar situation. If

Greg was their player, I have no doubt he would've played out the remainder of the 2008 season. Ultimately he was never convicted. He should've been treated as innocent until proven otherwise.

Back then there wasn't an ARL Commission or NRL Integrity Unit that had standards or benchmarks that could lead to certain players being stood down for one reason or another. There was no procedure. It was a reactive decision made at the time by a club under huge financial stress. The fear of sponsorship loss and a tattered image was considered more important than their player. It wouldn't have mattered which player it was—I don't think anyone in charge of the Sharks really sat down and analysed the impact of the situation thoroughly enough.

There was another casualty as a result of the widespread stress this entire period caused—the relationship between Birdy and me. Greg felt that I had betrayed him by failing to encourage strike action among our team. He accused me of not standing by him. So we stopped talking. It was hard. Bloody hard. As far as I was concerned, I had done everything I could to see him reinstated.

As I said, I spent every day discussing Birdy's return with Ricky, until the debate was moot. Ricky was my coach and my boss, so I urged him as much as I could to help overturn the decision. Would striking have changed the club's decision? Who knows . . . probably not.

Birdy's lack of faith in me—not knowing or believing how much I had urged the club to bring him back—wore away at my own loyalty towards him. I became angry because I was losing a mate.

We had formed such a tight bond since we lived together for twelve months in our early twenties. Back then, with both of us wanting to cement a permanent position in first grade, our professional footy careers were on a similar upward curve. Instead of going to the pub during the week, we would stay home and take turns cooking dinner.

We had travelled the world together, holidaying in Cancun, Las Vegas and Los Angeles. We had played together for New South Wales in State of Origin. We were as close as mates could be, and so when we stopped talking it hit me hard. I thought, 'Who does he think he is? I've done everything I can for him and that's still not good enough?'

We didn't speak to each other for several months. Until one day, an overseas number appeared on my mobile phone. It was Birdy calling me from France, where he had moved to pick up the pieces of his career, despite never having been found guilty of the charges laid against him. I answered, and we swapped small talk.

It was the phone call that broke the ice. We soon began chatting more frequently. As time passed, we repaired the bond that we had always shared. We went on to win an Origin series together for New South Wales. We won Test matches, the Four Nations and a World Cup for Australia together. We had so much fun winning some big matches together, but we also had a great time as mates together off the field.

A few years ago, I spoke to Birdy about how difficult the 2008 season and the months that followed were. I have told him personally what I have written here today—that I did everything I possibly could to get him back, but I wish I could have done more. He admitted that, emotionally and mentally, he was in a horrible place at the time.

It was a place I guess we've all been at least once before. A place where, due to the amount of stress he was enduring, it made him question even his closest friends and family. The fact that we could come back from that showed me that we shared a bond that was much more than just teammates.

It was a rare moment where life and rugby league actually did meld into one. Just like sometimes in life, when the chips are down, the first people you become angry with are those who are closest to you.

16

Standing Down

If I close my eyes, I can still see the torment written all over Ricky Stuart's face. And when you've never seen that type of anguish from someone close to you before, you never forget it.

Just over 24 hours after losing the 2008 World Cup to New Zealand, I could see Ricky walking towards me with more than the disappointment of defeat in his eyes. Standing inside our team hotel in Brisbane, I could sense that something wasn't right. 'I've stuffed up,' Ricky said, as he stopped in front of me. He then began to confide in me what had just unfolded. It was a tough conversation.

Two weeks later, Ricky would quit as the Test coach of Australia. He was forced to resign thanks to his outburst directed at referee Ashley Klein and match official Stuart Cummings in the lobby of our Brisbane hotel the morning after our shock World Cup loss to New Zealand. I was gutted for Ricky.

I knew the impact that this decision would have on him and his family. I was worried about his health, as I could see how much the incident was eating away at his pride. He absolutely loved coaching Australia. The resignation cut him deeply, and

I supported Ricky as much as I could. Ironically, I could never have imagined that, just six months later, it would be me seeking his support.

The 2008 World Cup loss to the Kiwis in Brisbane was a major upset. From the first day of the tournament, we had quickly united as a squad under Ricky. I'll never forget our first night in camp, when Billy Slater, Darren Lockyer and I were the last three to go to bed. We sat around the bar chatting, laughing and drinking a few cold beers together.

People have often asked me, given my passion for New South Wales, what my relationship with the Queensland players was like. I can only say that I always got on well with all of the senior Queenslanders. I never had a problem with Billy, Locky, Cam Smith, JT (Johnathan Thurston) or GI (Greg Inglis). They are all down-to-earth fellas, who I share so many wonderful memories with.

At the point in the season when we came together to play for Australia, we enjoyed each other's company. I underline the 2008 World Cup as the tournament where we first cultivated a bond and respect for each other. That mateship ultimately delivered results, as not surprisingly we cruised through our pool rounds—including a memorable moment when I was able to play against my brother-in-law from Papua New Guinea, Kevin Prior.

We were confident that, if we played to our ability, we would finish the tournament as World Cup champions. But against the Kiwis in the final, we fell at the last hurdle, losing by fourteen points in front of 50,599 fans at Suncorp Stadium.

We had already beaten our arch rivals 30–6 in the opening pool match of the tournament. But on this night, when it mattered most, we played well below our standard. Full credit to the Kiwis—they capitalised on our errors. 'I would rate it right up there with winning the premiership with the Tigers in 2005,'

New Zealand five-eighth Benji Marshall told the press after the match.

Personally, I was shattered by the loss. The subsequent drama involving Ricky the next day only made things worse. By the end of 2008—after the World Cup loss, all the drama surrounding Birdy and the way we bowed out one game shy of the grand final with the Sharks—I was mentally and physically cooked.

With my footy commitments over, I was happy to switch off from the game and take a short break before returning for the Sharks' 2009 pre-season. Little did I know, I would require as much energy as possible to navigate through the 2009 season, which was one of the most turbulent years of my career.

It would begin with one of life's greatest moments, when my partner, Anne, and I celebrated the arrival of our first baby girl, Charly, in February. The rest of my Cronulla teammates had travelled to Darwin for a trial match against the Gold Coast. I remained in Sydney to support Anne and witness the birth of our baby. I've never been more gobsmacked than on the day Charly arrived. That incredible emotion would be matched only by the arrival of Kody and Macy over the next few years.

Welcoming Charly into the world provided me with extra motivation ahead of the 2009 season with Cronulla. For the first time in my life, I had become a father—and suddenly I was a 27 year old with the incredible responsibility of ensuring that our baby girl was protected and cared for at all times. However, if I was hoping for a trouble-free first year as a father, I was in for a rude shock.

The torment began in Cessnock on the last Saturday of February, when in a trial match against Newcastle I suffered a knee injury in the first half. Unable to put any pressure on my knee, I needed to be chaired from the field by our medical staff. So, too, did new recruit Reni Maitua, who had sustained a leg injury in the trial match.

I had two weeks to recover before Round 1. With intense rehabilitation, I managed to make it back in time to be fit for selection for our season opener against Penrith. We won the match 18–10. We were not to know our victory song 'Up Up Cronulla' wouldn't be sung again for several months. In fact, it would be nine weeks before we won another game.

The positive vibe and belief internally at the club that we had a strong year ahead of us appeared to be dashed within a fortnight. In a major jolt for the club, we lost talented back-rower Fraser Anderson to a massive offer from Japanese rugby union two weeks before the season began. An emotional Fraser stood before the entire dressing room after training, explaining that he had to leave as the contract offer from Japan was too good to refuse.

The loss of Fraser impacted us greatly—as the loss of any player inside your top-25 squad always does. But then, during our Round 1 win over the Panthers, our victory would come at an even greater cost. Our starting prop, Ben Ross, was ruled out for the rest of the season after suffering a devastating neck injury.

Rossy's injury was a major scare for everyone involved with the Sharks. Instead of enjoying our win, the entire team was concerned for the welfare of one of our good mates, who had just been stretchered off in a neck brace. The injury changed Rossy's life, but it's with great relief that I regularly see him now living a full and happy life with his young family.

Not only did we lose Rossy to injury in the season opener, we also lost our starting fullback, Brett 'BK' Kearney, to a serious foot injury. Like Rossy, BK wouldn't play again during the 2009 season. So after just one match of the season, we had lost two starting forwards in Fraser and Rossy, and our first-choice fullback was also gone.

The arrival of Trent 'Baz' Barrett back from the UK Super League was widely regarded as the club's biggest off-season signing. However, as much as he tried, Baz couldn't overcome the team's lack of depth and its inability to gel due to the rotating list of players called into the side as injuries mounted.

It was one of the most painful and frustrating periods of my career. Sitting anchored to the bottom of the ladder, our finals hopes were as good as gone by the halfway point of the 2009 season.

In May, after our eighth consecutive loss—which occurred during a return match against the Panthers at Penrith Stadium—as captain I felt compelled to accept responsibility for how poorly we were playing. 'I take the game pretty personally, and I almost shoulder that loss on my own,' I said during the post-match press conference following our 26–22 loss. 'Senior players like myself can't afford to have a game like that when we're in the position we are in.' And it wasn't just on the field that the entire team were under the gun.

In the lead-up to our eighth straight defeat, the front office of the club was also in turmoil. The Sharks' administration was reeling as a result of revelations about a sexual assault allegation from our 2002 pre-season trip to Christchurch. While no charges were laid, the damaging headlines caused chaos at the club. Sponsors were threatening to rip up their contracts because of the allegation.

'It has affected us by corporate sponsors reviewing their position,' the Sharks chief executive, Tony Zappia, admitted to *The Sunday Telegraph*. 'It's probably as tough as the week after the Greg Bird incident.' Little did we know that the carnage had only just begun.

Three days before hosting our arch rivals, St George Illawarra, at Shark Park on a Saturday night in May, teammate Reni Maitua was stood down from all playing and training duties after testing positive to a drug test. It was yet another black eye for the club. We were already seen as the NRL whipping boy, but the suspension of Reni paved the way for more criticism—a lot of it justified—and left some of our fans disenchanted with and embarrassed by the way the club continued to lurch from one drama to the next.

Incredibly, despite sitting last on the ladder and with the club besieged by crisis after crisis, more than 15,000 fans provided unwavering support—as they had done on so many occasions throughout my career—in our home match against the Dragons. With our backs against the wall, I felt that we could snap our run of eight straight losses against the Saints.

The Dragons led 4–0 at half-time. Despite being close enough if we were good enough, we had no answer for Jamie Soward's kicking game. He sparked three second-half tries in the space of ten minutes. We lost our ninth straight game, 26–4.

The pressure I felt to lead the club during the 2009 season was immense. I can't say if it contributed to the drama that would soon engulf my career, impact my family and scourge my reputation.

With the Dragons marching their way to victory, I took a routine carry of the footy in the 73rd minute and was tackled by St George Illawarra forward Mickey Paea. The next 30 seconds would alter my career, challenge who I was as a person and leave me questioning the leadership of the NRL.

It was alleged that, during the process of being tackled, I racially abused Mickey. I'm not going to create a 'my word against his' scenario, as Mickey made it clear on the night that he didn't want the incident to go any further. I'll aim to respect him by fulfilling my end of the bargain.

The on-field referees asked Mickey and his captain, Ben Hornby, if they wanted to make a formal complaint against me. Mickey said, 'No.' We shook hands after the match. Mickey told the journalists, post-match, 'It was just a bit of push and scuffle— what was said out there stays on the field. That's all it was. It was a tough game, and in the heat of the moment it was a push and scuffle, there was nothing more than that. I'm happy to leave it there.' But there was no hope of that happening.

Two days after the match, propelled by widespread media coverage of the incident, the NRL launched an immediate inquiry. The NRL contacted host broadcaster Fox Sports to investigate if there was any evidence or audio that would reveal proof of racial abuse. Fox Sports indicated that there was no video or audio evidence.

'In the absence of any complaint and without any other evidence, there's really nowhere it can go,' NRL chief operating officer Graham Annesley said. 'You need a complaint to deal with it under the anti-vilification code, but there's obviously the match-review committee and the NRL code of conduct that can also come into play, depending on what evidence is available, but at the moment there really isn't any evidence.'

It didn't matter. By Monday afternoon, I had been hit with a $10,000 fine for what the NRL described as a breach of the player's code of conduct. Naturally, I was disappointed. If Mickey had been offended by comments and subsequently filed a complaint against me, I could've understood and accepted why the NRL needed to take disciplinary action. But having spoken to and shaken hands with Mickey after the game, I believed that any issue that may have existed had been dealt with.

As I said, it was a precarious period for the Sharks as a club. Compared to our rivals and other powerhouse clubs, we were seen as a little fish in a big pond. And the game's administrators were struggling against a tsunami of media pressure to do nothing less than ensure that action was taken against me. NRL chief executive David Gallop hit me with the fine. In turn, the penalty only heaped further stress on an already strained Cronulla board, which was under pressure from critics who wanted to see me stripped of the captaincy.

The entire drama wore me thin. It also wore down my partner, Anne. She was an emotional mess. A strong woman, Anne had managed to create a certain bubble or divide between our family life and my football life throughout my career. It helped her separate what was real and what was just someone else's opinion. But the Mickey Paea incident floored her. As it did me.

Despite the media following my every move, I visited Ricky Stuart's house early one morning. I sat there crying in his backyard. He would later advise me that I should stand down as captain before the Cronulla board made their move. So I sat down and wrote an email to the Cronulla board, informing them of my decision to stand down as captain. It was tough to put my decision into words.

Not one of the Cronulla directors replied to my email. Perhaps it was an indication of the level of leadership we had at the time, but none of the Sharks directors ever spoke to me about my decision to stand down from the privileged position as Cronulla club captain. I found that odd.

Privately, I felt aggrieved that the two people who were willing to leave the entire incident on the field had no influence on the administrators off the field, who wanted to pursue the issue. So Ricky organised a meeting between David Gallop and me. He felt it was important that I be given the opportunity to speak with David one on one.

Alongside Ricky and my manager, David Riolo, I sat down in David Gallop's office. 'You're abusing your power here,' I said to Gallop. 'You've got no evidence of me saying anything, you've got no complaint from Mickey, we've both spoken to each other and he's happy to move on.' It's worth remembering that, back then, there was no NRL Integrity Unit or appeals panel to dispute my breach notice.

Having grown up in the multicultural community of Western Sydney, I had plenty of friends and schoolmates who were of Asian, Maltese, Lebanese and Italian heritage. Anne's family is from Poland, and my brother-in-law is from Papua New Guinea. I have never cared about the race of a particular person or the colour of their skin. We are all equal.

My frustration with Gallop was that during the following season, in 2010, another NRL player would be accused of a racial slur, while one would be accused of a religious slur. The media focus on the two incidents, although well documented, was significantly less than what my case received.

It would be dishonest of me not to concede that the incident, while taxing on both my family and my hip pocket, aided my development as a player and as a leader of my club. But I stand by the belief that, during my time in rugby league, there was one rule for some and another rule for others.

In my opinion, the focus on a particular player during a crisis depends on who you are and how the media perceives you. And, having been involved in the Anthony Laffranchi incident less than twelve months earlier, my reputation was deteriorating whether I liked it or not.

It would be two weeks before the dust settled on the race row, but for me the pain from that match would linger. Lost amid all the drama was the fact that I had suffered a rotator cuff injury during the Round 11 loss to the Dragons. State of Origin I was just under a fortnight away.

I was ultimately chosen for Origin I in Melbourne by NSW coach Craig Bellamy, but I was always at long odds to pass the medical clearance every player must undergo before being declared a certain starter. On the Saturday before Wednesday's Origin I at Etihad Stadium, I could hardly run. I told the Blues' coaching staff that it wouldn't be fair to the team if I played. I was out.

Both Glenn Stewart (who was suspended) and I watched our NSW teammates go down to Queensland 28–18 in the Origin opener. I made it my goal to be back for Origin II.

At the Sharks, we had returned to the winner's circle with success over Parramatta and New Zealand. It allowed us to chase a third straight win in Round 14 against Canberra in the nation's capital. I scored two tries against the Raiders. My second try came late in the game and helped us to seal our 24–20 victory. Thankfully, Craig rushed me straight back into the Blues' starting line-up at lock for Origin II—a must-win match in front of our home fans in Sydney.

There have been too many games to recall during my career where I felt that I shouldn't have played due to an injury. In some of those games, although I've said to myself that 'I shouldn't be running out there today', I have finished as the man of the match. Sometimes, you can push through the pain. As a footballer, you learn to live with injuries after a while. But sometimes you can be out on the field, struggling with an injury, and you just know that every minute is going to be a battle. Origin II in 2009 was one of those battles.

I had nursed my shoulder right up until kick-off, skipping a couple of training sessions during the week. By game day, I felt that I could still contribute to the team. After my first hit-up with the football, I thought, 'You beauty, I'm sweet.' But fifteen minutes later, I was in a world of pain.

The shoulder just wasn't right, and in Origin you can't afford to play hampered or down even 5 per cent. I tried telling myself to block out the pain and just keep working for my teammates. We needed to win to keep the series alive. But we eventually lost 24–14, having rallied from eighteen points behind on the scoreboard to trail by just four.

It was the only game for New South Wales that I would play during the 2009 series. Due to my dull performance in Origin II, which was stymied by my shoulder injury, as well as the NSW selectors' desire for change, I was overlooked for Origin III. Despite watching from the sidelines, I was delighted that the Blues won 28–16, enabling them to avoid a 3–0 clean sweep by Queensland.

With the Origin series over, my focus now was to try to save our club from finishing sixteenth and receiving the dreaded wooden spoon. Somehow, despite failing to win a single match from Round 16 until the final round—a total of ten straight defeats—we finished second-last, just in front of the Sydney Roosters. As a team, we were relieved that we had dodged the wooden spoon and that the season from hell was over.

Despite all the drama of the 2009 season—including the personal disappointment of relinquishing the Sharks captaincy, the injuries and subsequent form slump of our side and playing just once for New South Wales—I clung to the hope of pulling on the green and gold of Australia during the end-of-season Four Nations tournament.

With great satisfaction, I was included in the Four Nations squad to tour the United Kingdom under coach Tim Sheens. I look back and cherish those memories of spending a month away overseas with so many champion players and forming relationships with many talented individuals.

In the Four Nations final against England, I was selected to start the match in the back row alongside Nathan Hindmarsh and Luke Lewis. Darren Lockyer became the first Australian in the history of the game to play in 50 international matches for his country. In addition, teammate and fellow Queenslander Petero Civoniceva became the most-capped forward, breaking Johnny Raper's record by earning his fortieth cap.

England boasted a powerful side that included Sam Burgess, Gareth Ellis, Adrian Morley, Sam Tomkins and James Graham. The home side were typically strong from the opening whistle, but eventually our class prevailed as we ran away to claim the Four Nations title, 46–16. Being part of the victory provided sweet relief after such an exhausting year on and off the field.

But just when I felt as though I could put a cap on 2009, I gave the headline writers one final Christmas present. In December, I was caught urinating in public after a few drinks with mates in Darling Harbour. It was hardly the crime of the century, but I knew—given my horrendous year—that it was a bad stuff-up.

I rang our chief executive at the Sharks, Richard Fisk, and immediately offered my apology. I was fined another $10,000—it remains the most expensive toilet stop I have ever made.

17
Sticky Situation

It was July, in the middle of the 2010 season, when Ricky Stuart's reign as Cronulla's head coach came to an end. He was leaving after just three years. I was gutted by the decision.

My first reaction was anger. I was upset because of how much I enjoyed playing under Ricky. He gave me direction and purpose at an important time in my career. His energy and intensity were critical in assisting my personal development and my ambition to elevate the consistency of my game so that I could play representative football.

Perhaps it was due to our similar personalities, but Ricky believed in me—not just as a player, but also as a person. When I was crying at his dinner table because it felt like the world was against me only six months earlier, Ricky had been able to pick my spirits up off the floor. But there was too much going on behind the scenes for Ricky to stay at Cronulla.

On the Sunday morning after we had suffered loss number twelve for the season, 48–18, in Round 19 against Manly, I drove to Ricky's house and knocked on his front door. I had a sense that all was not well with him. One week later, in his newspaper column, Ricky would explain in great detail how he knew that it was time to stand down when he looked across the dressing room moments before the kick-off against Manly. 'They just seemed dead in the eyes, as if nothing I said was reaching them,' Ricky wrote.

Long before Ricky informed the Cronulla board of his decision to resign after the Manly defeat, there was intent among some members of the board—which the players were aware of—to see Ricky axed. In the few weeks prior to Ricky's exit, selected members of the Sharks' board had made contact with me, asking if I could meet them. I found the meeting request odd.

Throughout the entire Mickey Paea drama, I had never received a single phone call from any of the Cronulla board members. Not even to lend an ear or a quiet word. The same board members who were now trying to meet with me to discuss 'the club's plans going forward' were also the same individuals who had led an internal charge to see me stripped of the captaincy during the height of the Paea drama. So it's fair to say that unity and support when faced with a little bit of adversity weren't their greatest attributes.

Of course, please don't read this as though I'm condoning any of the off-field drama I experienced during my career. But footy clubs aren't like working at the ANZ Bank or for Telstra—there are times when your club, by the mere definition of the word, needs to come together as one around the most important commodity: the players. However, the only phone calls I had previously received from the board at that time were to tell me that I had to explain myself, at the risk of a $10,000 breach notice.

Despite never before hearing of players at the Sharks, or any other clubs for that matter, being asked to meet with board members, I agreed to their meeting request out of respect. I met a member of the board at a cafe in Brighton Le Sands.

I don't believe a player should have to answer, worry about or deal with the questions that I was asked about Ricky that day. You look at the major clubs in the NRL—and I've spoken to many senior coaches and players from the biggest clubs in the game about this—it just doesn't happen. It's not the responsibility of a player, albeit a senior one, to have a say on the positives and negatives of the head coach or what direction the club is going in.

At the end of the day, a captain or senior player at a footy club is an extension of the coach. The captain and senior players need to be led by the coach—they are the person we report to first. The coach needs to be led by the club's chief executive officer.

Before Lyall Gorman arrived in 2014, the Sharks had experienced seven different CEOs in just over ten years. Every one of them, including Richard Fisk, Steve Noyce and Tony Zappia, were hard working and passionate about taking the club forward. But that level of change and instability made it extremely difficult to cultivate success.

I'm not sure that the two board members I met with received the news that they wanted to hear anyway. I told them why I thought Ricky was such an important person for our club.

Ricky is too smart not to have known about the politics that the board were investing their time into, so after the Manly loss he decided enough was enough. Unexpectedly, his resignation left me facing a dilemma of my own.

A clause in my contract stated that I could leave the club at any point after Ricky was no longer the Sharks' head coach. So, with Ricky gone, I was a free agent. All of a sudden, seeing my contract with the Sharks through to the end of 2013 meant nothing.

Knowing how eager Manly was to have me in 2007, my manager, Dave Riolo, made a phone call to inform the Sea Eagles' administration of my new situation. Ringing in my head at the same time were Ricky's words. Before he packed up his office, Ricky had turned to me and said, 'Gal, in this game, you look after yourself. You're not here for a long time, and you can't trust anyone.'

The Sharks' board was well aware of the 'Ricky clause' and that, while it existed, there was always a possibility I could up and leave the club. I was made acutely aware that the Sharks' management didn't want me to activate the clause. A couple of the Sharks' board members at that time phoned Dave and explained that the club was planning to reinstate me as captain. They also suggested that the club would name the newly built southern grandstand at Shark Park after me: the Paul Gallen Grandstand.

The latter was a stunning gesture and a carrot that had never previously been dangled before me. Well aware of the many great players who had pulled on the black, white and blue, I knew that it was an incredible sign of recognition by the club and something that my family and friends could be proud of, well after I had retired. However, it only served to add yet another layer of complexity to my decision—even though, as the years passed, the grandstand carrot never became a reality.

What I couldn't escape, though, was the sense of discomfort with the way we were playing as a group through 2009 and 2010. I was also concerned with how far off the pace our recruitment was compared to that of our rivals. It left me certain that as much as I felt comfortable with the elevation of Ricky's assistant, Shane 'Flanno' Flanagan, into the head-coach role, I just didn't think we had the roster to be playing finals footy consistently, let alone win an elusive premiership. Moving to Manly and playing with the Sea Eagles became a real and legitimate option.

People who have struggled to leave their job to join a rival organisation will understand when I say that I really can't pinpoint any one overriding factor that ultimately saw me stay at the Sharks.

Primarily, I believe it was a fear of change. Having arrived at the club as a teenager with nothing, it was now a significant part of my life.

The same factors that had contributed to my decision-making previously still hadn't changed. I loved the area and the fans, and the lure of winning the club's first premiership was also a huge factor. And how would I feel if, after leaving, Cronulla was able to achieve that dream? Let me tell you, it would prove much more difficult than watching Manly achieve their grand final success. And that's not too say I haven't thought often about the Sea Eagles' premiership glory in 2008 and 2011.

The one thing I always come back to is this: I know that there was no guarantee that Manly would've won in 2011 had I been there. Anything could've happened. There are so many variables to winning a competition, and playing well yourself is just one of them. You also need luck across the entire playing squad. You only have to look at what Melbourne did to us in the 2008 preliminary final, by knocking us out of the premiership race with a team that was formed outside the legal parameters of the salary cap.

The day before I needed to make a decision on my future at the Sharks, I sat down with Lance Thompson, the former St George Illawarra and Sharks forward, who I had played with only two years earlier. Lance was one player who, even when he was playing, always had one eye on life after footy.

As I sat there explaining my dilemma to him, he interrupted and said, 'Gal, you've created who you are at this club. Forget about what everyone else says. Your time at Cronulla—you've put so much time and effort into the club. That legacy as a one-club man is rare.' What Lance said hit home.

The blood, sweat and tears I had spilled in the black, white and blue would seem almost worthless if I were to up and leave now.

And I knew that by staying, it would also make Dad happy. He rarely offered much advice when it came to footy, but one thing he always said was that he wanted me to be a one-club player.

I had also spoken at length about my dilemma with Flanno. All along, he wanted me to stay. Despite Ricky moving on, I was positive that Flanno would handle the elevation to the role of first-grade coach. I liked Flanno's attitude, his ideals and his desire to never give the opposition an inch.

He had worked hard under Ricky and previously as Craig Bellamy's assistant coach for New South Wales, so he deserved his shot. With Flanno, you always knew that no matter the standard of players we had at the club at any one given time, he was always doing his best to make us a better team with what he had at his disposal. And what he was able to achieve, given his resources and ability to recruit players, was impressive. I decided to stay.

Flanno had just shaken hands on a deal to bring Wade Graham from Penrith to the Sharks in 2011. He also told me that the club was in deep negotiations with St George Illawarra and New Zealand Test forward Jeremy Smith. The signing of Wade and the prospect of adding Jeremy to our 2011 squad excited me.

Jeremy was exactly the class of player we needed at the club. I called Jeremy myself. I was relieved when he told me he had decided that he was heading to the Sharks. The acquisition of Jeremy ensured that we now had a forward pack to challenge our rivals, with myself, Anthony Tupou, Luke Douglas and Kade Snowden providing us with plenty of starch up front.

'Adding [Smith] to it makes it a pretty formidable pack, but we've got to score some points,' I told Australian Associated Press at the time. 'That's probably our big problem at the moment and probably will be next year if we don't get some outside backs, too—so fingers crossed we get an outside back or two as well.'

Winning just two of our last seven matches of 2010 and finishing fourteenth on the ladder, little would soften the blow of such a tumultuous season—even being named the Player of the Year and Player's Player at the Sharks' end-of-season awards function. However, I was hopeful—rather than confident—that I had played enough quality football for the Sharks to be selected for Australia's Four Nations team to face England, New Zealand and Papua New Guinea here at home in Australia with matches also played in New Zealand.

Wearing the green and gold and playing under Tim Sheens brought out the best in me. Tim created an environment where you never felt secure about your position within the team. You were constantly on your toes, especially at training. If you told Sheensy that you felt like you needed to sit out a certain training session due to a niggle or minor injury, he would simply pick another player to train in your position. You always needed to be at your best under Sheensy, and that worked for me when he was in charge of the Kangaroos.

In that 2010 series, I picked up the man of the match award in our final pool match victory over New Zealand. However, less than a week later, we were beaten 16–12 by New Zealand in dramatic circumstances during the Four Nations final at Suncorp Stadium.

In the last play of the game, Kiwi winger Jason Nightingale threw a Hail Mary pass that resulted in Nathan Fien scoring the match-winner. Nightingale's pass was at least 6 metres forward. Somehow the officials missed it.

The defeat shocked the entire camp, and the tears streaming down Brent Tate's face after he had suffered a third torn ACL only cast a further pall over the entire dressing room following the match. As a result, it would be almost six weeks before I received one of the greatest honours of my career—the prestigious

Harry Sunderland Medal. The award was supposed to be presented after the Four Nations final, but team officials decided to delay the presentation due to the bitter disappointment of losing to the Kiwis.

It was after a pre-season training session at the Sharks that *The Daily Telegraph*'s Phil Rothfield contacted me to break the news. 'I'm that happy and feel so privileged to win it,' I told him when I heard the news. 'I can't believe it. It's the biggest award I've got. It's an honour to play alongside so many great players, let alone win anything like this.'

The award was judged by Test coach Tim Sheens, his coaching staff and team management. Since its inception in the 1960s, it has been won by many of the true legends of the game, including Wally Lewis, Darren Lockyer, Johnny Raper, Billy Smith, Ron Coote and Billy Slater. I know all this because I researched the medal after it was awarded to me.

I was blown away to learn how highly regarded the award is within the game. Considering the players I was playing with during that 2010 Four Nations, I was unbelievably proud to have received that award.

18

Blue Leader

Wayne Bennett and I are very dissimilar, but there is one thing we have in common. We can both polarise a room. As is the case with me, rugby league fans tend to like Wayne, or they don't.

'Whether he is playing for the Sharks, New South Wales, Australia or the NRL All Stars, what you see is what you get with Paul,' Wayne wrote in a 2012 newspaper column. 'You might not support his team, but you have to love the way he plays. He is a bloke who gives his best every time. There is no fuss about him; he doesn't let anyone down. He gets the job done, and you know you can count on him.'

The first time I met Wayne was in the pre-season of 2011, when I was chosen to play under him for the NRL All Stars side against the NRL Indigenous All Stars. My first impression of Wayne was that he was nothing like I expected. Before that, I had only ever viewed him as the opposition coach, in a press-conference situation, where I saw what most supporters saw—someone with an uncanny resemblance to Clint Eastwood.

As the entire 2011 All Stars squad climbed onto the bus for the first time during our five-day preparation for the match,

I positioned myself where I always did throughout my entire career—in the fourth row of seats on the left-hand side. And Wayne? Well, he walked straight down the aisle of the bus, before planting himself on the back row of seats.

I can say that not once in my entire career did I see a coach sit anywhere else but the very front seat of the bus. But on this day, there was Wayne on the back seat, sitting back, arms folded, with a little grin on his face. It was as though he was just another one of the boys.

Wayne said more from the back seat in the first two minutes of that bus ride than I had heard from him my entire life. From the back of the bus, he sang out and threw barbs down the aisle at different players, which left the entire bus in hysterics. Not content to let Wayne have all the fun, team manager Chris 'Choppy' Close grabbed the microphone.

Choppy was sitting at the front of the bus and, with the microphone in hand, he began to make sure the entire bus was aware of the size of Wayne's ears and his elongated neck. Wayne endured the ribbing with good humour. Smiling to myself, I sat there almost in disbelief. I couldn't believe that this was the same Wayne I had seen in opposition dressing rooms. It was the perfect icebreaker for the group.

When it came time to selecting the 2011 All Stars team positions, we were allowed to basically pick the side for ourselves. This was far from a masterful strategy that the 'supercoach' had devised. The backs chose themselves, and then the forwards went about divvying up their jumpers. Nathan Hindmarsh, Dave Taylor and I had to work out who would wear what jumper in the back row.

Too quick for me, Nathan put up his hand to play in the middle of the field, with the '11' jumper. Dave picked the left-edge position, so that left only the right edge for me. From the corner of the room, Wayne piped up. 'You're kidding—you can't play right edge,' Wayne said in front of the team. You could've knocked me over with a feather. I didn't know what to say.

You've got to remember, this was an All Stars team so I only knew half a dozen of the blokes—the ones I had played with for New South Wales or Australia. Wayne had just singled me out, saying that I wasn't capable of playing a role for this team.

As the room fell silent, it was Darren Lockyer who then spoke up for me. 'He can play there,' Locky said. 'I've played with Gal in that position before for Australia—he can do the job.'

The right edge was a position I didn't really enjoy. I preferred the middle forward position more than playing on an edge, and on the left was where I had predominantly played in the past. It wasn't until later in the week that I would learn why Wayne was reluctant to see me play in that position. It was because he still held memories of me playing on the right in the 2009 State of Origin series. While I was on the right edge for New South Wales, Queensland left centre Greg Inglis had scored the first try of the match after I had overread the play, providing him with all the room he needed to score.

'Well, if Locky backs you—I'll back you, too,' Wayne said. The next day, we were on a team walk and once again Wayne was throwing out one-liners at everyone, including me. He took a shot at me about the Sharks, because at that time the club still had not won its elusive first premiership, despite entering the competition in 1967.

So I fired back, 'Righto Supercoach, if you're so good, why don't you come and coach Cronulla?'

He just smiled and said, 'I'm a good coach, but I'm not a miracle worker.' Everyone laughed.

I enjoyed getting to know Wayne during that short period in the All Stars squad. In that time, he made a point of speaking to me about surrounding myself with good people, and we also spoke about how to be a better father.

The trick, I believe, to Wayne's coaching is that he has a way of making things sound so simple. After an hour of chatting about football and life with Wayne one day, I left his room feeling calmer than when I had arrived. Wayne had made me realise that my only job was to focus on football. He said, 'All you can ask of people is to give their best all the time.'

Nothing sums up the way I played rugby league more than that simple statement. If ever there was a motto I lived by throughout my career, it was this one. It's the same message I give to kids any chance I get. Your skill level doesn't matter, and neither does what you do in life or where you come from—all that matters is that you do the very best you can. It's so simple.

I doubt anything else illustrates that more than my 2011 season. On an individual level, I left nothing in reserve that year. With Shane 'Flanno' Flanagan in charge and the arrival of Jeremy Smith, there was a sense of great optimism at the club.

Despite a shocking Round 1 start against Canberra, losing 40–12, we were able to steady the ship by beating the 2010 premiers, St George Illawarra. We then followed that up with a 44–12 demolition of Penrith and, for the first time since Round 1 in 2009, we were sitting inside the top eight on the competition table.

My form and that of my Cronulla teammates enabled me to gain a sixteenth Test jumper for Australia, when I was chosen for the ANZAC Test against New Zealand on the Gold Coast. In one of the strongest performances of my career, I played 69 minutes and produced thirteen runs, 38 tackles, three off-loads and two tackle busts. In a career highlight, I was named man of the match. But it was a match I almost didn't play in.

Had it not been for the patience of Kangaroos coach Tim Sheens, I would've been watching the match from the sidelines as I had carried a calf injury into the week-long preparation. I was able to train for just one session, prompting Tim to call Beau Scott into the squad as my shadow player. Nervous, I rang Ricky Stuart, who was coaching New South Wales at the time. He suggested that I pull out. 'You've got a long year ahead of you,' Ricky said.

Six hours before kick-off, I knocked on Tim's hotel-room door and said, 'I'm going to pull out.'

Tim replied, 'Just settle down, mate.'

'I don't think I can get through the game,' I said.

'Don't stress, we've got Beau Scott here. Just go and read your game notes, and you'll make it,' Tim assured me. I took a deep breath and listened to Tim.

I'll never forget Cameron Smith's face as he looked over at me during the pre-game warm-up. He could tell I was battling. Luckily, adrenaline got me through the match.

It didn't matter if it was for New South Wales or Australia—I just loved playing in that big-game arena. I loved the planning and preparation that went into pulling apart New Zealand or Queensland. An example of that occurred in 2011.

Almost five months before game one of the 2011 State of Origin series, Ricky took the first step towards attempting to dismantle Queensland's five-year dominance. Locked away in a room at Cronulla's Rydges hotel for three hours, Ricky held a meeting with me and six other leading Blues players—Kurt Gidley, Greg Bird, Luke Lewis, Jarryd Hayne, Mitchell Pearce and Todd Carney. The theme? Restoring state pride.

All of Ricky's support staff—including trainer Ron Palmer, assistant coaches Wayne Portlock and Trent Barrett, team manager Craig Young, physiotherapist Andrew Gray and doctor Martin Raftery—were in the room. Ricky sat at the head of the table.

He wanted us—the players—to take ownership of the team and create a culture of passion and pride in the Blues jumper. Ricky also spoke about creating a stable environment in which to commence our preparation.

With so much discussion and debate focused on whether or not I was worthy of the NSW captaincy in previous years, I had a sense that if I was ever to have a chance to lead the state, it was in 2011 under Ricky. To be honest, though, I can't say that captaining the Blues was ever a goal of mine. Playing for New South Wales was definitely something I wanted, but captaining the Blues? No, that was beyond my control.

The very first indication I had that I could be named captain of the NSW Blues was when Trent 'Baz' Barrett phoned me in March 2011. Baz had retired from rugby league following the 2010 season, but I had stayed in touch with him after his retirement. 'Stay in the headlines for the right reasons,' he told me. While he never said that I was the frontrunner to be named captain of the Blues, I understood what he was saying.

I took Baz's advice on board and became hell-bent on avoiding any penalties on the field and staying on the straight and narrow off it. I just wanted to put my head down and play my game. I even met with NRL referees' boss Robert Finch to discuss how I could work with the referees to ensure that largely penalty-free seasons followed. I would like to think that this conscious effort worked.

So when Ricky told me he wanted me to captain New South Wales for the first time in Origin I, 2011, I accepted the role with great pride and appreciation. I understood that Ricky had chosen me because of the way I had performed on the field—and, there-fore, I shouldn't change the way I played just because I was now the first to emerge from the tunnel.

After informing me of his decision, to my surprise Ricky told me to ring Darren Lockyer. I had to check if Ricky was joking, given that Locky was the Queensland captain at the time. Ricky knew how much I respected Locky, having coached both of us as we played for Australia during the 2008 World Cup. He wanted me to chat with Locky about what is required to be the captain of your state, what that role involves and how to handle the demands that the honour of leading your state can make.

I didn't think it was such a bad idea to chat with Locky, but deep down I didn't want to be like anyone else. I wanted to be myself and, as captain, I wanted to lead the Blues my own way. So I explained to Ricky why I wouldn't be calling Locky.

Something changed dramatically between the 2010 and 2011 State of Origin series, because when we arrived for Origin I, I had no doubt that we could beat Queensland on their home turf of Suncorp Stadium. Our Origin I camp was one of the best I'd ever been involved with. It's not every night that you are fortunate enough to listen to old Origin war stories from NSW legends such as Laurie Daley and Tommy Raudonikis. And I certainly never thought I'd be sitting down to dinner with then NSW premier Barry O'Farrell. But that was my introduction to life as the NSW skipper.

On day one of camp, Ricky addressed the team inside our hotel meeting room at the Coogee Crowne Plaza. Some of us in the playing group had never met, but I swear you would never have known. We hit it off immediately.

Ricky spoke about one thing—and that was enjoyment. He wanted every player to leave this camp with no regrets or ill feeling, no matter the result. He spoke to us about savouring the moment together, working towards something special and ensuring we walked out of camp with memories to share for the rest of our lives.

In a typical Origin arm wrestle, we went down 16–12 to Queensland in Origin I at Suncorp Stadium. Like so many other Origin matches I was involved in, it was a match that we could quite easily have won. As disappointed as we all were, we decided to quickly move on and ensure we squared the series in front of our home fans in Origin II.

I'll never forget running out onto ANZ Stadium for the first time as Blues skipper. For the rest of my life, I'll remember that feeling. There were 81,000 fans, all decked out in sky blue. The first glimpse of that blue followed by the spine-tingling roar of the crowd as they spotted my boots stepping out from the tunnel in the bowels of ANZ Stadium . . . wow.

I was always fairly calm in the countdown before Origin, or any match for that matter. My demeanour really didn't change for this game. My final words as captain were straightforward and simple. The most important point I wanted to ram home to the boys was the simplest one—know your role and do your job to the best of your ability.

As the Sydney Children's Choir delivered the national anthem for Origin II, I did what I have always done—I looked for my family in the sea of blue. Dad was holding Charly up above his shoulders, so that I could see her among the thousands of faces staring down at the stadium turf.

I love singing the national anthem. I always have. Whenever I stood for a national anthem, I would rarely be thinking about the game or about the next hit-up. I would just be savouring the moment and reserving my energy for what was about to unfold.

For sure, there were times, too, when I felt scared. There were many things I was scared of before a big match. I was scared of getting hurt. I was scared of failing. I was scared of not doing my job, or letting down my teammates with an error. When you're about to play in front of over 80,000 people in the stadium and four million people watching at home, I can tell you that it's a hugely daunting situation.

As we waited for the referee's whistle to signal time-on, memories of my childhood came flooding back. I always wanted to watch the first hit-up of an Origin game, and I wondered if there were kids at home waiting to see who would take the first hit-up and, if it was me, whether or not I would get smashed.

The first five minutes of an Origin is like no other game of rugby league. In a club game, you can pick guys in the defensive line to target and run at. You know there are weak links in different teams, but in Origin there's nothing like that. Every player will hit you as hard as the next.

There were Origin games when I'd look up at the clock and only eight minutes had passed. Then I'd glance up again, feeling as though ten minutes had passed since my last look, and there'd be only five minutes remaining in the match.

Bravely, we levelled the series 1–1 with an 18–8 victory in Origin II. It was Queensland's lowest score in any Origin match since game three, 2007. And it meant that we now had to head to Brisbane to try to wrap up the series.

Proudly, I was named man of the match. Chosen in the front row by Ricky, I played the entire 80 minutes and finished the match with 234 metres and 32 tackles. The reaction from the media typified the impact Origin has on the two states—it bordered on hysterical.

Even Ricky, I thought, went a little over the top with his praise after the match. 'Everybody laughed at me when I picked him in front row,' he said during the post-match press conference.

'There is only one other player who has played 80 minutes of Origin football in the front row—that was Glenn Lazarus, and he was the best front-rower ever to play the game of rugby league.

'Paul Gallen has equalled that: 80 minutes playing front row, in that intensity, at that high speed and style of football, is freakish. That is the level of a Slater, a Thurston, a Lockyer, a Cameron Smith.'

As I said, I felt like it was a little too much from Ricky to compare me to those great players. Without wanting to ever sound like a show-off or a bighead, I have never understood the fuss. I was honestly just so happy that we were able to level the series—and we were now heading to Brisbane for the decider.

It wasn't as though the statistics I managed to accumulate in Origin II were like nothing I had ever achieved before or would achieve again later in my career. If you ask me to explain how I played, or the style I played, the best explanation I've ever heard is from Tim Sheens, who once told me I reminded him of a stock car: they get banged and bashed, but they just keep going.

There were players who would outperform me every day in fitness tests at the Sharks. In any sprint test, I would be in the last few over the finishing line at the club. But give me a footy and an opposition, and I'll run for you all day. In a match, those same players who had left me in their wake during the week at training would be blowing harder than a southerly at Shark Park during the heat of battle. Competition is what drives me. And I love physical sports.

I couldn't swing a golf club if you asked me to. I couldn't think of anything worse than riding a bike from the suburbs to the city. But ask me to run through that defender, and I will. Ask me to jump into a boxing ring, and I would do that, too.

So, while I felt like I had played to the best of my ability in that Origin II, I didn't think it was anything out of this world.

It sounds so boring, but to me, I'd done my job. Frankly, I found the headlines and press interest embarrassing.

As I said, the best thing was that the result meant we had levelled the series 1–1.

* * *

Having chipped away at Queensland's resolve to win Origin II, we arrived in Brisbane confident of ending the Maroons' reign. However, our chances of victory were all over by half-time.

In the first half, they put four tries on us, leading 24–0. And although we salvaged some pride on the scoreboard, we lost Origin III 34–24 and the 2011 series 2–1. I was gutted. You can't give Queensland a 24–0 lead and expect to win an Origin game.

Sitting in the dressing room after the match, I felt like I had put more effort into that game than into Origin II. I made 50 tackles and 165 metres. It only added to the pain.

By Round 18 with the Sharks, I was broken physically and mentally. During our 26–12 victory against Canberra at Shark Park, I couldn't take the punishment to my body any longer. We had strung four consecutive wins together and were on track for a finals berth, but I couldn't go on. I walked off during the match without any feeling in my right arm.

'My neck's sore, my whole body's sore, I need a rest,' I said during the post-match press conference. 'It's the first time I've ever admitted I need a rest. I've just played too much footy and, like Flanno said, it's catching up with me.'

I backed up the next week against St George Illawarra with a calf injury, but missed the next two games for Cronulla. After that win over the Raiders, we never won another game in 2011.

We lost eight straight matches, missing the finals again and finishing twelfth on the ladder.

Shattered that we had let yet another opportunity to make the finals slip by, it was a cold reminder to me of how much of an emotional roller-coaster the life of a footballer can be. Needing a break, I took two weeks off training before Tim Sheens chose me for the end-of-season Four Nations tournament.

For the ARL, it was an important trip as we had surrendered the Four Nations trophy the previous year. Intent on returning the trophy to Australia, we advanced through our pool matches undefeated before beating England 30–8 in the final.

After the game, we gathered for a post-match function in Leeds. We weren't informed why we had all been brought together in a function room. I was presented with my second Harry Sunderland Medal. We were the number-one rugby league nation in the world at the time, and to be voted the best player among superstars such as Johnathan Thurston, Darren Lockyer and Billy Slater was incredibly humbling. It was truly a privilege and an honour to claim those two prestigious medals in my career.

I returned to Sydney, excited to see my little girl, Charly, and my baby boy, Kody. Upon my arrival home, I was offered the opportunity to step inside a boxing ring for the first time.

Two successful sporting promoters from New Zealand, Dean Lonergan and David Higgins, invited me to be part of a rugby league versus rugby union Fight For Life charity boxing night in Auckland. Exhausted and needing time to switch off with Anne and my two beautiful babies, I said, 'Thanks, but no thanks.'

I really had no desire to step into the boxing ring. But one thing is for sure: the seed had been planted.

19

Star Power

The first time I ever spoke at length to Todd Carney was during a phone conversation in September 2011. Previously, I had made similar phone calls to players whom the Sharks were attempting to sign. Jeremy Smith and Wade Graham were two players I contacted before they made the decision to join Cronulla. And as influential as those two players had been for the club, Todd promised to be a player of true star power.

A skilful five-eighth with the ability to create something out of nothing, Todd was the type of player we hadn't seen at the Sharks since the likes of David Peachey and Preston Campbell. He was without a club for the 2012 season, after parting ways with the Sydney Roosters at the end of the 2011 season.

Having secured my own future—extending my contract at Cronulla until the end of 2015—I picked up the phone in a bid to encourage Todd to sign with Cronulla. I had met Todd during the 2010 Four Nations tournament played in Australia and New Zealand. I liked him.

Sure, he had some baggage after being let go by the Sydney Roosters and the Canberra Raiders, but I knew from my time with him during that camp that, although he may have been rough around the edges, he had a good heart. And with what would most likely be his last chance to play in the NRL, I felt that at the Sharks he could have an opportunity to finally take hold of his career.

After the phone call, I began pursuing Todd's recruitment to the Sharks with the administration of the club. I spoke to head coach Shane 'Flanno' Flanagan, and I also began to support Todd publicly—which, I had noticed, not many people were doing. 'I know he's had a few chances, but when you look at what he has done recently, he hasn't done too much wrong in terms of general society,' I said during an interview with the press. 'He did a few things wrong when he was younger, but you haven't seen him going out beating up women or fighting people, and it's good that he's playing for us.'

When Todd signed a two-year deal in October 2011, his arrival was the boost of confidence we desperately needed at the club. His skill level with the footy was outstanding, and his impact at training was immediate. During that pre-season, we just needed to keep his mind on the job. And wow—that was the toughest task I had ever been involved with.

Early on after his arrival at the Sutherland Shire, Todd couldn't go out without people wanting a piece of him. He reminded me of a little puppy dog you see in the street—everyone just wants to pat him. There were girls, young women, teenage boys and even men who wanted to have a crack at him—I have experienced interest from fans before, but I have never seen anyone attract so much attention publicly as Todd did.

At five-eighth, he joined Jeff Robson as our halves combination. While we lost our first two matches of the 2012 season—a golden-point loss to the Wests Tigers at Leichhardt Oval in searing heat, and an 18–6 loss to Newcastle at home—we then won our next six matches.

Such was the immediate impact that Todd had on our side, it culminated in increasing calls for Todd to be chosen as five-eighth for New South Wales. 'If he keeps doing that over the next six weeks, there's no reason he couldn't get a Blues jumper,' I said to the media. 'I think the biggest thing for Toddy is he has to defend well, because that's a huge part of the Origin arena, and I think he's done that pretty well the last couple of weeks. He had the biggest, toughest bloke in [Canterbury player] Tony Williams against him a couple of weeks ago, and he handled himself really well.'

Todd was rewarded for his form by playing in all three matches for New South Wales during the 2012 State of Origin series. It was ultimately a series we would once again surrender to Queensland, but one that I still believe we should've won.

With seven minutes remaining in the Origin I match at Etihad Stadium, the Maroons were awarded a controversial try that should never have been allowed. Greg 'GI' Inglis lost control of the football as he touched down, but video referee Sean Hampstead flashed the green light, ruling that the boot of NSW hooker Robbie Farah had dislodged the ball as GI regathered to score. We lost the match 18–10.

After the match, GI didn't deny fumbling the ball. 'It was pretty much pure luck,' he said. 'I didn't know the ruling on it. I knew I had fumbled it. I didn't know the foot was underneath, to be honest.' The defeat meant we needed to win game two in Sydney to save the series.

While Greg Bird would finish as man of the match for New South Wales in Origin II, Todd was influential in our 16–12 victory, with his break of the Maroons defensive line. He then sent our fullback, Brett Stewart, away on a 50-metre sprint to the tryline, proving the difference.

If we felt unlucky as a group after Origin I, then the decider at Suncorp Stadium was something else. I have never felt more robbed of a result than after our one-point defeat in Origin III during 2012.

Once again, the Maroons were awarded a try that they should never have been given. This time it was Queensland centre Justin Hodges. As Blues forwards Beau Scott and Robbie Farah were being obstructed by Queensland's Ben Hannant, Hodges ran behind his Brisbane Broncos teammate to score. Up in the commentary box, former NSW captain Brad Fittler and Queensland great Wally Lewis both slammed the decision. Cooper Cronk's field goal with six minutes remaining allowed the Maroons to hang on for victory.

I couldn't fault the efforts of my teammates. As with every Origin series, we had worked hard as a group to get ourselves in a position to win that series. We only needed one of those two controversial calls to go our way and we could've been holding up the shield. It was the last match Ricky Stuart would coach for New South Wales, bowing out after three years at the helm of the Blues.

In the second half of the decider, I tore my hip flexor. It was a painful injury that would have an impact on the promptness with which I could return to the field for the Sharks. Incredibly frustrated, I was forced to wait until Round 22 before being declared fit to return against the New Zealand Warriors at Mt Smart Stadium. We had secured just one point from our previous four games. After three successive losses, it was a must-win game.

In one of Todd's best performances for Cronulla, we were too strong for the Warriors and won the game 45–4. Returning from his own injury, Todd scored 25 points from two tries, eight goals and a field goal. The seven-try romp reignited our season—but ultimately the spark was short-lived.

During our four remaining matches of the season, we could only beat South Sydney. In my 200th first-grade game, we lost 30–22 to the Wests Tigers. We won just two of our last ten matches, leaving us to limp into the finals in seventh position.

For our do-or-die semifinal, we were drawn to tackle the Raiders in Canberra on a Sunday afternoon. The match is remembered for three things: the Raiders ending our season, Todd injuring his Achilles tendon in the pre-game warm-up before completely rupturing it in the 48th minute, and the battle between me and young Canberra forward Josh Papalii.

We would learn after the post-match press conference that, prior to the semifinal, Josh was handed a mission by Raiders coach David Furner to keep me quiet throughout the match. And, to his credit, Josh did what was asked of him—not that I agreed with the way he went about his business.

In a contentious moment during the match, Josh hit me from behind after I had passed the ball. I called it a 'dog shot' after the game. 'I really don't care about Papalii,' I told a gathering of journalists after the loss. 'He hit me with a dog shot with a swinging arm once in the back without the ball. Other than that, I don't think there was too much to it.'

Being the competitor that I am, who despises losing, I was emotional when I made those comments. Although our season was over, I probably could've chosen my words better that day. In that moment after the match, I overreacted. Sure, Josh had got me good, leaving me with a shoulder 'burner'—which he would do once again the following year in Origin. But my biggest issue was the fact that the contest was portrayed as though Josh had physically dominated me—when the replays clearly showed he had hit me from behind without the ball.

I would get to know Josh well during the Kangaroos tour the following year and, funnily enough, we became friends on the tour. We shared a common interest in boxing, and on several occasions we would train together, one on one. That's the thing I always liked about footy—grudges were rarely held between players. It was certainly the case between Josh and me.

With our 2012 season over at Cronulla, disappointment quickly turned to delight both on and off the field.

I made my boxing debut in the Fight For Life charity event in New Zealand. And while playing for the Kangaroos in an end-of-season Test match against New Zealand in Townsville, I channelled Benji Marshall with a flick pass to help set up the winning try. It was just one of those moments when, as a footballer, you try something and it comes off. It could've so easily gone the other way. Safe to say, I never tried a similar pass again.

The victory put a full stop on my 2012 season, but away from the game my life with Anne was just beginning. The highlight away from footy without a doubt was marrying Anne in front of our family and friends in the Sutherland Shire. It was a day I had never pictured, but one I will never forget for as long as I live. It was a time in my life where I couldn't have been happier.

Anne and I travelled to New York—my favourite overseas destination—for our honeymoon, and it was awesome to spend a couple of weeks together on our own. As I said, life was great. I was married to my best friend, I was the father of a beautiful girl and a healthy little boy, and I was the proud captain of my club and state.

Then on 7 February 2013, something happened. It would be the beginning of the most tormenting 561 days of my life.

20

The Darkest Day

I didn't want to include the most difficult period of my life in this book. With only the last few chapters to be written, I wanted to walk away from the entire project. I just didn't want anything to do with that time of my life or the sickening emotions attached to it. By reliving it, I felt like I was digging up the past and picking at an old wound, when in reality I have moved on, eager to strive towards a better future.

Still to this day, I've found it too difficult to discuss certain elements of the most gut-wrenching period of my career. The mere mention of the 2013 supplements scandal makes my stomach churn. There are personally challenging days that occurred at the time and in the wake of the eventual ASADA (Australian Sports Anti-Doping Authority) ban that I haven't shared with even my own family.

I have worked hard on tempering my emotions ever since those incredibly dark days. But I will never completely forget the torment, and I never want to experience the indescribable feelings of uncertainty, distrust, emptiness and anguish ever again. I wasn't the only person dragged through this mess, but, without question,

I was the most high-profile rugby league player. And with that profile came challenges of the toughest kind—and also the greatest of consequences. I unwillingly was, because of my high profile, forced to confront a greater level of responsibility.

Indeed, had I known—way back when I signed my first contract with Cronulla as a teenager—of the mental and physical anguish that would begin in 2011 and culminate in 2014 with our ASADA ban, I doubt I would have ever committed to chasing an NRL career. The pain would not have been worth the pursuit. I have come a long way since 2011. But I will never overcome the mental and emotional torment I endured during the eighteen-month period of the ASADA investigation and its consequences. Sixteen members of the Cronulla Sharks playing group were breached by ASADA after they determined—according to their official records—that we 'may have used a prohibited substance between around March and April 2011.'

I don't know if I was duped or doped—I probably never will. But what I do know is a four-week period where supplements were introduced, supplied and administered by my club changed my life and those of my teammates forever. That's something I have also come to terms with. The overriding motivation in sharing this chapter with you is to tell my story. Even my harshest critics will concede that I am not one to shy away from putting forward my side of the story. Second, I want to help you understand my actions, the actions of others and how, without a shadow of doubt, I took every possible step—as I had always been professionally advised—to ensure my career could never be tainted like it was.

The first time I heard the word peptide was in 2011. It was on a Sunday morning, 20 March, the day before our Round 2 match of the 2011 NRL season against our arch rivals, St George Illawarra. I had played for the Sharks in our Round 1 season opener against the Canberra Raiders, finishing with a disappointing loss and a strained calf muscle. The calf injury was still nagging several days later. As a result, the tightness in my calf was just enough to limit my preparation leading into our clash with the Dragons.

To minimise the chance of aggravating the injury further, I sat on the sideline of Shark Park and watched my teammates complete the final training session ahead of our match with the Saints. Out on the field, the first-grade squad completed the short, sharp session with a light stretch before returning to the dressing rooms. Or so I thought.

Alone, I made my way back into the Shark Park locker room. Something wasn't right. The entire place was virtually empty. I didn't think too much about it, other than the rest of the boys must have been having a chat out on the field, as they warmed down.

I took a seat under my locker and waited a few minutes before thinking, 'Where is everyone?' Only a handful of players had wandered through the locker room. The scene was nothing like the typically boisterous vibe of a footy team's locker room the day before an important match with one of their greatest rivals. 'Where is everyone?' I asked one of the few teammates who had found his way back to his locker.

'Upstairs, getting that supplement,' he said.

'Right,' I said, pretending that I knew exactly what he meant. The reality is, I had no idea what he was referring to. I decided to take a walk upstairs to find out.

I climbed the stairs that travel up inside the Andrew Ettingshausen grandstand at Shark Park, before finding a few players inside a room that the club used outside of game day for rehabilitation and physiotherapy. Our head trainer at the time, Trent Elkin, was in the room chatting with a few of the boys. 'Hey boys, what's going on?' I said, announcing myself.

Trent explained that, because the calf injury had forced me to miss our regular training sessions during the previous few days, I had also been absent from a meeting that had been organised to explain that the team would be undergoing a new supplement regime. My absence from these meetings has since been documented and proven as fact.

'What are the supplements?' I asked. Trent explained to me that the supplements were amino acids and vitamins.

He added that Stephen Dank would be able to help me better understand what the supplements were. Dank had been invited to work at the club in a bid to assist our level of physical performance ahead of the 2011 season. In the wake of the supplements scandal, many believe that Dank's role at the Sharks was only ever associated with the controversial supplements program. That's not entirely true.

Dank also introduced an increased level of sports science technology that the cash-strapped Sharks had never been able to afford before. In 2011, the Sharks were on the breadline; the club was financially stricken, and there were stories that it would be relocated or dissolved. So, at the time, the arrival of Dank—who had worked at Manly from 2006 to 2010, where he played an integral role in making the club a leader in sports science—was considered a coup for the Sharks.

One addition to our training that Dank made was the introduction of GPS for the first time at the club. It monitored and assessed the training load of every player. This piece of technology immediately brought us up to speed with the fifteen other NRL clubs that already had the system in operation.

Dank also devised a player-specific training schedule that was individualised so that players from different positions—for example, forwards and backs—were no longer training with a 'one size fits all' mentality. At that time, Dank also overhauled the way the club handled a player's rehabilitation from injury. The implementation of oxygen masks for injured players in a bid to increase the flow of oxygen around the body and hasten their recovery was an example of the level of sports science he delivered to the Sharks.

I followed Trent along a corridor, inside the Andrew Ettingshausen grandstand and behind the game-day corporate suites, to a separate room where Dank was sitting. Trent asked Dank to explain to me what amino acids and vitamins were. Dank said they were a form of peptide. 'What's that?' I replied.

Dank said a peptide was a group of amino acids joined together. I then asked what the peptide is called. Dank replied, 'GHRP6—it's a type of secretagogue.' If you're reading this and have no clue what a secretagogue is, don't worry—neither did I.

Seeing that I was confused, he added, 'Let me explain it a little better.' He turned around to face a whiteboard and began writing, while explaining the intricate workings of an amino acid by drawing circles, numbers and lines. As you would expect, some of the information being put forward was sinking in, but a large majority of it flew well over my head. But, without any doubt, I realised the importance of what was being proposed.

I continued to pose questions to Dank and Trent, attempting to be certain about what was being explained. I finished the conversation by saying, 'I want to check the ASADA website first.'

Dank nodded his head and said, 'Sure, no problems.'

I walked back downstairs and into our locker room. I searched for the ASADA website on a computer that, as a team, we were permitted and encouraged to use. Then I searched for the list of banned substances related to rugby league at that specific time. I looked up the supplement that Dank and Trent had discussed, but the exact name of the peptide failed to appear on the search query.

I then telephoned our club doctor, David Givney. My phone records show that I called the Doc at 11.39 a.m. Due to legal advice, I can't reveal what was said during that phone call.

From the age of eighteen, when I arrived at Cronulla, I had been lectured by our club—and by the NRL and ASADA—on how to search for banned substances on the ASADA website. At the beginning of every season, ASADA officials would organise a presentation and information pack for every player, explaining how best to check for illegal and banned substances. Checking the WADA (World Anti-Doping Agency) website was never mentioned by the ASADA staff members. Not once. Yet this is an important—in fact, critical—point, which I would only discover in the coming months.

With my ASADA website query failing to deliver a positive match to the peptide I had searched for, and having spoken to our club doctor and asked questions of Trent and Dank, I felt comfortable that what I was about to consume was legal. I trusted the combined advice from my superiors.

Trent had been our head of high performance at the Sharks for the previous seven years, which is a long time to be associated with a coaching staff member in any professional sport. He was one of the most thorough and hard-working head trainers I had ever been associated with.

There's a bond that forms between a player and the club's head of high performance. During a season, a footballer will work just as closely—if not more closely—with the head trainer as with the head coach. Each day that you go to work as a professional rugby league player, you are constantly assessing how your body feels, which part of the body needs attention and why you may need to increase your level of conditioning or, alternatively, rest from a training session. And aside from the individual, no one at a footy club understands a player's body better than the head conditioner.

Trent was renowned for working incredibly long hours on a shoestring budget at the Sharks, researching different training methods and always looking to improve our health, diet, strength and conditioning. He may have been considered an authoritarian, but I knew that Trent's focus and preparation towards our training was A1. He would leave no stone unturned, so I knew that—given his diligence—it simply couldn't be feasible that he would put the players' careers, health and lives at risk.

Confident in my own checks and the faith I had in my superiors, I accepted the supplements. It wouldn't be until Round 12 of the 2011 season—ten weeks later—that, for the first time, I had my first sense of uneasiness.

During a recovery session in Melbourne, having been beaten 14–8 by the Storm, I was approached by our club doctor, Dave Givney. He asked if the players were still receiving Stephen Dank's products. I said yes, but only because we were being provided with vitamins and sports drinks (both found to be legal) by the club. But sensing that the Doc wasn't happy, I asked, 'Why, what's wrong?'

I'm paranoid at the best of times. I've been known to stress about the smallest of runny noses and to demand an X-ray for a sore big toe. So I immediately felt concerned by the Doc's line of questioning and the way he was describing Dank's character. As a result of this conversation, I asked if he would personally test my blood for 'absolutely everything'. Half of the team had already been urine-tested by ASADA agents throughout the previous three months. But the way Doc was talking alarmed me.

The next morning, a Monday, I drove to the Doc's surgery at Cronulla. He took a blood sample from me and said to wait a few days for the results. Ironically, around the same time, I was urine and blood tested by ASADA officials at training.

The Doc said all my results were clear—showing no abnormalities in testosterone or growth hormone. Further, I failed to receive any correspondence from ASADA, or information that the supplements we had consumed were on the banned list.

As history shows—and I now know—according to ASADA, the supplements were indeed on the banned list. I ended up accepting, with the most incredible reluctance, a backdated twelve-month ban on 22 August 2014. I was stood down immediately from all playing and training. I was banned from the final three matches of the 2014 season and was also deemed ineligible for Australia's end-of-season Four Nations squad.

Was I duped or doped? It's a question I know I'll never answer. I understand the widespread belief that every athlete is responsible for what they put into their body. But at what point did I not show responsibility?

I queried my superiors and asked for the specific name of the supplement, so I could search for its legitimacy. I called our club doctor. And I also did exactly what I was trained to do—by ASADA—from the very first ASADA briefing I had as a seventeen year old. I searched the ASADA website for the supplement being put forward, and the name provided to me by Dank failed to be displayed on the banned substance list.

After we were suspended in 2014, I received a phone call from my lawyer, Andrew De Celis. He'd called to tell me that the word 'secretagogue' was now on the WADA banned list. It had never been before. This appears to be the loophole that Dank used to explain why the peptides weren't on the banned list in 2011 and weren't illegal.

I can't change what happened, but I'm 100 per cent confident that I took the necessary steps within my power to ensure that any supplement I did take wasn't illegal at the time. I'm also 100 per cent confident that all the people involved would not have knowingly given any player at our club anything illegal. I had no problem taking supplements at the time. But I was disappointed at the actions of certain individuals who left the players' careers to be tarnished after it was those individuals who introduced the supplements to the players.

It wasn't until 2013—two years after receiving the supplements—that we were informed that the supplements fell under what is called the S2 clause in the WADA code. Throughout my entire career, I had never been taught about the S2 WADA code—in fact, until 2013, I had never even heard of it. I knew WADA was the World Anti-Doping Agency, but not once was I ever told to check the WADA banned list or to find out what an S2-class drug was.

Ironically, it wasn't until I had explained to ASADA representatives the amount of research I undertook on their website to ensure the legality of the supplements that the entire website was redesigned.

Was I duped or doped? I'll never know. But in the next few chapters, I'll attempt to detail how those torturous eighteen months ripped the heart out of not only every player involved, but also families and an entire community.

21

The Meeting

On 13 February 2013, six days after the infamous 'darkest day in sport' press conference had been held in Canberra, Cronulla Sharks chairman Damian Irvine gathered every player who had been part of the 2011 squad together inside the high-performance centre beneath the Monty Porter grandstand of Shark Park.

Damian and our football manager, Darren Mooney, had just returned from a meeting with the NRL, which had been chaired by Tony Whitlam QC, the head of the NRL's Integrity Commission. The meeting, which also involved NRL CEO David Smith and representatives from five other NRL clubs, was called to provide a better understanding of the investigation being undertaken by ASADA at that time. Following the meeting with the NRL, Damian and Darren then attended a separate briefing with ASADA representatives.

'From those meetings, the Sharks can confirm that none of their players have tested positive to performance-enhancing substances and that ASADA are focusing their investigation on a short period of time in 2011,' read a Sharks statement, which was sent later that day to every media outlet.

Having returned to Shark Park from the meetings with the NRL and ASADA, and now standing in front of the entire 2013 Cronulla playing squad, Damian told every player who wasn't at the club in 2011 to leave the room. Half a dozen players made their way to the exit.

Damian then explained to the remaining players in the room that the club would be providing legal defence for every player. The atmosphere in the room was tense and increasingly volatile. Some players were visibly emotional. Others were obviously frightened, firing questions at Damian that he couldn't—or wouldn't—answer.

After more than 40 minutes of emotion—especially anger—pinging across the room, Damian said that one of the directors on the Sharks' board, solicitor Peter Kerr, would help us better understand our road ahead. Kerr was also a member of the International Swimming Federation (FINA) advisory panel for doping, which gave him a deep understanding of the process of an ASADA investigation.

Inside a room where uncertainty, fear and pressure reigned, we saw Kerr as someone with a legal mind who would help us. So we, the players, told him our story. 'Why do we need to confess to taking something that we were only ever advised was legal?' one of the clearly shaken younger players in the team asked.

'And if it is illegal, all we can admit is that we have only ever taken what we were told too,' another said.

Looking back, Kerr was ill equipped to handle the situation. His answers carried little depth or understanding of our situation. He did little to allay the immense state of concern and fear that had filled the room. 'Look boys, I don't believe you've done a lot wrong, so you need to tell the NRL and ASADA what has happened,' Kerr said.

Just over 24 hours later, the shock, overwhelming confusion, fear and uncertainty were only to be exacerbated. On the lower level of the Cronulla Sutherland Leagues Club, every member of the 2011 playing squad sat quietly, waiting for another meeting to begin. It was Valentine's Day, 14 February 2013. Despite the absolutely serious nature of what was unfolding around us, the majority of the players were hopeful that this whole 'drama' would fizzle away without any serious impact.

During the meeting in the leagues club, we were introduced to Richard Redman, a lawyer appointed by the Cronulla board to represent the players. As he stood in front of us, Richard began asking questions about what had happened from the pre-season of 2011 up until Stephen Dank was told to leave the club on 29 May that same year.

The players reiterated what they had said less than a day earlier to Peter Kerr: none of them had any knowledge of ever taking an illegal substance. Richard then said, 'In situations like this, ASADA relies heavily on admissions.' And he emphasised the word 'heavily'.

In conclusion, Richard said, 'This is a waiting game—it won't be over quickly.' He wasn't wrong. The majority of the players were expecting the inquiry to be finalised in 'a few weeks'. It would take almost two years.

Once the meeting was over, I purposely stayed back as the rest of the group left. Looking back, I probably did this for two reasons. I was the player with the highest profile at our club, and I was certain that I could escape this tangled web because of the lengths to which I had gone to understand the legality of the supplements.

I waited until everyone had left the room before approaching Richard and asking if he had a moment to talk. During the group meeting, some of the players had come forward to give their version of events. But I wanted to talk with Richard, one on one, and explain everything that had happened from my point of view.

I told him how I had checked the ASADA website and how I had questioned Trent and Stephen before being given any supplements. Listening, Richard nodded and then began to explain about WADA's S2 category of prohibited supplements. He said that, even if a supplement is not listed on the ASADA website, it does not automatically mean that the substance is permitted for use—anything WADA classifies as an S2-category drug is also prohibited by ASADA.

My education and advice from the Australian Sports Anti-Doping Authority (ASADA) from the age of seventeen were only ever to do with ASADA. There was never any mention of searching or contacting the World Anti-Doping Agency (WADA). I knew the latter was the governing body for anti-doping in sports worldwide. But as far I was always told, our sport—rugby league in Australia—was governed by ASADA.

In all the meetings and information sessions with ASADA, there was never any mention of using WADA as a contact to assess whether a form of medication or supplement was illegal. And never had I ever heard of the S2 category. How can that be? I was a professional athlete who had played at the highest level of rugby league—played over 200 first-grade games—and not once had I been told to contact WADA, or research what the S2 category meant.

It was on that bottom floor of the Cronulla Sutherland Leagues Club that Richard broke the news to me for the first time—I would be fighting to explain why and how I had been administered an illegal supplement. I didn't know how to respond. I actually didn't believe what Richard was saying. At least, I didn't want to believe it.

Over the next fortnight, confusion underlined our every waking hour. Our greatest insights into the latest developments or direction of the inquiry were discovered through the media. Without any doubt, the media had more information than us, and they had it before us. The media knew what was going to happen to us next, before we had even been informed ourselves.

As the confusion continued, we were advised that Richard would now be acting solely as the lawyer for the players, while the coaching staff and club would be represented by their own legal team. What that did, intentionally or otherwise—I could never say—was instantly create a division within the club. Unwittingly or strategically, a sense of 'us versus them' had been formed. It only increased the tension, angst and discomfort we felt towards the club.

Upon being told the news that a separate legal team would be representing the players, I asked head coach Shane 'Flanno' Flanagan, 'What's going on here—aren't we supposed to be one club?'

He shook his head in confusion before responding, 'That's what I thought, too.'

22

Drug Test at the Dinner Table

I would find it extremely difficult, almost impossible, to place an actual number on how many times I was required to undergo a drug test during my entire playing career. However, if I were to include Cronulla's own in-house drug-testing policy, which was separate to that of ASADA's urine- and blood-testing procedures, the number would be over 100.

My first drug test by ASADA occurred when I was eighteen. I had just commenced my first-grade career with Cronulla and, like every other NRL-contracted player, I was tested randomly. The tests for Sharks players were only ever conducted at Cronulla's home ground of Shark Park after training. At least, that was the way the testing procedure was for the first four years of my career.

In the pre-season of 2006, just five years into my first-grade career, I was tested over the course of three consecutive training sessions: a Thursday, a Friday and then a Monday. At the time, I thought this was a bit odd. Wasn't the testing supposed to be random? There are 30 other players in our pre-season squad, and ASADA had 'randomly' chosen me over three consecutive working days. That's different, I thought.

There was nothing I could do about it or complain about, so I provided the samples and forgot about it.

While it was a small inconvenience, I never had an issue or problem with the ASADA agents who collected a sample from me. I was always forthcoming and polite with the officials in charge of overseeing each test, as I knew that they were merely doing their job. But in 2012, when blood testing began, things changed. At the time, ASADA's sample-taking process bordered on insulting and ridiculous. The entire process was anything but professional; in fact, it was demeaning and amateurish. It's why in 2019, under the direction of ASADA CEO David Sharpe, ASADA has made such a significant effort to work more closely with athletes, including providing more information than ever before to allow players to seek advice.

Following a morning training session during the 2012 season, I walked from Shark Park to be tested at 11 a.m. No big deal, right? Of course not. The issue was that by 8 p.m. the same night, in the pitch black of winter, knocking on the front door of my house was none other than a fresh team of ASADA agents. I vividly recall opening my front door and questioning in my own mind, 'What's going on here—why two tests in ten hours?'

As I have said previously, I have never had an issue with being tested for drugs. First, it's part and parcel of being a professional athlete. And second, I never had anything to hide. But to be tested twice, in the space of ten hours—this was anything but normal or 'random'.

My suspicion that I was being 'target tested' by ASADA was laid bare in a meeting with lawyer Richard Redman during the ASADA scandal. When we were alone in a room together, Richard became the first person to tell me that I was, indeed, a target of ASADA. What he said didn't come as a great surprise to me.

It had become blatantly obvious to me that ASADA wanted my scalp, given the frequency with which I had been asked to provide samples.

For the first time in my career, I became agitated by ASADA's obvious motives. As time went by, I gained a deeper insight into ASADA's deliberate attempt to claim a scalp big enough to ensure that the infamous 'darkest day in sport' press conference was something more than just white noise. A close friend, whom I trust, told me that when members of the Cronulla coaching staff were interviewed by ASADA, I was the focus of the investigators' line of questioning. 'What do you know about Paul Gallen?' the ASADA investigators asked.

As I said, my opinion of ASADA changed following that meeting with Richard. It was clear that all they wanted—and needed—in the wake of that Canberra press conference was a scalp. So the testing continued, and so did the negative drug readings—even during the times in my career when I couldn't play due to injury.

After injuring my ankle in the opening round of the 2014 season, I was sidelined for six weeks. I was out of action and unable to contribute to the Sharks' start to what would be a horrific year. Even while I was sidelined for all those weeks, I continued to have my urine and blood tested at my home and also at training.

The doorbell would ring as early as 7 a.m. or as late as 9 p.m. I would produce everything that was asked of me. Such was the frequency of the agents' visits to my house that they spoke candidly with my wife and children, using their first names. They would regularly ask how Charly or Kody were going with dancing or at school.

While it would have been easy to become upset and frustrated at the invasion of my family's privacy, I knew that—as a professional rugby league player—I had signed up for this, so I had to cooperate and do what was asked of me. But what did concern me greatly was what I considered to be a disturbing level of gross unprofessionalism from the entire group of ASADA testing agents.

Because of the disgraceful lack of professionalism in how the ASADA officials requested a sample from me, it got to the point where I would only supply that sample if I had a witness. My request—concerning the greatest invasion of privacy you can ask—was for a Sharks official, family member or close friend to be standing beside me while I provided the sample.

I had every reason to propose such a gross level of self-preservation, because of a frightening example of the level of unprofessionalism that I endured and, most likely, other athletes did, too. In 2012, two ASADA testing agents arrived at my house requesting a urine sample. Yet again, it was my second 'random' urine test that day, having already completed one earlier that morning at training.

I remember this night well, because shortly after the ASADA officers had said goodbye and I had closed my front door, I sat down at my dinner table to unwind after another long day of training. As I sat there, I couldn't believe what my own eyes were seeing. Sitting on the middle of my dinner table was the box that held the A and B urine samples, which I had provided only a few minutes earlier.

As I said, I was exhausted from a heavy day at training. But I was by no means delirious. I could only wish that I were imagining such things. In an indication of how improper and careless the ASADA agents were in the performance of their daily duties, they had failed to carry out the simplest of tasks: taking my sample with them.

They had forgotten to take the box of urine with them. Can you imagine this? Their one job is to collect thousands of samples each year from athletes across the country. We're talking about the greatest Australian athletes of our time, Olympians and world champions. Athletes with multimillion-dollar sponsorship deals and rewards for sporting excellence. And here was the country's official drug-policing agency, walking out my front door without the single most important part of their job. It's not like they forgot their car keys or wallet.

I just sat there completely stunned. And then my blood began to boil. It would be up to ten minutes before the same ASADA agents would return, knocking on my door and asking with embarrassment to retrieve the box of A and B urine samples. It doesn't matter if it was one minute, or ten minutes. They obviously tried to apologise, but I was furious as I willingly handed the tests over.

I immediately sat down and wrote an email to the Rugby League Players Association (RLPA), demanding that both samples that had been left on my dinner table be regarded as null and void. In my email, I reiterated that my entire career sat inside those two small jars, and that the sample box had been left out of the sight of the ASADA agents for more than ten minutes. As far as I was concerned, those two jars were contaminated.

I'll keep saying it—I have never had any issue with being tested. Test me every day—I couldn't care less. It's the process that I have never agreed with. That night, the thought of those A and B samples sitting on my dinner table illustrated more than ever before that the level of governance from ASADA's end didn't equal the damage that one dodgy test could do to an athlete's career. How many other samples have been left in locker rooms or in the homes and offices of other high-profile athletes?

The disturbing level of incompetence continued in the years that followed. In 2015, at my house, I was left in no doubt that ASADA was an agency being policed by officers who either didn't care about how incredibly important their role was, were incapable of doing their job or who were part-time operators, not qualified to fulfil the requirements of their position.

This time, I was asked by one of the ASADA drug-testing agents to fill a testing jar with urine to the level of 120 millilitres. Unfortunately, with my bladder dry, I could only muster 115 millilitres of urine. Physically, I just couldn't release any more. Now, given my entire career was in that jar, I was prepared to keep trying or at least wait twenty minutes in order to try to urinate again so that I could reach the level that had been asked of me.

Instead—and I remain stunned to this day that this happened—the drug officer said simply, 'Just shake it.' Sorry, what did you say?

'Just shake it, because if the bubbles go to 120 millilitres, that's enough,' he said.

Pardon me? Did this agent just explain how to fudge the sample? I wasn't sure if he was being serious. I instantly felt sick to my stomach.

This organisation has the power to ensure that all sport is played on a level playing field. They are undeniably powerful and can ultimately shatter lives and end careers. Yet here I was being told, so simply, how to fudge the system.

The naivety and lack of care were as consistent as my front doorbell ringing. It was the work of amateurs in a field that should display the highest regard for professionalism. I make no apology for saying as much.

23

The Options

Four days before the opening game of the 2013 NRL season, the Cronulla players who had been caught up in ASADA's tangled web gathered together inside the Shark Park gym. Waiting for us was lawyer Richard Redman. This meeting was exclusively for the players, because, as I've already mentioned, the coaching staff had been provided with a separate legal team.

'Look, I haven't got good news,' Richard said matter-of-factly. 'You are all facing a six-month ban. If you sit down with ASADA and explain what happened, they will offer you a deal or potentially less than six months, due to what is called "substantial assistance".' We all looked at each other, with our hearts somewhere in our stomachs.

As if sensing the anger, emotion and confusion rising from inside the small room, Richard then grabbed a whiteboard marker and wrote on a nearby whiteboard: 'OPTION A' and 'OPTION B'. The first option was the scenario he had just explained: tell ASADA what had happened, take the six-month ban, have the club pay your legal fees and continue to receive full pay throughout the duration of your suspension.

Then Richard said, 'There's Option B—you're on your own. You face the possibility of a provisional suspension by the NRL as you wait for your hearing, which means you're at risk of no longer being paid. You'll have to pay your own legal fees, and you'll also face the possibility of being found guilty of knowingly taking a banned substance and [be] suspended for two years.'

Looking up at the whiteboard, you only needed half a brain cell to determine which option held more appeal. However, as I stood there staring at the two options that would change my life and career, something just didn't feel right.

I thought about the information that Richard had already supplied to us. For over a fortnight now, we had gained what felt like a fairly detailed and comprehensive insight into the legal process. Richard had spent a lot of time with us, explaining in depth that for ASADA to distribute suspensions to players, they would need to be able to prove exactly what illegal supplement we had been given and when it had been given, or they would need someone to declare that what we had been given was, indeed, an illegal supplement.

Standing in front of the whiteboard, I reminded Richard of the advice that he had offered on the day we had first been introduced to him, on the lower level of the Cronulla Sutherland Leagues Club. In situations like this, Richard had stated, ASADA relied heavily—and he repeated the word 'heavily'—on an athlete coming forward with an admission of guilt.

It seemed as though now, standing inside the team gym, Richard was pushing an option that in every sense declared we were guilty of knowingly taking an illegal supplement. It definitely didn't sit well with me.

As we listened to Richard describe our predicament, a few of the players—including me—suggested that we call our managers or agents. My manager, David Riolo, and one of rugby league's longest-serving agents, Wayne Beavis, demanded an emergency meeting with Richard, to be held at 5 p.m. that same afternoon.

Our Round 1 match of the season against the Gold Coast Titans was scheduled to be played in five days. It was the furthest thing from our minds; in fact, we couldn't have cared less.

When our respective player managers arrived to meet Richard later that afternoon, we moved to an upper-level corporate suite inside the Andrew Ettingshausen grandstand. The open-air suite boasts expansive views of Shark Park, stretching out to the peaceful blue waters of Botany Bay. But with our managers now gathered in front of Richard, this was not the time to admire the scenery.

'We didn't ask for this—where's Elkin?' was the overriding argument the players put forward to Richard. The involvement from our agents was crucial. They provided a level of sanity to the room, as the players were far from calm or stable.

After arguing back and forth for several hours, eventually Wayne turned to Richard and asked, 'Do you have Option A and Option B in writing from the NRL or ASADA, as a guaranteed offer?'

'No,' Richard replied.

'Do you have it in writing that, while sitting on the sidelines suspended by ASADA, the players will continue to receive full pay?' Wayne asked.

'No,' Richard said.

'Well, this is bullshit then,' Wayne fired back. 'Until you have the two options in writing from the NRL, stating that the players will be paid while provisionally suspended, no one will be taking either Option A or B.'

One of the players then asked, 'Where do the coaching staff fit into this? Are they being offered a deal like us?'

Richard said simply, 'No, they're all gone.' The room fell silent—what did he mean?

'They won't be at training tomorrow,' Richard affirmed.

As a group, we advised Richard that we wouldn't be accepting either option. 'Okay then, until I hear more, just turn up to training tomorrow as normal,' he said.

Mentally drained and emotionally exhausted, we made our way out of the meeting. I felt as though I was trapped inside a nightmare, and I desperately wanted answers about how and why we were in this predicament. I felt that our former head trainer, Trent Elkin, was one person who could provide some sort of clarity about the situation. He had left the club to join Ricky Stuart at Parramatta in 2013, but he still lived in the Sutherland Shire.

After the meeting with Richard, two Cronulla teammates and I drove to Trent's house. In all the previous meetings with Richard and our chairman, Damian Irvine, we had asked if Trent could assist with the dire predicament we were in. Consistently, we were told that Trent had appointed his own independent legal team and that he would be handling his own matters his way. I was confused and upset, and I wanted to know why he was unable to help us through this crisis. So the time had come when we needed to find out Trent's position and hear his understanding of the state were in.

It was later that night when my two teammates and I knocked on Trent's front door. He invited us inside. We sat down at his dinner table and explained to Trent the options that Richard had broken down on the whiteboard for us. Trent was highly emotional; he repeatedly told us that he was sorry. 'I don't know what to say, boys . . . I don't what to say,' he kept stating over and over again.

As we posed more questions to Trent, hoping that he would be able to help us, he picked up his phone and began dialling a number. Who was he calling? We weren't to know. I can only presume it was his lawyer, because no less than six minutes after knocking on his door, we were walking back out again. Without ever saying it in those exact words, he had asked us to leave. (Due to the staggering emotional and mental toll the situation took on our lives, it would be three years before I spoke to Trent again.)

Having left Trent's house more confused than when I arrived, I returned home to Anne and the kids. The next morning, a Thursday—three days before our 2013 season opener against the Gold Coast—I arrived at Shark Park, passing through a sea of TV cameras, to begin training. Well, if you could call it that.

Given what Richard had revealed to us about the coaching staff—that 'they're all gone'—the players had no idea if head coach Shane 'Flanno' Flanagan and the rest of the coaching staff would even be there. To our surprise, Flanno and our football manager, Darren 'Moons' Mooney, walked into the dressing room and said, 'Righto, let's go and train.'

We literally had to stop ourselves from breaking out into a fit of laughter. 'Don't you know what's going on?' one of the players asked both Flanno and Moons. 'We've been told that the coaching staff have been stood down.'

They both replied, 'No one has told us that.' Moons pulled out his phone and called a Cronulla board member. After he hung up from the conversation, Moons turned to us and said, 'Okay boys, we've been told to carry on as normal.'

The playing group and coaching staff walked out onto Shark Park for our second-last training session before tackling the Titans. Training that day—and there would be similar days to come—was a complete and utter waste of time. Footy was the furthest thing from any of the players' minds.

During the session, we would be working through a particular training drill, when suddenly a teammate would simply drop the football and walk off the field. Then another one would wander off, his head held low. Then another and another . . . Physically and mentally, such was the burden of carrying the weight and pressure of the unknown that we just couldn't deal with the simple task of passing a football, especially when our careers sat precariously in the balance.

I have no clue how long that second-last training run before our clash with the Titans went for. To this day, it remains a complete blur.

The next day, the club formally stood down Flanno, Moons, trainer Mark Noakes, Dr David Givney and physiotherapist Konrad Schultz from all duties. Given the forecast we had received from Richard, the news of their suspension, while devastating, was far from a major shock. I phoned Flanno, Moons and the Doc to see how they were holding up. 'We'll be okay, just worry about yourself and carry on as normal,' was their reply.

Assistant coach Peter Sharp was immediately promoted to the head-coaching role. Later that afternoon, with the club seemingly in freefall, the entire 2013 playing squad was summoned to meet inside a room of the Rydges hotel, opposite North Cronulla Beach. This was two days before playing the Titans.

Once inside the conference room, four Cronulla board members faced the playing group and explained why the coaching staff had been stood down. I had a feeling that the board were expecting a vastly different response to the one they received— the players' reaction was best described as irate, bordering on out of control. 'We're supposed to be a club, and you're letting this happen,' one player shouted.

'What a joke! This is not a game—we're talking about people's lives here,' another yelled.

Players were shouting, swearing and demanding to know why the club wasn't sticking by them and the staff. Some of the players pressing for answers weren't even involved in the scandal, as they were contracted to the Sharks after 2011. 'Why aren't we united on this?' another player demanded. It was a sentiment that was still with me when I woke the following day.

I have no great insight into how we beat the Gold Coast Titans in the opening match of the 2013 NRL season on a Sunday afternoon at Shark Park. Never again in my career did I experience a preparation prior to an NRL match like the one the 2013 playing squad was forced to endure before this match. For example, I have no recollection of how I got to the ground that day. I have no clue at all if I drove or if someone else drove me. It was as though life was moving as normal around us, while we stood looking from inside an imaginary bubble of numbness and disconnection.

Inside the dressing rooms that day, it was quiet and subdued. It felt nothing like the preparation required to play in the NRL. The decision to scribble the names of our suspended coaching staff on the strapping around my bicep was made in the dressing rooms prior to our warm-up. I wanted to make a statement of support. Just as the players and I had demanded to see unity from the board, I thought it was imperative that we—the players— displayed a united front.

Flanno, Moons, Noaksey, Konrad and the Doc had begun the week doing everything possible to prepare us for the Titans. But as we got ready to run out onto Shark Park before an emotional crowd of faithful supporters, Moons was admitted to hospital due to stress. The remainder of the suspended staff sat watching the match from a nearby pub, the Gymea Tradies. I have been told that tears were streaming down their faces as we ran out.

The names of our coaching staff strapped to my arm got an obvious and immediate reaction from the TV broadcasters that televised our pre-game warm-up. However, as soon as I returned to the dressing rooms after our warm-up and prior to kick-off, an NRL official told me in no uncertain terms to rip the strapping from my arm.

I look back now and have a sense of regret for taking the stance of displaying this obvious visible support, because as the days, weeks and months passed, I learned that the entire affair was a situation where every individual involved was only focused on defending themselves. I'll never forget Richard Redman saying to me, 'Be careful who you choose to defend. I've seen these situations over and over, and self-preservation always prevails. No one will be there for you.'

Again, I have no idea how we won that game. In front of 17,541 passionate, loyal and vocal Sharks supporters, we held on to beat the Titans 12–10. I would like to offer a detailed account of how we scored, how we tackled and how we worked as a team to win that match. But I can't. It's as though my brain and body switched to autopilot for 80 minutes that afternoon.

After the match, I would learn that, from his coaches' box, our stand-in coach Peter Sharp had been texting Flanno for instructions during the match. It was both an indication of the respect that Sharpie had for Flanno and also an example of how ill-prepared we were as a team to play a game of football.

Apparently, I conducted an interview with Fox Sports immediately after the match. I have no memory of this interview occurring. 'It was [a] tough [week]. But once you cross that white line, it doesn't matter what happens off the field,' I told Fox Sports. 'You've got to get out there and do your job, and that's something I said before the game. It's emotional, but the emotion is shed after 30 seconds. Fortunately, we stuck to what Flanno [Flanagan] trained us to do the whole pre-season and that's play tough football.'

Our victory, during such a turbulent time, blanketed every major newspaper and news bulletin in Sydney.

* * *

The next morning, I woke to a phone call from one of Sydney's longest-serving and most highly respected talkback radio hosts, Alan Jones. 'Paul, you need to come and see me,' Alan said.

I had spoken to Alan on only a handful of occasions during my career. But that afternoon, I drove to Alan's lavish apartment overlooking Sydney Harbour. Given the media attention that the ASADA inquiry had consumed, Alan was well aware of our predicament. Within two minutes of chatting to Alan about our situation, Andrew Coleman SC was knocking on Alan's front door. 'I'd like you to meet Andrew,' Alan said to me. 'He's the best man to represent you and the rest of the players.'

Before I left, I thanked Alan for his support, his concern for our welfare and the opportunity to meet with Andrew. I explained that I would need to talk to the rest of the playing group about Andrew taking a deeper interest in our predicament.

Leaving Alan's apartment following our fifteen-minute discussion, I drove home struggling to digest how it was that I had got to this point in my life. The pressure that I felt on my own career, my credibility and my character was too much to bear. But as the captain of our club, I felt a responsibility to ensure that the other players who were caught up in this drama received the best possible advice they could.

The following morning, I organised for Andrew to introduce himself to the players. The meeting concluded with the players appointing Coleman SC as our barrister and with Richard Redman remaining on as our lawyer.

It was ahead of our Round 2 match—a 42–4 loss to the Canterbury Bulldogs—that we held one-on-one meetings with Richard. In each of these meetings, the question originally proposed by our player managers—about compensation from the club due to the impact this mess would have on our careers—became the discussion point.

Richard asked me if I had considered requesting compensation from the Sharks. I had given it no previous thought. I hadn't been thinking straight for almost a month. However, I had heard what other players were considering with regard to compensation, which helped me as I pondered my own dilemma.

I explained that my priority was to be able to maintain the lifestyle that I had worked so hard to achieve. I added that, instead of filing for damages against the club, I wanted a twelve-month extension of my current contract and I wanted my sponsorship deals at the time with Harley-Davidson and Toyota—which I would eventually lose as a result of the ASADA scandal—covered as a loss of earnings.

In fact, of the five sponsorship deals I had with companies, only clothing and shoe supplier Blades continued to align me with their brand. My association with the scandal would result in the loss of just over $200,000 in sponsorship earnings. I have since discovered—and I found these quite amusing—some of the other proposals that a few of my teammates put forward to the club. One of my teammates asked for the remaining mortgage on his house to be paid off. Another asked for permission to commence UFC fighting.

In the end it all meant very little, as compensation was dependent on us accepting Option A—a six-month suspension.

What disgusted me most about this period and this process was that everything I have just written here was being reported in the newspapers at the time. I can only assume the information was being leaked by some members of our Cronulla board.

Physically and mentally exhausted from not knowing if we would be suspended for six months or two years, three of my teammates approached me after training one day to explain that they had had enough and were going to admit guilt to ASADA. 'We're going to accept the six-month deal,' the trio said.

First of all, I queried why they would do that. 'What are you going to admit to?' I then asked. I was confident that the three players hadn't been aware of what they had taken, other than the fact that they had been told the supplements were amino acids and vitamins.

They said, 'We just want it to be over.'

'Don't be ridiculous,' I said. 'This is your life we're talking about.'

A couple of days later, they had changed their minds.

It shows the state of confusion and lack of transparency forthcoming from ASADA during this period that over 12 months later one of the three players that had contemplated the life-changing deal was overlooked when we were suspended in 2014.

The weeks and, indeed, months that followed were surreal. Our lawyers kept saying, 'Until you hear from us, live your normal lives.' But there was nothing normal about what we were enduring. Having your face splashed across the front and back pages of the newspaper, or on the nightly news, for weeks and months is not normal.

Our emotions were being controlled by the speed at which the media filed their stories—which, at times, was a daily occurrence.

As time passed, the media reports slowed down to the point where there would be weeks when we wouldn't see a single line about the investigation reported. But as soon as each new development of the story appeared, it meant that for the next seven days, journalists and TV cameras would be camped at Shark Park. And the entire time, we—the players—wouldn't know any more than what had been reported.

Once a month, a new report would emerge claiming that ASADA was going to ramp up their investigation. A resolution was coming. And then, nothing. We'd work ourselves into a panic for no reason. This same process would occur over and over again.

In May 2013, teammate Wade Graham was the first player to be interviewed by ASADA. I wouldn't be asked to answer questions from ASADA until August 2013. By the time my final interview was conducted in August 2014, it had been fifteen months since Wade was first questioned.

I can say matter-of-factly that the entire interview and investigation process were a farce. Our lives were placed on hold as we waited for ASADA to do whatever it was they needed to do— break our spirits, fray our friendships and splinter our families—in order to gain an admission of guilt from us. It was the only way they could 'win'.

By Round 5 of the 2013 season, the frazzled Cronulla Sharks playing group had reached its lowest ebb. After we had been beaten 13–6 on a Saturday night by the Parramatta Eels at Parramatta Stadium, Flanno—who had been reinstated as head coach—walked into the dressing room. As he did after most losses, Flanno began breaking down our performance, surmising how we were beaten.

I let him speak about the match, until he then began talking about the importance of preparation. I spoke up. 'Are you serious? We can't prepare,' I snapped. As if I had provided a green light for the rest of the playing group, frustration and anger began spilling freely across the room. Even those players absolved from the ASADA scandal began venting.

Ultimately, the criticism and anger weren't directed at Flanno or the club—they were directed at the NRL. 'Why are they [the NRL] allowing this to happen? Why don't they tell ASADA to put up or shut up?' one player asked. 'Can't they stop this death by a thousand cuts—someone is going to hurt themselves.' And with that one line, the room fell silent. What the player had said was spot-on.

The demise of the health and wellbeing of some players had become visibly frightening. Aside from players walking off the field in the middle of training sessions, incapable of finding the energy to run, pass or sprint, several players also needed to be formally medicated. I was one of them. I was prescribed antidepressants, which I continue to take to this day.

And that's another point. While the game moved on in the wake of this scandal, we as players have carried the burden—some longer than others—every day since. So low was the point I had hit that, one night at home, I told Anne to ring Mark 'Noakesy' Noakes, the Cronulla Sharks' long-serving trainer. 'Ask him to come around now,' I told Anne. Deep down, I knew that if anything were to happen to me that night, Noakesy was the type of person who could calm me down. I was going to harm myself.

Thankfully, Noakesy listened to Anne. He sat beside me for a few hours, until my Mum drove from Penrith to also be by my side. Concerned about my wellbeing, Mum stayed with me for an entire week. Instead of her going to work, I covered Mum's weekly wage just to have her with me at a time when I wasn't sure what I was capable of doing to myself.

Steve 'Noycey' Noyce was in the dressing room that night at Parramatta Stadium. It was his first game as CEO of Cronulla.

He had been appointed to the position by the NRL, which had stepped in to guide the club through the ASADA crisis. What an unbelievably daunting introduction it was for Noycey.

He was actually the second person placed in charge of the Sharks by the NRL. The first person was Bruno Cullen, who showed little interest in assisting the players, explaining to us that his only focus was to be in and out of the role within six weeks.

At first, I was sceptical of Noycey, largely because he had been appointed by the NRL, which at that precarious time had shown little compassion for the players. It would take several weeks before I would feel comfortable about opening up to him. But the longer and deeper the investigation went, the more I began to notice Noycey's genuine concern and willingness to support us.

Each morning, Noycey would drive for almost an hour from his home in Sydney's west to arrive at Shark Park. Most mornings, he was the first one at training. He would make sure he was at training every day, speaking to us individually—with no player considered more important than the player he was speaking with at the time.

His care was authentic, and his priority was the players. Not a day went by that Noycey didn't attempt to keep us updated and informed of the progress of the investigation, as opposed to learning about what was to hit us next via the media—as was the case when Bruno was in charge.

In the days after our loss to Parramatta, I knocked on Noycey's office door. 'My situation is different to the other boys, Noycey. Not only do I know that I did more than anyone else to ensure those supplements were legal, but I feel like I've got more to lose,' I said. 'My situation is different because I'm the face of this. It's not him or him or him, it's me on the front page or 6 p.m. news— it's me. Like it or not, that's the case.'

The longer the investigation dragged on, the more I learned to understand why I was the one ASADA wanted. Richard Redman had suggested to me that, because of the magnitude of the 'darkest day in sport' press conference, 'they needed a scalp'. Richard had also told me that, during the interview process with ASADA, I would be the last of the players to be formally interviewed—a tactic commonly used in many criminal cases to form evidence against the person they are intent on bringing down.

I told Noycey that I wanted to look at the possibility of appointing my own legal team—separate to the rest of the playing group. Some of my teammates had stopped attending meetings—some had been told to stop attending again.

What had begun with twenty-five players, had been cut to twenty, then 19 and 18.

'What's going on here?', I thought. If what Richard Redman had told me was true, that I was the scalp they wanted, I could stay with the current legal team—who as far as courtroom victories go, would've been happy to have 17 of the 18 players at the time escape suspension.

I didn't want to take the chance of cutting a deal, without being able to defend myself and tell my side of the story.

Noycey said he would need approval from the NRL and RLPA for me to change my legal team.

Just like a number of other Cronulla players who were involved in the investigation but were now playing with rival clubs, I appointed an independent lawyer to act on my behalf.

During those eighteen months, I relied on a small circle of only my closest family and friends for support. They were people I was certain I could trust and confide in. One person who I felt I could turn to was an old schoolmate from Parramatta Marist, Andrew De Celis. Andrew and I were mates well before rugby league became my full-time profession. He was also a lawyer, who worked for one of Sydney's leading law firms, Gilbert + Tobin.

In the months that followed my decision to appoint my own legal team, Andrew's legal expertise became invaluable—but what was of greater influence was his day-to-day counselling on a human level. He kept my spirits up on the dark days.

It was through Andrew that I was introduced to Gilbert + Tobin partner Steven Glass. Steven would take up my representation, while I also appointed former Supreme Court judge Greg James QC as my barrister.

Amid all this, I was chosen to represent Australia in the 2013 ANZAC Test against New Zealand in Canberra. For the first time since the pre-season, I felt like I could switch off from the ASADA drama.

24

The Punch

Inside the NSW Origin team hotel, Blues coach Laurie Daley stood in front of the entire playing group prior to game one of the 2013 State of Origin series. 'By looking at this, it appears to me that they want it more than us,' he stated.

In his hand, Laurie held a TV remote control. Pause and rewind; pause and rewind. Laurie replayed the embarrassing footage on the TV screen in front of us over and over again. The video showed one thing: Queensland players were treating us like their playthings.

We watched vision of past Origin matches, dating back two years. We winced as Queenslanders—including Cameron Smith, Billy Slater, Sam Thaiday and Nate Myles—intentionally landed late on the limbs of our Blues teammates, clipping us with an elbow or diving on our backs or heads as we crossed the tryline.

It was Origin, so the niggling tactics were hardly shocking. But sick of losing series after series, Laurie had had enough. He was challenging us. So there and then, I decided to take a stand. As captain, I would do what I had to do to put a stop to the thing that the Maroons were more willing than us to do for victory.

After watching the footage, I told myself and nobody else that if the Queenslanders implemented the same tactics during Origin I in front of our home fans at ANZ Stadium, I would show them that enough is enough. My intention was never to throw a punch—it was to show my teammates that no longer would we be treated as pushovers.

Due to a knee injury suffered in a one-point victory over Newcastle in Round 8 with the Sharks, I needed every bit of the next four weeks leading into Origin I to recover. Even then, I was only 90 per cent fit going into the opening game of the series. In front of just over 80,000 passionate Blues fans, we prevailed 14–6 to take a crucial 1–0 lead in the series. But it would be my confrontation with Maroons forward Nate Myles that would, quite incredibly, forever change the way that rugby league was played.

The strapping on my right knee must have seemed like a red rag to a bull because, just moments before NSW teammate Michael 'Jenko' Jennings scored a try close to half-time, Nate grabbed my leg and twisted my still-recovering knee as he tackled me to the ground. The pain from the wrenching action raced all the way up my right leg to my hip. If nothing else, Laurie had a new clip to show at our next video session.

However, in that moment, I thought about what I had told myself only days earlier. As I played the football, I looked at Nate and took a mental note. Then, walking back past Nate after Jenko had scored his try to give us a 14–0 lead, I said to Nate, 'If you do that to me again, I'm going to put one on your chin.'

Maroons forward Sam Thaiday overheard what I had said. For what it was worth, he offered his own two cents on the situation. I told him where he could go.

With 41 seconds remaining in the first half, Queensland was on the attack and Nate was carrying the football towards the halfway line. My Blues teammates, Anthony Watmough and Luke Lewis, met Nate together in defence before I arrived as the third man to complete the tackle. Wanting to make a point of the tackle, I tried to cheap shot Nate by swinging my right arm heavily into him. My forearm hit him just under his chin.

As Nate and I began to get up for the play-the-ball, he gave me a shove with his elbow and forearm while asking, 'Is that all you've got?' We then stood together, rapidly firing a repertoire of obscenities at each other.

Nate then rolled the footy under his foot, before giving me a final heavy shove, this time in the chest. He followed it up by walking towards me. He asked again, 'Is that all you've got?'

A split second earlier, in my head, I had told myself, 'If he comes at me, I'm going to hit him.' So that's exactly what I did. I jabbed at Nate's chin with my left fist before swiping at him with my right fist. I then reloaded with an uppercut. However, the swarm of jerseys, with arms and chests pulling us apart, ended any chance of more punches being thrown.

It would take over a minute for the mess of pumped-up big men to be separated. As the dust settled, referee Ashley Klein called me out. He placed me on report for my original swinging arm, but not for the fight. I then asked Ashley, 'Can I say something? He's grabbing my knee and twisting it every time I get tackled. Every time.'

Ashley replied, 'We'll keep an eye on it, but you can't take it into your own hands.'

I responded, 'He's been doing it series after series, head butt after head butt and twisting after twisting.' However, the second

I walked away from Ashley, Nate was no longer my concern. It was that Queensland might score a try.

There were just over 40 seconds remaining in the first half. We had worked hard to gain a 14–0 advantage, but the Maroons now had a full set of six tackles on our 30-metre line. It was with relief that they were unable to break our defensive line.

Back inside the NSW dressing rooms at half-time, the punch was hardly spoken about—unlike on social media and on TV and radio. It wouldn't be until after the match that Laurie found me at my locker and whispered into my ear, 'Well done for standing up to them, not only for yourself but for all of New South Wales.'

Like most issues I encountered during my career, that fight took on a life of its own. Mums began phoning talkback radio shows, declaring that they would never let their son or daughter play rugby league. I was labelled a thug, out of control and reckless. It was as though nobody had ever seen a fight on a football field before.

Despite Maroons coach Mal Meninga telling the press after the match, 'It's Origin, we're comfortable with what happened,' the NRL used the punch as the catalyst for immediately intro-ducing a 'no-punch rule'. I had heard that the NRL had been considering banning the punch for some time. But such was the publicity the incident between Nate and me had received that the NRL had now decided to act.

The one thing that disturbed me most was the hypocrisy from so many people involved with the game. Origin was and contin-ues to be promoted for its brutality. You can say it isn't, but it is. The fans are aware that when they watch State of Origin, they are seeing the fastest, fittest and strongest rugby league players in the world. They also know that, without hesitation, those 34 players will be doing anything and everything in their power to ensure that their opposition is not only beaten on the scoreboard, but also physically. It's a huge reason why State of Origin is the most watched sporting event on TV.

In front of all those impassioned fans at ANZ Stadium, in that split second, I wasn't thinking about mums and dads watching the match at home. But the backlash and commentary were incredible. I'm adamant it ballooned into something much more significant largely because it was State of Origin and also because of the polarising figure I was in Queensland.

If you listen to or read any interview since the punch, Nate has never once complained about the incident. We both know what happened, and I've got so much respect for Nate for the way he has never said anything otherwise.

'My thought process wasn't really on how the game was going to handle it. I've always been a believer in what happens on the field stays on the field. I would have been happy for it to all finish after that,' Nate said. 'People want to see fighting. Now, maybe they're watching the wrong sport. It's different. When it was all about the fans, they just wanted to see a free-for-all. It's not that way anymore. It's about changing the image, and the players have to be responsible for that.'

Nate is correct and it's why in the wake of the incident, we partnered for an advertising campaign for depression awareness.

Not long after Origin I, I took up an invitation to speak with students at a NSW country primary school. Singleton Heights Public School headmaster, Simon Mulready, had contacted the Sharks' front office to ask if I could address a couple of Year 5 students via telephone hook-up, as they had punched each other during a schoolyard rugby league game.

The boys were called into the headmaster's office, and I was placed on the loudspeaker. I spoke on the phone to the boys for about ten minutes, and told them that I wasn't proud of my conduct. I said that my actions were in a completely different environment to a schoolyard. I wasn't excusing my behaviour, but providing context—a rugby league field, especially State of Origin, is where emotions often spill over.

I'm aware of the impact that the incident had because even until the final days before my retirement, I would be asked about Nate and 'the punch' during school visits. It's funny—not one student has ever asked me about ASADA. But that punch? Absolutely. I suppose it's further proof of how huge State of Origin is.

Is the game better for stamping out fighting? The politically correct thing to say is 'yes'. And sure, I'm pleased that the game will be played into the future without the need for wild punches to be thrown. But that doesn't mean it won't happen.

Even after the one-punch rule was introduced, players still couldn't resist lashing out with their fists in the seasons that have followed. And that's the thing—the rule might be in place, but if someone is going to throw a punch during a match, they will.

25

The Dreaded Spoon

In March 2014, Shane 'Flanno' Flanagan's appeal against a twelve-month NRL ban was denied, resulting in Sharks assistant coach Peter 'Sharpie' Sharp taking full control as head coach of the NRL squad. Sharpie took on the role in the belief that he would be the interim coach until Flanno was successful in returning at some point during the upcoming 2014 season. But that never happened.

The ASADA investigation remained ever-present. We were no closer to discovering what the investigation would bring. All we knew was that, as far as the 2014 season was concerned, Sharpie was now in charge. 'Look boys, we know that Sharpie didn't ask for this, we know he's not our head coach, but unless we try and put in for him and ourselves, we're not going to get anywhere,' I told the players prior to Round 1.

The response from the boys was, by and large, positive. However, that sentiment of digging in together and for each other lasted no more than a few weeks. On the back of injuries— including a syndesmosis ankle ligament injury that I suffered in our 2014 opening-round defeat to the Titans—the losses quickly mounted as the level of care and focus plummeted, and the season turned into a farce.

In an attempt to handle the deflating lows I would confront each time a new media report or development emerged in the ASADA case, I sought professional psychological counselling. I also committed to continuing with antidepressant medication, which I had begun taking twelve months earlier.

Counselling isn't something I enjoyed. I have no doubt that counselling can be an unbelievably beneficial tool for anyone who is suffering from depression. But my problem was that I revolted against the one vital element required at each counselling session: opening up. I despised talking to anyone, largely because I refused to trust people outside my immediate family.

The media reports on the ASADA investigation would consist of four days of extensive coverage, and then—just like a rolling set of waves—they would be gone. Four weeks later, there would be another four more days of cameras and press following your every move . . . and then they would be gone again. For those players caught up in the scandal, this in-and-out, up-and-down life felt like you had a monthly illness or virus that would flatten you and leave you not wanting to leave the house. And there wasn't a single thing you could do about it.

Climbing out of that once-a-month hole became extremely difficult. This was largely because deep down, despite the head-lines, you knew that the investigation was nowhere near complete, and therefore it would only be a matter of time before the waves of fear and uncertainty would return.

At the time, I had the overwhelming feeling that the public had a clear opinion about the investigation. Either way, they wanted the NRL and ASADA to just get it over and done with, and to put the players out of their misery. And, certainly, I wanted it over, too.

I wanted my life back, and I wanted my wife and children to live without a cloud over their heads. But I didn't want the investigation to be over at a cost or penalty to me. Because, as far as I was concerned—and still am—I had done what I had been taught to do by ASADA since I was seventeen years old: I had checked the banned substances list.

* * *

Cronulla won a total of five matches and lost an embarrassing nineteen games in 2014. Had you witnessed what I had seen at training that year, you would have been like me—still scratching your head as to how we managed to win one game, let alone five.

Training wasn't the training you would expect from a multi-million-dollar sporting organisation. Training was simply turning up. From an NRL first-grade point of view, there was nothing— and I mean nothing—remotely physical, intense or strenuous about what we were doing at training.

By the halfway point of the 2014 season, with our season already in freefall, I attempted to offer an insight into the current problems at Cronulla during my co-hosting role with Triple M radio. 'I don't want to sit here and bag Sharpie, because Sharpie has been thrown in the deep end,' I said. 'Because he came out on day one and said he doesn't want the job.

'To me, players are like schoolkids. If you can turn up Monday and the coach isn't going to rouse on you for not having a good game, I don't think you're going to put 100 per cent in. I think that's been the problem throughout the year. I don't think players have been putting 100 per cent in because they're under the impression Sharpie isn't putting 100 per cent in. I just think we've lacked direction there throughout the year.'

On reflection, I am extremely disappointed in myself for making those comments. It was never my intention for the comments to be perceived as placing blame on Sharpie for that horrid 2014 season. The comments weren't fair to Sharpie at all. He knows I'm sorry for the way I communicated that insight.

Unfortunately, it took time before both Sharpie and I could put our egos aside to discuss what I was attempting to say. It was during a phone call not long after I made the comments when I apologised to Sharpie for portraying him the wrong way.

Those comments were just another black eye for the entire 2014 season, which was essentially a write-off for our loyal fans. Everywhere you looked, it was ugly. Sharpie was doing his best. It wasn't like he was turning up and twiddling his thumbs, but the players had such disinterest in the entire season that it created an environment of little care or responsibility from their point of view.

Not only did we begin the season without Flanno, but Todd Carney would also be sacked by the last weekend of June. Two days later, Sharpie handed in his resignation. From the NSW Origin camp in Coffs Harbour, I phoned him to make sure his reason for quitting had nothing to do with my comments. He assured me that it didn't. He needed to stand down for his own health reasons, he explained. I'm pleased that Sharpie remains someone who I have great respect for and happily speak to whenever we bump into each other at a game or around the Shire.

So, not only had we lost our head coach, Flanno, but our assistant coach was gone, too. With few options remaining, James 'Shep' Shepherd—Sharpie's assistant coach and the Sharks' under-20s coach—was then promoted and handed the reins to the NRL squad.

Sharpie's exit, with ten rounds remaining in the 2014 season, was just another crisis that the club could ill afford. In the

48 hours after Sharpie stepped down, the Cronulla board asked me to contact then Test coach Tim 'Sheensy' Sheens, who had been let go by the Wests Tigers in 2012. The Sharks' administration wanted Sheensy to take over for the final ten rounds of the season, in the hope that his experience and leadership could help restore pride and respect for our performances and also the Cronulla jumper.

My relationship with Sheensy dated back to when he selected me for Australia in 2009. The board thought I could convince him to join us and help salvage what was a sinking ship. But with only ten matches remaining, Sheensy wasn't keen to take on the role for such a small window of time. He thanked me and the club for thinking of him, but he said that, unless the job was more permanent, he couldn't commit to it.

Looking back, Sheensy would've been on a hiding to nothing. We were a club involved in the ASADA scandal, we had just sacked our playmaker in Todd Carney, we had players dropping like flies with injuries and we were sitting in last position on the competition ladder. After Sheensy, I then spoke with former champion halfback Brett Kimmorley about the coaching role, but he wasn't interested, either.

There's no denying that Shep deserved his crack at the head-coach role. To his credit, he delivered one of the club's greatest upsets, against the Sydney Roosters in Round 17. I watched the incredible victory from Coffs Harbour, inside camp with the NSW State of Origin side. Without Luke Lewis, Chris Heighington, John Morris, Andrew Fifita and me, Shep's Sharks trailed the defending premiers 24–6 before rallying to record an amazing 30–28 win at Allianz Stadium.

'Let's put it all in perspective. With Gallen, Lewis, Fifita, Morris and Heighington all out, a coach who is a replacement for a replacement, being behind 24–0 after 30 minutes, ASADA hanging around and add to that the appalling act by Todd Carney, I'll tell you how I describe it. I've been around for 50 years at this level, and I'd say this is the best win in the club's history,' Rugby League Immortal Bob Fulton said during his commentary for 2GB. 'Outside of the win by Balmain over Souths in the '69 Grand Final, I think it's maybe the best win under the circumstances for the last 50 years.'

The victory dance was short-lived, as the calamity off the field and within the coaching ranks would continue. Prior to the Melbourne Storm thrashing us 48–6 in Round 23, John 'Bomber' Morris—who had announced that he would retire at the end of the season—was forced to coach the team, after Shep was bedridden by a virus. Our embattled season degenerated into an unimaginable case of last man standing, with Bomber—who only weeks earlier was our starting hooker—having to take control of a spare-parts NRL side.

The list of unavailable players was like nothing I had ever seen from a professional sporting outfit. In total, fifteen of the Sharks' top-25 NRL squad that began the 2014 season were unavailable for selection. Eleven of those fifteen players—including representative forwards Luke Lewis, Andrew Fifita and Wade Graham—had been ruled out for the season with injury.

Here's the list of unavailable players from our top-25 NRL squad ahead of our Round 23 loss to Melbourne: Luke Lewis, Wade Graham, John Morris, Andrew Fifita, David Fifita, Siosaia Vave, Beau Ryan, Sam Tagataese, Bryce Gibbs, Eric Grothe Jr, Jacob Gagan, Todd Carney, Anthony Tupou, Ricky Leutele, Isaac De Gois and Nathan Stapleton.

Although it was gut-wrenching, it was hardly surprising that our season ended with the club's first wooden spoon since 1969.

It's the one 'trophy' I desperately wanted to avoid during my NRL career. However, even the most successful clubs would've struggled to perform with as much resolve as we did in 2014— especially considering the stress, distraction, crisis meetings and casualty ward of players that we experienced during that season.

26

History in Blue

History has amplified the task and the significance of New South Wales winning the 2014 State of Origin series. The record books show that the 2014 three-game series resulted in the first shield presented to the Blues in eight years, or a total of 24 Origin matches. It would take a further four years for New South Wales to claim their next series victory—in 2018.

The Queensland era of State of Origin domination—winning eleven of the twelve series played from 2006 until 2017—is unlikely to ever be repeated. Never before had the game of rugby league witnessed the collection of champions and future immortals that the Maroons' team boasted during that period of dominance. Cameron Smith, Johnathan Thurston, Greg Inglis, Billy Slater and Cooper Cronk were responsible for inflicting years of gut-wrenching disappointment on New South Wales.

The damage caused during Queensland's period of dominance was far-reaching. It cost coaches their jobs and cut short many NSW players' Origin hopes, dreams and careers in the sky-blue jersey. It's impossible not to consider that the bloodletting, perception of players, intense criticism, pressure and embarrassment that followed the Blues after every series loss during that period may never have occurred had Queensland not been armed with such a special group of talented players. This is why the achievement of the 2014 NSW State of Origin side should rank as one of the greatest series wins in Origin history.

The gap between Queensland and New South Wales had been closing since 2011. For example, in that year, the series was locked up at 1–1 when both teams arrived in Brisbane for the decider. Queensland claimed victory and the series by beating the Blues 34–24. It was a lot closer in 2012—Queensland won the series in the game-three decider by a solitary point, 21–20. And in 2013, Queensland won the series in the game-three decider, 12–10.

So in 2014, when NSW coach Laurie Daley gathered the Blues in camp at Coffs Harbour—our training base for this series and for the next three years—there was a collective belief among the coaching staff and playing group that we could end the pain. From day one in camp, there was a different and noticeable feeling of desire within the group. With the exception of Luke Lewis, not one player selected for the Blues had ever won an Origin series, which to me was part of our drive—because you simply can't put a value on want and desire. In rugby league, so many results are determined simply by which team wants to win more.

Training during the opening camp of 2014 was short, sharp and intense. We didn't need to get on the drink together, or 'bond'. We already got on well. And, as a group, nothing binds you together more than a common goal.

We had a new halves pairing in Josh Reynolds, our five-eighth, and Trent Hodkinson, our halfback. Trent was untested in the Origin arena, while Josh had only played from the interchange bench in the 2013 series. It was a significant show of faith from Laurie—and to the two boys' credit, they refused to let him or their state down. Trent and Josh ran the majority of our video sessions, standing at the front of the room before we hit the training paddock each morning, explaining how we were going to train and play.

There was a real sense of belief and buying into the plan. It was obvious that, to end Queensland's dominance, we needed to come together like never before. Above all, there was a huge focus on winning game one in Brisbane. I had never experienced a greater intention to finish victorious in game one than I did in the 2014 series. We knew that, if we were going to win the series, we had to take the points first up in Brisbane before then returning to our ANZ Stadium home in Sydney to try to wrap up the series.

I'd always enjoyed going to Brisbane's Suncorp Stadium for State of Origin. I love the Queenslanders' passion for Origin and their hatred for New South Wales. The Queensland players can propagate their belief that they're more passionate than NSW players as much as they like. It's rubbish. But what I will give them is that their fans are incredibly passionate and vocal.

I loved going for a walk through Brisbane's Queen Street Mall on the day of an Origin match. I'd always cop verbal banter and abuse left, right and centre—but that's exactly what I love about rugby league and especially Origin. Remember, I didn't grow up supporting a particular NRL team. I supported New South Wales and loved everything about them. So as NSW captain, I loved the passion associated with the fans at Origin time.

Game one was everything we expected: tight and against the odds. Had one player swayed from our simple game plan to work unrelentingly for each other, we wouldn't have finished victorious on the scoreboard, 12–8.

For me, game one will forever be remembered for the heroics of the Morris twins, Brett and Josh. Brett pulled off a match-saving tackle on Queensland's Darius Boyd with a dislocated shoulder, which he'd carried for almost an hour. Josh went down with a knee injury while playing in the centres. Seemingly on his way off the field, Josh brushed aside the Blues' medical staff to get back into the defensive line and make an important tackle on Greg Inglis. Scans the next day would reveal that Josh's injury was serious, and he would miss the next nine matches for his club, the Bulldogs.

Those two extraordinary efforts from the Morris boys typified who we were as a team in 2014. For the last twenty minutes of game one, with the scores tight, Queensland threw everything at our 'Blue Wall' of defence. But we made tackle after tackle. 'Blue Wall' is what I remember my NSW teammates yelling as the Maroons muscled towards our tryline. We simply failed to relent. Although there was so much work still to be done, I felt that we had taken a huge step towards ending Queensland's reign.

For game two, we were at home in Sydney. Due to the Morris brothers' injuries, Laurie chose Will Hopoate, Josh Dugan and Greg Bird for the series-deciding clash. Changes to any team always left me slightly nervous. I remember thinking prior to Origin II, 'Why do we have to change a winning team?' But they were injury-enforced changes—and, like in life, nothing ever follows the script in sport, particularly in State of Origin.

Timing is everything. I mean that. The Blues' 2018 series win was as much about perfect timing as it was about guts and courage, as a new era of young Blues players capitalised on a Maroons side struggling for consistent polish and finesse after years of dominance. In game two of the 2014 Origin series, Trent Hodkinson nailed his timing.

Once again, our 'Blue Wall' had stopped the Maroons from crossing our tryline. However, by the time the game was inching towards the shadows of the finishing post, Queensland had pinched a slender 4–0 lead through penalty conversions. By and large, the match was an ugly tug of war with plenty of pushing and shoving but very little expansive attacking football. But the history books never show the glamour. I wish they showed the grit and desire behind the scoreline.

In the 71st minute, with just nine minutes left in the match, we were still trailing on the scoreboard when the football found its way into Trent's hands. Trent will freely admit that he is not the most gifted ball-runner with light feet or a dazzling step. But on this night in 2014, he might as well have been Johnathan Thurston.

As Trent moved to his left, with teammates around him in motion, for one of the few times in the match, the Maroons' defence looked tentative. They began to slide and back away, fearing that the Blues' halfback would shift the ball out wide to his most dangerous attacking teammates. Instead, Trent showed to pass wide, dummied, swerved, accelerated and darted over the tryline to level the scores. He pointed to the hysterical sea of Blues fans as he planted the ball down.

Patiently and with incredible poise, Trent then piloted the ball through the goal posts to give us a two-point lead. It was the most important goal kick of his entire career, and he soaked up the pressure magnificently. The final scoreline of 6–4 is one that we will remember forever.

There were nervous moments in the final few minutes, though. Queensland is never dead until the final siren sounds. With 40 seconds to play, we had the ball and couldn't have been better placed, attacking the Maroons' tryline. Unable to beat the clock to full-time, we had a choice to make on our last tackle. Hoping to end the match by forcing Queensland to receive the ball from inside its own in-goal, Josh Reynolds kicked towards the Maroons' line.

Typical of Billy Slater, he read the kick well. He ricocheted the ball off his knee before darting forward to collect it as it bounced away. Instantly, I had visions of him retrieving the football and racing 80 metres to score. But Josh—and I'm so happy he did this—tugged at Billy's jersey. It was a blatant penalty for Queensland, but knowing Billy's footy prowess, it's a penalty I'm glad Josh conceded.

The penalty required one more defensive set, with a visibly gassed Queensland needing to score from inside its own half—and there were only 31 seconds in which to do so. 'Keep working for each other,' I screamed. Nobody could hear me above the deafening sound of 83,421 fans—the largest crowd at the venue since the Sydney 2000 Olympics.

We just had to rely on each other. We couldn't allow our 'Blue Wall' to break now. As the seconds ticked away, Queensland tried to beat us by spinning the ball out wide. But wherever there was a Maroon jumper with the footy, two sky-blue jerseys would appear. Cornered and out of room on the wing, Queenslander Chris McQueen had the final play. He pumped a hopeful kick down field and over the head of our fullback, Jarryd Hayne. Jarryd collected the footy as the full-time siren sounded, running famously towards our legion of supporters dressed in blue wigs, Blatchys Blues.

It was fruitless. We'd won. We'd done it.

It's a moment I'll never forget. I cherish it more and more as the years pass.

I need footage from the night to help me recollect what I did at the exact moment the siren sounded. Relief is the closest word I can use to sum up that initial feeling. Then excitement kicked in. I ran towards my players at the northern end of the stadium. My embrace with Robbie Farah and Greg Bird seemed to last for hours.

Although I was incredibly emotional, one of the first things I did was to leave my teammates and head back towards the halfway line to give my thanks to Cameron Smith and the Queenslanders. However, because they had gathered in a circle, I was unable to shake any of their hands. I wasn't about to push my way into the huddle. So I waited for what seemed like an eternity, about 20 metres away. That's when Laurie found me. We hugged in relief, and the pure adrenaline of the moment left me virtually collapsing in his embrace.

I was so happy for Laurie and so proud to have played under a loyal and passionate New South Welshman, who had literally made himself sick in his pursuit of State of Origin success for the Blues. I was also fortunate to be named man of the match that night. It's a special acknowledgement that I was obviously honoured to receive at the time, but I'm more proud of the award upon reflection.

I would've loved lifting the State of Origin shield in front of our loyal supporters, but the trophy presentation is always held at the completion of Origin III. As a team and as a state, we would have to wait three weeks.

Some games you just can't remember. Others you just erase. I've erased Origin III from my memory, obviously because of the 32–8 victory by Queensland.

As a group, we had arrived in Brisbane with every intention of becoming the first side to win the series 3–0 since 2000. But we played poorly, without smarts or attention to detail, gifting the Maroons too many opportunities. With their own pride on the line, they put us to the sword in front of their home fans. While disappointed with the result, as a group we had achieved what we had set out to do, which was to give New South Wales back its pride. We lifted the shield in front of several thousand loyal supporters, but largely an empty stadium. I promise that it didn't make the moment any less satisfying.

I had been made aware of the Wally Lewis Medal after I had been named man of the match in Origin II. A reporter had asked me what it would mean if I won the award named in the Queensland legend's honour. Inside my head I thought, 'Geez, that would be nice to win.' I was acutely aware of the impact Wally had had on State of Origin, and although I had been fortunate enough to receive many major individual playing awards throughout my career, I couldn't get away from the thought of how special it would be to win the Wally Lewis Medal.

I witnessed firsthand from a young age that in New South Wales we had a cheeky way of showing our respect to Wally. Dad took me to Parramatta Stadium when I was about eleven to watch Wally play. The Eels were playing Wally's Brisbane Broncos on this day—but, at the time, I didn't really know who Wally was.

During a period of the match, the entire stadium began chanting, 'Wally's a wanker, Wally's a wanker . . .'

I looked up at Dad and said, 'Who's Wally?'

He replied, 'He's the greatest thing since sliced bread.'

'So why is he a wanker?' I asked.

Dad answered, 'Because he's just too good.' I suppose, deep down, that's why I always loved the banter and abuse from the Queensland crowd. While I would never compare myself to 'The King' Wally Lewis, the reason he copped abuse from fans in New South Wales was because, by and large, he was just so good that, as a Blue, you could do nothing but hate him.

I was overwhelmingly humbled when I was called up on stage to collect the Wally Lewis Medal. I truly believed that Jarryd Hayne would win the award. He'd played well in Origin I, and in a tight Origin II contest he hadn't put a foot wrong. I was proud

of how hard I had worked through all three Origin matches—
and, lucky for me, it was enough for me to be handed the
prestigious medal.

After captaining New South Wales to a series victory, winning
the medal capped off a period of my life that I will never forget.
On the night of Origin III, I actually slept with the medal around
my neck and the shield by my bedside.

No matter where I am in my life for the years to come, I'll
always share a special bond with my Blues brothers.

27

The Hammer Blow

NRL CEO Dave Smith delivered the smoke signal. The hammer was about to drop. Days before our Round 23 clash with the Melbourne Storm in 2014, Smith called me on the phone. 'Gal— Ben McDevitt [ASADA CEO], you and I . . . we need to all sit down,' Smith said.

He claimed that Ben understood our situation and knew what the players were being put through. 'However, don't worry about it, don't stress, just go play your game this weekend,' Smith said finally. I never heard from Smith again after that phone call.

Two days after being crushed 48–6 by the Storm, the headlines were back. And this time, it wasn't smoke—it was fire. The timing of Smith's phone call now made sense.

In the ensuing days, ASADA relayed information to my legal team that a life-changing deal would arrive by no later than 6 p.m. on Thursday, 21 August. I spent the afternoon of 21 August pacing the floor of my lounge room, gripping my mobile phone tightly and waiting for the ring tone to shrill.

The moment that I never wanted to imagine finally arrived. My phone rang, and I was asked to attend a meeting in the city.

Also there were two legal representatives from ASADA, NRL Integrity Unit boss Nick Weeks and my own lawyer, Steven Glass.

I sat down and was taken through the breach notice ASADA was preparing to level against me. ASADA added that Steven would be provided with a 'summary of the evidence'. I couldn't understand why they would be so brief with something so critical. 'A summary? Aren't you supposed to provide the evidence in full?' Steven asked.

ASADA simply said, 'If you want to go to trial, we'll supply the evidence in full.' A warm and weak sensation trickled through my body. I felt like I was going to pass out.

I tried to make sense of what was happening, reiterating what I had stated from day one. 'I went through the correct procedures, which I had always been advised to follow,' I said. 'I did everything you taught me to do.'

And they knew it. Given the level of technology they had at their disposal, they would have had all the records of me logging in to the ASADA website and checking the banned substance list— as I had explained in my original interview with ASADA in 2014.

They also had my phone records after customs officers confiscated my phone as I arrived at Sydney airport following a 2014 season game in New Zealand against the Warriors.

ASADA's response was simple. 'We can't be responsible for putting everything on the banned list.' Now I was really going to faint.

Adding to the state of confusion and mental anguish were the phone calls and emails I had received throughout this entire period. It was incredible how many experts and lawyers, from both Australia and overseas, reached out to me. Each of them had a theory or reason why I should avoid at all costs accepting any deal with ASADA.

At one point in the meeting—and, to me, this was a crucial question—Steven asked, 'Have you proven that these substances are illegal?'

ASADA responded, 'You can prove they're not, if you want.' They were challenging us to go to trial. This only added to the confusion I had been experiencing for the duration of the entire scandal.

Not a month went by when I didn't receive some form of correspondence—letters, emails and text messages—or phone calls from people who suggested we had done nothing wrong. The most telling email came from a university professor, who provided written documentation and a chain of emails detailing how the Court of Arbitration for Sport (CAS) was yet to ban the peptides in question. I wanted to believe the professor; I wanted to believe every minor piece of correspondence I received. But seriously, how was I to know? How was anyone to know?

The meeting was over without any clarity. Steven told me to sit tight and wait for ASADA's formal offer to be sent through. As I waited, I contemplated why—despite vehemently denying, which I still do to this day, ever knowing that the substances provided to us were illegal—I was now planning to accept a deal.

Across town, my Cronulla teammates were locked away with their own legal team inside a city boardroom, so I decided to visit them. I needed only to take one step inside that room to realise their decision had been made. A vivid and overwhelming calmness exuded from the entire group. I knew immediately that they had decided to accept a deal from ASADA. 'What else are we going to do? We've had enough,' one of the boys said. I could relate to their sense of just wanting it all to be over.

My legal team was also present, so they openly discussed each player's position with the other lawyers. The three sets of legal teams all agreed that the evidence was 'weak' at best. I left the meeting with a media scrum following me out of the building.

The advice from my legal team was that ASADA would forward the deal through by 6 p.m. You could only imagine the level of stress that washed over every player when the 6 p.m. deadline passed and no offer had arrived from ASADA. Seven o'clock, nothing. Eight o'clock came and—surprise—ASADA had moved the goal posts. They were now saying we needed to first plead guilty to knowingly taking a banned substance before any deal would be offered and subsequently ratified by WADA.

This was ridiculous. Stuff them, I thought. I'm sick of them controlling our lives. The deal is off. Confusion and anger reigned as we—the players—began ringing and messaging each other. 'We're not taking any deal—they are torturing us on purpose,' one player said.

Furious, upset and unable to deal with ASADA's tactical mind games, I received a phone call from my legal team. 'Calm down, it's okay—the paperwork is coming through any minute now,' I was told. The deal arrived at 10.35 p.m.—four and a half hours after ASADA had promised.

I am convinced ASADA delayed the delivery of the deal as a form of strategy. It was a legitimate ploy to pour one last layer of anxiety, stress and anguish over us, in a bid to ensure they got the bans they wanted without ever proving a single thing.

The deal would mean that we—the players—would accept a reduced twelve-month suspension. The ban would be back-dated to 1 November 2013. It meant that we would miss the remaining three games of the 2014 season, and I would also be disqualified from representing Australia during the end-of-year Four Nations tournament. But why was ASADA willing to compromise?

The Daily Telegraph reported, 'It's believed ASADA was willing to compromise because of the inordinate delay in the investigation, as well as the fact players might have been misled into believing they were taking permitted substances.'

My opinion? ASADA was acutely aware of the embarrassment they had caused not only to their organisation but also to the players by the inordinate delay in the investigation. They also knew, as reported, that we—the players—had been misled into using prohibited substances.

ASADA also knew that I had followed their exact guidelines, as advised by them, to determine if the supplements were listed as a banned substance on the ASADA website. They knew I had followed their very instructions. So, as a result of an almost eighteen-month investigation following what was said to be the 'darkest day in sport', ASADA came up with what was effectively a three-match ban. I have received a longer suspension from the NRL for a high tackle.

I was advised that I had until 9.30 a.m. the next morning to formally accept the deal. I didn't sleep a wink that night. By 5.30 a.m., I was in my car, driving towards Gilbert + Tobin's towers on Park Street in Sydney. On the way, I phoned Cronulla chairman Damian Keogh. 'Will the club stick by me if I don't accept this deal?' I asked Damian. He simply said he wanted to work with me and help me.

Sitting inside the office towers of Gilbert + Tobin, I again played the waiting game. As a playing group, we had told ASADA that we would only consider accepting the deal if they could ensure WADA would not appeal the suspension for unknowingly taking a prohibited substance. Not long before ASADA's deadline of 9.30 a.m., the paperwork from WADA arrived. I turned to my legal team one final time.

My lawyer, Steven Glass, wrote down on a piece of paper the pros and cons of the decision I was about to make. He was reluctant to provide a recommendation, one way or the other. My barrister, Greg James QC, said, 'Take the offer, Paul. My job is to mitigate loss, and as far I can see your life has been screwed for the past eighteen months. I can make this go on for years, if you want to pay for it. You'll be long retired by the time we finish fighting it for you. But do you want that? Do you want to keep living your life like this?' And that was it. ASADA had beaten us. In this game of life, ASADA had won.

They had the admission—the same admission that Richard Redman had warned me about almost eighteen months earlier. An admission, he had said at that time, is what their whole case depended on. In reality, it's all they had. They were unable to prove that I was guilty of taking a prohibited substance. If they had any evidence, why then would they slap me with just a three-game ban? It made me sick to the stomach.

Before signing off on the deal, I asked my legal team for one more thing. I wanted the NRL to explain in their press statement the many lengths to which I had gone to ensure the supplements provided to me weren't on ASADA's banned substance list at the time. I wanted them to recognise that I had repeatedly asked my club superiors at the time if the supplements were legal. And I wanted the NRL to make it clear to the public that I had done everything I had been trained to do by ASADA and the NRL when it came to checking for banned substances. But the NRL wouldn't do any of those things.

Due to my profile, I was the unwitting face of this scandal. When it was reported—be it online, in the paper or on TV— I was the one splashed across the screen or pages. I felt, given how much I had been used as the face of this story, that the NRL could recognise the efforts I had made to avoid this situation. But they wouldn't. And it was this lack of support, I can now declare, that was the genesis for my angry Twitter message directed at the NRL only two months later.

With my signature on the ASADA paperwork, I put an end to the long-running scandal. Instantly, I felt a weight lift from my shoulders. I jumped in my car and drove home. I have never experienced, before or since, such a surreal feeling. It was as though I was numb.

I had slept a maximum of two hours in the last two days, and I had only eaten one piece of toast in that time. I had consumed more medication—the same course of tablets for my depression that I had been on since 2013—than actual food.

It was mid-morning when I turned the key in the front door of my home. I walked inside. It was empty. Anne had taken the kids to school. I sat down and cried. I thought of what I had become. My entire life, I had worked so hard for everything I had received. I thought about Mum driving me to the trial matches with Norths. I thought about the extra gym sessions after school with Jason Cayless. I thought about my NRL debut, playing for New South Wales and my love of playing for Australia. It was all gone—replaced by an emptiness.

I felt let down. I felt like I had let other people down. For the first time in my life, I felt worthless. How would I ever recover from this? I was convinced I couldn't. I considered harming myself. But I couldn't do that to my wife and beautiful kids. The weight of eighteen months of pressure and confusion spilled freely onto my lounge-room floor that day.

Despite the gathering of TV cameras on my front lawn, I wanted to show Charly and Kody that their dad was okay and life would go on. Later that afternoon, I decided to step outside and take them to a local park in Cronulla. On reflection, I was kidding myself. I was in a state of complete shock, pretending that everything was just fine. 'It's pretty tough, but you've just got to get on with life,' I told the Channel Nine reporter who had followed me to the park. If only I had taken my own advice.

For the next week, I lay in bed. I only got up to use the toilet, before returning to my darkened room. I didn't shower, I didn't eat, I didn't change my clothes and I didn't put one foot outside the front door of my home—not even to check the letterbox or put the rubbish out. At night, Anne would bring me a glass of milk. I switched my phone off and stayed in bed for seven straight days.

* * *

After four days of lying in my dark, stinking room, the sound of my kids talking out in the kitchen broke my heart. 'Why isn't Daddy getting up? Why isn't Daddy having breakfast with us?' My heart was shattered, but I still stayed there. Physically, I couldn't face my own house, let alone the rest of the world. My body and mind had simply shut down.

After six days, Anne's concerns for my health led her to phone the newly appointed club doctor for the Cronulla Sharks, George Pitsis. He dropped by and asked me if I had been taking my prescribed medication, before saying, 'Gal, you can't do this to yourself. You have to find a way to get up and get moving . . . besides, your bedroom stinks.'

I replied abruptly, 'What's the point?' I didn't care about life. I didn't care about anything.

Anne also had my manager, Dave Riolo, call me. 'Anne is worried; she's scared. You've got to get out of bed,' Dave said.

After seven days, I recall dragging myself out of bed and walking down the stairs to our living room. It sounds odd now, but even that small amount of movement made me feel better.

The following morning, I did the same thing: I woke up and went downstairs for a glass of milk. The tracksuit pants that I had worn for the past seven days were slipping from my waist. In one week I had lost 5 kilograms.

Downstairs, realising that I needed to escape the hole I was in, I turned to Anne said, 'Let's get out of here.' Within 48 hours, we were on a flight to Fiji with the kids.

28

You Shouldn't Be Here

Before November 2014, I had never met sports psychologist Steven Johnson. Yet in that first workshop session, I sat in his office, crying my eyes out.

The quotes below have been lifted directly from a profile feature about me which was written by *The Australian* sports journalist Brent Read. They are from Steven.

Paul is an incredibly resilient and emotionally tough person. Part of that is because he didn't have an easy upbringing. I can honestly say I don't think I have worked with an athlete that has been more dedicated to the cause. He totally committed himself over the three months to doing everything that was asked of him, even when it was incredibly tough.

The other thing people don't understand about him is because he plays the game so hard, people assume that is him by nature. But underneath that ruggedness and toughness is a very kind and generous individual. You never see that and the public doesn't get to see that. Compared to a lot of athletes I have worked with, he is an intelligent and at times articulate guy.

There are some fundamental principles I operate when I work on things, and I guess the starting point is I start with what is right with people not what is wrong with them, and try to work with people's strengths, not their weaknesses. It's pretty hard to make sense of who you are as a young man unless you can make sense of the key influences that influenced you to become a man. Clearly that is about your relationship with your parents and particularly your own father. What I have found is helping athletes and young men understand themselves, it is fundamental they understand masculinity and fatherhood themselves. In some cases, that is having a reflection on what their father was like for them and what sort of father they would like to be for their children.

You have to be open to learning, and you have to be open with yourself. In other words, you have to be willing to confront your own truth. Some of the things I get them to do are pretty confronting. So, for example, I will spend a couple of hours going through their family history and ask them some pretty blunt and direct questions. Then I will get them to do some things on the back of that. In some cases, it is making peace with someone. In some cases, it is apologising to someone. In some cases, it is going and expressing gratitude to someone for something they did who had a major impact on their life. That was the case with Paul, for instance. Someone in his life made a real difference. There is a growing field in psychology called positive [psychology], and part of the evidence of that field is getting people to express their gratitude to others has a very positive effect on people's emotional wellbeing.

It was a pleasure to work with him because he is bright, he gets things quickly and he is not afraid of speaking his mind, either. He's a good guy, and not everybody would see that. You have your parochial clubs and your parochial states. He is probably on the hate list for fifteen of those clubs. He is so honest, and he is not afraid.

He is authentic to himself and other people, extremely trustworthy, very loyal. There were times there I walked away thinking to myself that he could do whatever he put his mind to when he finished playing league.

I'm forever grateful to Steven for the insightful words. But, most of all, I'm forever indebted to Steven for the impact he had on my life.

'Are you in a position of authority to do this to people?' I asked Steven, while wiping away tears from my face. He pointed to the wall behind him, where his degree hung. A sports psychologist who once taught at Harvard Medical School, Steven is the managing director of Transformation Partners. He had been employed by the NRL to oversee a three-month leadership accountability course that I was ordered to undertake after posting eighteen words on Twitter: 'Steve Noice [sic] actually cared about players from Cronulla's feelings. Couldn't say that about any other c*** from NRL.' I posted this stupid rant complete with offensive language during an overseas getaway to Hawaii with Anne—after we had been to Fiji with the kids—in October 2014.

As I've previously declared, the tweet stemmed from my belief that the NRL had done little to support the players throughout the entire ASADA scandal. Grown men had been on the verge of suicide. And sure, the NRL welfare department would make a phone call to offer the players a free lunch, but what did that actually mean? What the players wanted was a leader to stand up and acknowledge that we never once asked for this predicament. And that's what Sharks chief executive Steve Noyce did.

He understood that we—the players—were part of a program that should never have been discussed, let alone implemented. So when Cronulla chairman Damian Keogh called me in Hawaii to explain that Noycey had been relieved of his duties, I was gutted. Noycey was a good man, who I believe did everything he possibly could to put the players' welfare first in an extremely difficult situation.

So, with a belly full of alcohol and a fragile mental space—where my focus was far from anything to do with football following our ASADA suspension—I keyed in my thoughts on social media. I wrote the tweet in the foyer of my hotel in Hawaii. By the time I had taken the elevator up to my room, opened the door and told Anne what I had just blurted out to each of my many thousands of followers—whereupon she told me I was an idiot and demanded that I delete the tweet—no more than five minutes had passed. But the damage was done. It was only a matter of time.

I didn't know what to expect, but—even though I pulled the post after just a few minutes—as my history shows, I was always going to get a reaction. However, when I checked my social media channel before jetting out of Hawaii the following day, there was nothing to report.

Arriving back in Sydney twelve hours later, I turned on my phone. I had over 30 messages from friends and family, including 'What have you said?' and 'Why did you post that?' I immediately tried to call NRL CEO Dave Smith and Damian Keogh. Neither answered.

Within the next few days, the NRL bowled me over with a $50,000 fine for a breach of the code of conduct. My subsequent apology, where I described my language as 'unacceptable', did little to calm down Dave Smith, who was intent on showing me who was boss.

I felt that the fine was excessive to say the least. Particularly when the penalty included the threat of me being overlooked for the 2015 ANZAC Test match, should I refuse to complete the leadership course with Steven Johnson.

There were also immediate calls for me to be stripped of the NSW State of Origin captaincy. Thankfully, the NSWRL, led by chief executive Dave Trodden and chairman George Peponis, recognised where my error in judgement had come from. 'Poor old Gal has been to hell and back in the last twelve months. It's inappropriate what he said [but] he feels like he didn't get a lot of support,' Dr Peponis said. 'I actually feel sorry for the bloke.'

On appeal, I managed to have the fine reduced to $35,000—still a ridiculously over-the-top figure compared to that paid by other players for their indiscretions both in the past and present. Players proven guilty of physical assault get away with less. Still, I had little option—I accepted the penalty and began meeting with Steven.

The meetings were originally something I didn't want to do. But with each session, I began to enjoy the process. As Steven indicated in his quotes, he took me back to when I was a boy, growing up in Western Sydney. This was extremely difficult on a personal level, but it was a way of understanding who I was as a person and why I am the person I am now.

The majority of our character stems from who we were as kids growing up. How did you relate to people? Who were your role models? Was there a father figure in your life? Did you have mentors outside your family circle? This is particularly important, especially for boys through their teenage years. Steven explained that a lot of teenage boys between the ages of twelve and fifteen have mentors or idols that they look up to and who they try to follow.

In one of the early sessions, Steven turned to me and said simply, 'You didn't have any idols. You didn't have any mentors. Your dad—as much as you loved him and he loved you—was distracted by living the life of a single man.' And then he said something to me that Wayne Bennett, whom I had confided in during previous NRL All Stars camps, had also said to me before. 'You actually shouldn't be where you are.' Steven was amazed at who I had managed to become, given where I had come from. It floored me. I sobbed like a baby.

One of the other insightful and key moments during the course was when Steven asked me to interview someone whom I considered to be a significant leader in the sporting community and who could assist my own development as a leader. The easiest thing I could've done would've been to pick up the phone and call my old mate Ricky Stuart, my former Test coach Tim Sheens or champion boxer Daniel Geale, with whom I had come to form a solid friendship. But I wanted to give Steven's task the respect it deserved.

I took two days to decide whom I wanted to interview. Before deciding, I sat down at my kitchen bench with a notepad and pen and began writing questions I wanted to ask my chosen person. What has led to you being perceived as a good role model off the field? What do you do to develop more as a leader? What is one characteristic you believe every leader should have? What are some sacrifices you have had to make, particularly in your personal life with your family and friends? How do you communicate team values to your team? Does being a role model sit well with you? How do you deal with players not doing the right thing in relation to off-field behaviour or at training? There were twenty questions in total.

In the end, I chose three individuals whom I admire greatly: two-time AFL Brownlow medallist and former Sydney Swans champion Adam Goodes, former Australian cricket captain Steve Waugh and cycling's Anna Meares, the four-time Olympian and two-time Olympic champion. I was required to personally phone, text or email the trio of sporting royalty.

I met Adam Goodes face to face. He answered every question I asked him before detailing his role in maintaining and leading the Swans' famous 'Bloods' culture. 'Treat everyone the same,' he told me. That stuck with me. The Swans' culture is about everyone buying into the system where nobody is treated differently. Adam drove that as a leader of the Swans, he steered their culture. It was compelling advice.

As for Steve Waugh, I listened as the former Test batsman spoke about leading by example. If anyone reminded me of myself, it was Steve. He led by his actions, and I'd like to think that I tried to do this, too. I can't speak highly enough of Steve Waugh and the way he spoke to me in our meeting. I found him so honest, and there was no bullshit in the advice he gave me.

From Anna Meares, I gained a rare insight into sacrifice and resilience. She is a cycling champion whose world is agonisingly defined by a single performance every four years at the Olympics. Anna's mental strength is something I admire greatly; you can't help but listen and learn when someone of Anna's standing is talking to you. From our conversation, I took away with me a new respect for her incredible fortitude and focus.

While my interaction with these three wonderful leaders was undoubtedly beneficial, it was the process of self-reflection during Steven's course that hit home the hardest. I learned more about myself in those three months than I ever did during 26 rounds of a rugby league season.

During the course, Steven asked me to focus on how I wanted my children to grow up and what I wanted for my son, Kody. He proposed that I write a letter to my son, who was three years old at the time. In the letter, I explained how I would help and nurture his growth into a respectful, well-mannered, caring and protective young man. I stated how, one day, I hoped that Kody, too, would be a father to a son, so that he could feel the same joy that he brings me every day.

Did the course change me? I believe I'll only know the answer to that as my life continues. Certainly, it aided my desire to be a positive role model, father and husband.

Long after I had completed the course, and a couple of days before the 2016 ANZAC Test, I thought about the journey I had undertaken more than twelve months earlier with Steven. Kangaroos coach Mal Meninga had gathered the entire playing group into a circle and had said that the way you play your footy is the way you live your life. I understood where he was coming from. But I didn't completely agree with him.

I would never hurt someone in the street, but in every match I played I wanted to hurt the opposition. Those who know me outside of footy appreciate how soft I can be. Something extremely serious would have to happen for me to become angry or riled up in real life.

I would never hurt anyone. If anything, I'm calmer now than I was when I ran onto the football field. I'm proud of that. I'm also proud that the competitive footballer I was is different to the dedicated father, husband and friend that I'm striving to be.

29

Letters from Death Row

Phil Rothfield, *The Daily Telegraph*'s sports editor-at-large, is an avid Cronulla Sharks supporter. He is someone who always encouraged me throughout the majority of my career. But every now and then, he would phone and begin chatting with a tone that suggested all was not well—or he had something, a story angle perhaps, on his mind.

In early April 2015, I received a call from Phil that led to the most extraordinary and unexpected opportunity on a personal level that I've ever experienced. Phil had been in regular conversation, via social media, with Bali Nine drug smuggler Andrew Chan, in the lead up to his eventual execution on 29 April 2015.

Chan, a rugby league lover who followed the Penrith Panthers, had asked Phil if there was any way possible that he could 'chat to Paul Gallen'. 'I love Gallen's style—he's as hard as a machine,' Chan had told Phil during one of their conversations.

Phil explained to Chan that he would happily ask me if I would be willing to trade a few text messages. 'Will you do it, Gal?' Phil asked me down the phone line, one afternoon. I'll be honest— I didn't know what to say.

Usually Phil would call to chat about how the Sharks had played the previous weekend or how my latest injury was going or what I thought of a particular player ahead of an Origin series. So never did I expect the left-field proposal of chatting with a prisoner on death row. I was completely taken aback by the question and, feeling apprehensive, I didn't know what to do about it. 'What do you say to someone on death row?' I thought. 'What could I possibly say to lift Chan's spirit?'

I finished the phone call by explaining to Phil that I would think about it. Phil said okay, before reminding me that time wasn't exactly on Chan's side. It took me two weeks before I found certainty and reason to accept Chan's request to chat via the mobile phone application WhatsApp.

I met Phil at a Cronulla cafe, and we used his mobile phone to speak with Chan. He asked about the 2015 season signing of Trent Merrin to his beloved Penrith Panthers. 'He's a good bloke. I really like him, but it's a long way for his missus [his partner at the time, professional surfer Sally Fitzgibbons] to go to the beach,' I wrote to Chan. 'I think he will help u [sic] guys. He has a good work ethic around training, and he will help the younger guys coming through.' Chan then began to tell me about his own playing days for the Enmore Feds, an A-grade competition team. He had played with the brother of former Canterbury winger Hazem El Masri.

On three separate afternoons, I sat with Phil to trade messages with Chan. With one of Australia's most publicised convicted criminals, we talked footy, life, leadership, love and seizing the day. Much to my surprise, Chan also sent me two letters, which I have held on to.

Dear Gal,
    Hey Champ how are you? Happy Easter, btw [by the way],
I'm sure it's not a week to forget after bashing the Roosters, ha ha.

Well as you know I have moved over to a new place, mate there's more animals and bugs here then Taronga Zoo. I have managed to ask for the footy updates every week from my fiancé [sic] she hates the game but she'll still give me the rundown of weekly scores. Now I'm sure winning last week was a huge high, I can tell you a thing or two about losing, however I guess we are all searching for a constant win. One of the things I have learnt is that each time it gets rough and you feel like giving up, or you even get frustrated, during that moment I look to see around me where ever I am, that I have Jesus within my heart.

As long as I am still alive, I'll learn to seize the day (Carpe Diem).

Now I know you are a great leader on the field, I guess we all can become great leaders.

If you like to read, I suggest you read a book called 'Five Levels of Leadership' by John Maxwell.

Actually I suggest you get all the boys to read it, one thing it will show you and the boys is the gelling of leadership is not just in one person and one person alone, however they also need to do the hard yards. Well champ hope all is well, hopefully I'll hear from you soon.

Till then,

Be Blessed.

Andrew

Then six days before his execution, I received a second letter, dated 23 April 2015.

Dear Gal,

Hey mate pumped to hear from you, thanks for the mail. Now I heard you boys are building momentum on your wins, that's actually really good to hear.

I predicted that you boys would be playing in the September finals, you have a killer squad and I guess everyone else needs to eat yards up, not just a few. I'll be praying for you that you can play Test [football for Australia], I'm sure it means heaps for you as you said it could be the last time you play a test.

I know you guys are playing Penny [Penrith] this week, I don't think Penny will win with the injuries we have, but hey [Ivan] Cleary has a week to put the best 17 together, if you can't do that then Penny need a new coach ha ha. Congratulations on signing up another year, I know you said nothing solid yet, however let me tell you that every club would want you playing lock or front row for them. As for me I'm doing well, I have just learnt to value things more.

You have to have the attitude within you, learn not to be stressed, you just gotta ask yourself what's really important.

For me each day is a diamond all I can do is appreciate what I have and see the value of it, or I can just lay around.

I know what is precious to me, I'm sure you also know what is precious to you. Origin will be on soon, bash the Maroons, as you said this could be your last season of rep [football] so I say 'Carpe Diem' to seize the day.

Well mate hope to hear from you soon and seriously hope you're feeling better this week.

Be blessed.

Andrew

The night before Chan and fellow Bali Nine member Myuran Sukumaran were moved to the prison island of Nusakambangan to be executed by firing squad, I sent Phil a text message. 'If you get the chance, tell Andrew I'll remember him and it was good to chat.'

Andrew replied to Phil. 'Tell him I'll be praying Sharks win this week.'

Many things that Chan spoke to me about during our brief interaction will stay with me forever. Even the things that seem trivial. For example, how much State of Origin means to so many people, from so many walks of life. 'Gal, all through my life I've been shot at, stabbed and bashed, and I've never cried once,' Chan told me. 'I've never shown any emotion my whole life, but when we won the Origin last year [2014], I cried.'

However, the overwhelming sentiment I feel towards Chan following my brief association with him is that lives can be so easily wasted. From an early age, growing up in Western Sydney, Chan had experienced a rough upbringing but, unlike me, he had never managed to escape his vicious circle. It wasn't until he discovered Christianity that he found a devotion in his life. Until then, drugs were his life.

Sometimes people become trapped in that life, and he obviously couldn't break free. I wonder what would have happened if he had had support—a close friend or family member. Would it have saved him from a life unfinished? It wasn't until he was on death row that he realised what else there was in life—but by then it was too late.

Chan told me that he would wake every day in prison treasuring every second because, for the first time in his life, he understood what it meant to cherish something special. It was an acute reminder for me—and it remains so for us all today—to make the most of this one life we have. Carpe diem.

30

Wise Words

'Sorry Gal, I've never seen this before, but I can't see you ever playing football again.' I turned to my wife, Anne, with a look on my face that she had seen many times before. In fact, over the past few years, she'd seen it all too often. It was one of shock and disbelief.

In my head, I didn't know whether to burst out laughing or flop on the ground and start rolling around in tears. Because seriously, what else? After everything we'd been through, now this? My life had already descended into the type of movie script that most Hollywood producers would turf into the bin, certain that the audience would find it impossible to believe. And if what the specialist holding scans of my purple hip was saying to Anne and me was true, the time had come to start rolling the credits.

With our ASADA bans lifted, I wanted only to begin a new chapter. Yet here I was, six weeks into the 2015 season, at Miranda's Kareena Private Hospital with Anne, after Cronulla club doctor George Pitsis advised us both to meet with a specialist. The fact that the Doc had said Anne should go with me to the appointment was the first indication that this could be serious.

The Doc had been at a loss to diagnose the hip injury. To this day, I still don't know for certain how it occurred. I first felt pain while training at Shark Park during a contact session, ahead of our clash with the Melbourne Storm in Round 3 of the 2015 season. Such was the aggravation caused by the pain, I reported it to our club medical staff after the session. They said to let them know if it got worse.

By the time the captain's run came around, the day before playing Melbourne, I could hardly run. One of our staff members told me it would be okay, 'we'll try some painkillers for the game'. Prior to the warm-up, I was given the painkiller. But even after twenty minutes of warming up, every time my right foot met the turf, I felt a sharp pain running down my right leg. The painkiller clearly wasn't working, so I had another one. I needed to play.

Disappointingly, we'd already lost our opening two home games of the 2015 season, to the Raiders and Broncos, so beating Melbourne at AAMI Park was of huge importance. It wasn't to be. We were beaten by the Storm, 36–18.

After the game, I received a cortisone injection. Athletes commonly use cortisone to treat inflammation. The pain subsided— but only momentarily. The following week, I received more pain-killers before running onto Shark Park for our Round 4 clash with the Gold Coast. We lost to the Titans, 24–22. Now we were 0–4 and off to Allianz Stadium, fighting for our first win of the season against the Sydney Roosters.

During my career, critics—and even a section of my own Cronulla fans—accused me at times of putting my state before the club. If only they knew the lengths to which I went to run out each week for the Sharks.

I tried to rest my hip before the match against the Roosters, limiting my training load. To make matters worse, Anne needed to rush five-week-old Macy to hospital after she suffered an asthma-like episode the night before the game. On five hours' sleep and in immense pain, I blocked it all out for the 80 minutes against the Roosters.

Thanks to the NRL arrival of Jack Bird, who scored two tries in just his second first-grade appearance, we beat the Roosters 20–12 and collected our first win of the season. Not wanting to let the opposition know I was in immeasurable pain, I was relieved and pleased to contribute 211 metres from 23 hit-ups and 28 tackles. *The Daily Telegraph*'s Paul Kent surmised my situation well at the time, writing, 'This is the way it is for footballers, a side we don't see. They live on a diet of work and painkillers.'

Ahead of our next match against Newcastle, I was given another painkiller. Then, halfway through the warm-up, I had to go off for another one. We beat Newcastle, 22–6. After the match, the pain was like nothing I had previously experienced. My eyes were watering as I struggled to buckle my seatbelt around my hip, which was now swollen and purplish pink. This is what led me to meeting with a specialist.

And so here Anne and I sat, with the specialist holding scans of a 3-centimetre tear along the tendon of my gluteus maximus, the body's largest muscle, where it attaches to the iliotibial band—the tendon that connects the hip to the knee. 'You need surgery to reattach the tendon,' the specialist said. 'The recovery will be long and, even then, I can't see you playing again.'

George Pitsis had already contacted everyone he knew, including doctors at several AFL clubs, to discover if anyone had treated a similar injury. Nobody had seen an injury of this severity before. But I wasn't giving up there.

I had the number for Sydney's leading hip and knee specialist, Professor Craig Waller. 'Can I come and see you urgently? I've got this problem,' I said. Thankfully, Craig generously made time for me, and I arrived with my scans. However, the news was hardly inspiring.

'I don't know if your career is over, but you're going to have a long recovery after surgery,' Craig said.

Knowing how desperate I was, the Doc then spoke with a specialist in the field of plastic surgery, who felt that he might have a solution. I drove to his office on the North Shore of Sydney. His response gave me some hope. 'Your season is over with surgery, and you don't want that, so just leave it to rest,' he said. 'The body has an incredible ability to repair itself.' So that's exactly what I did.

I stopped all cortisone injections and painkillers. We introduced platelet-rich plasma (PRP) injections and, aside from that, just let it be. We allowed one day a week for an MRI scan, to determine if, indeed, the injured tendon had begun to self-heal. Incredibly, a week later the tear had closed up, ever so slightly.

As the weeks passed, it began to improve, little by little. After five weeks, it got to the point where the tear had all but completely healed. I told the Sharks' coaching staff that I felt like I could commence running.

I had wanted my Test jumper back for the annual ANZAC Test in May, having been suspended by ASADA from the 2014 Four Nations tournament. Even though Kangaroos coach Tim Sheens had phoned me to confirm that he'd pick me if I were right to play, on this occasion my head wanted more than what my body could deliver. So, with the Test match out of reach, my obsession became returning for the Sharks and in time for Origin I with New South Wales.

Having led the Blues to our first series win in eight years in 2014, I desperately wanted to defend the series in 2015.

But preparation for an Origin match can't be rushed. You need all seventeen players fit and firing for the entire week-long build-up. Unfortunately, I was never going to be able to achieve such a goal. I hadn't played since Round 6 against Newcastle and, while I was nearing a 100-per-cent recovery with my hip, I just wasn't right for one of the biggest games of the year.

When I broke the news to NSW coach Laurie Daley, he insisted I still travel into camp with the team at Coffs Harbour to assist with the Blues' Origin I preparation. I was grateful that he wanted me there but, truth be told, I didn't want to go. Robbie Farah was selected to skipper New South Wales, and I didn't want to step on his and others' toes. I also didn't want the attention to be on me, when the fact was that I had no chance of playing.

Out of respect for Laurie, I flew to Coffs Harbour for one training session so I could give the NSW debutants my best wishes, then I returned home. I rode every play from my lounge room as we lost Origin I 11–10 at ANZ Stadium. It was excruciating to watch. We blew a chance to kick a field goal right at the end and, once again, it was close but not close enough for New South Wales.

That loss was significant—I was adamant that we had to snag the Origin I result if we were to have any chance of winning the series again. I felt it was imperative, because that was the end of any home-ground advantage for us. Our next two matches would be on the road, in Melbourne at the Melbourne Cricket Ground (MCG) and then at Suncorp Stadium in Brisbane.

I had set a target to return to the field for the Sharks in our Round 13 home game against the Sydney Roosters. It was a huge relief to not only make it back onto Shark Park after being told I may never play again, but also to be able to return in the black, white and blue with a hard-fought 10–4 victory. I was pleased with my own performance and confident that my contribution of 214 metres and 41 tackles was enough to show Laurie that I wouldn't let him down ahead of selection for Origin II.

Thankfully, Laurie named me at lock and captain for Origin II. The other changes for the Blues from Origin I included Brett Morris being rushed into the side on the wing for Daniel Tupou, and Josh Jackson shifting from lock to the bench, forcing Andrew Fifita from the final seventeen.

There was plenty of excitement about the first State of Origin game being played at the MCG in eighteen years. But within our playing group, there was a focus and determination to ensure we keep the series alive.

From the moment we arrived at the MCG, I loved every minute of the experience. There had been suggestions that the atmosphere could be diluted by the mere fact that we were playing on a rectangular field inside an oval-shaped stadium, but that wasn't the case. However, the fans were closer to me than other players, because no sooner had we kicked off than I was back standing alongside them on the sideline, gasping in pain before I jogged awkwardly back down the tunnel.

In the opening three minutes of the match, my old sparring partner, Nate Myles, hit me hard in the back as I was passing the football. Two ribs instantly snapped. In obvious discomfort, I told long-serving NSW trainer Ronnie Palmer that I would play on for as long as I could. I ultimately succumbed to the pain fifteen minutes later.

Off the field and inside the dressing rooms, I immediately received a painkilling injection and then an additional dose at half-time. Thankfully, I was able to return for the second half to enjoy what became a memorable 26–18 victory for the Blues. No sooner were we high-fiving our series-saving victory than our focus switched to Origin III—the decider.

Our preparation for Origin III was flawless. Externally, the press was fixated on a thumb injury suffered by Robbie Farah while playing with the Wests Tigers prior to game three. Farah spent every day in camp with the Blues at Coffs Harbour, but not for a second was he ever going to play at Suncorp Stadium in the decider. It was nothing more than smoke and mirrors and games-manship from Laurie Daley.

As far as the press was ever told, my Sharks teammate Michael Ennis had been called into camp as cover for Farah, who would need to pass a fitness test for his thumb on the Sunday ahead of the Wednesday decider. That was never the case. Laurie hood-winked the entire Sydney media.

Due to Ennis receiving a one-week suspension for a high shot while playing for the Sharks, Laurie couldn't name him in the Blues team until his suspension elapsed on the Monday morning before the decider. So that's exactly what Laurie did. 'Robbie is out; he's not playing. Mick is playing hooker, and Robbie will merely warm up for the cameras before training,' Laurie told the entire NSW playing squad on day one. 'Once the cameras leave, Mick will train the entire session with us at hooker.'

It appeared to be a masterstroke from Laurie, because while the press fixated on playing a guessing game, we got down to business. And it was all business. Which is why the hiding that Queensland handed to us in the decider remains one of the greatest shocks of my entire career.

Without a doubt, it was the best preparation before an Origin match that I had ever experienced. At training, we hardly dropped a ball and, physically, we didn't leave anything behind. After what was a record 52–6 caning by the Maroons in the decider, I remember saying to the media, 'Maybe we trained too well.' That's the only thought I had, because everything else was spot-on. But we were never in it.

There had been a lot of hype in the lead-up to the game about NSW prop David Klemmer targeting Corey Parker after they had traded words in Origin II at the MCG. I admit, I was nervous about the amount of media exposure our young forwards received after Origin II, so much so I addressed the team about refocusing and forgetting all about game two. 'This will be totally different. We need to move on and not rest on our laurels. We need to reload and go again,' I told the group. It wouldn't have mattered what I said, as we were beaten by a red-hot Queensland side that ran straight over, through and around us.

The media tried to suggest that a *60 Minutes* feature on Alex McKinnon on the Sunday before the decider, which had portrayed Queensland captain Cameron Smith in a controversial light, played into the hands of the Maroons. I'm not sure about that. However, I did send Cam a text message after watching the story from my Brisbane hotel room. 'I feel for you with the way this has been portrayed. You've got my word we won't be using any of this as motivation for our side,' I wrote in the message.

Cam replied with a text message the next day. 'Thanks, see you out there.'

If Cam was feeling the heat before the decider, I was on the receiving end after the series-deciding loss, albeit not for the first time, from Channel Nine commentator Phil 'Gus' Gould. After the match, Gus delivered one of his typically abstract broadsides, saying he'd been astonished by the Blues' 'domineering' and 'selfish' leadership group over the past few years. Given that I was the captain, it could only mean that the criticism was directed at me. However, one can only guess and wonder, given that Gus refused to name whom he was actually referring to.

As those close to me are aware, if someone has a problem with me, I would prefer it if they tell me to my face, or at the very least communicate with me what I've done wrong. It's for that reason I attempted to contact Gus not long after Origin III. I'd only met Gus once previously, at a charity event back when Ricky Stuart was coaching Cronulla. Other than that brief encounter, surprisingly our paths had never crossed. However, that was of little concern to me when I tried to ring him after Origin III.

I phoned him because I was quite interested in what he had to say and, believe it or not, I thought it was important to understand his point of view. My phone call to Gus went unanswered. So, I texted him. 'G'day mate, it's Paul Gallen. Can we try and have a chat?' Gus replied that perhaps it would be better if we met face to face.

We were scheduled to meet but ultimately our attempts failed to eventuate due to the hustle and bustle of the footy season.

I was hoping to learn exactly what Gus was trying to say when he made his statement about the NSW leadership to a huge national TV audience.

He'd coached the Blues before, so he has an acute understanding of and appreciation for what's involved in being the NSW captain. And because he knows the requirements, I wanted to know if there was something I could do better. Fair enough, we weren't winning. I'm the first to acknowledge that with any loss comes criticism. But let's put it into context.

New South Wales had won the 2014 series, during which I was fortunate and privileged enough to be captain. As explained in this book, my hip injury prevented me from playing in Origin I, 2015. In Origin II, where I was NSW captain—and with the pressure on us to save the series away from home at the MCG—we squared up the series 1–1. To a man, inside that NSW squad we felt like our Origin III preparation was perfect. So when Gus added a personal tone to his post-match comments, I wondered where it had come from. What had I done to him? Where was the issue? To not want to meet with me and have that conversation, which could've been quite positive, was strange to me.

The thing with Origin is, as I maintained throughout my career, if someone is better than me, then please pick him. No problems. That's why, despite the criticism, I wasn't prepared to retire from representative football in the wake of the 2015 Origin series. Laurie always said that he would be honest with me if he ever felt that my time with the Blues was up. But that day never came.

I moved on from Gus's comments quickly, yet it took me at least a week to get over the disappointment of the Origin series loss. Returning to the Sharks provided me with a new and exciting focus, as I was confident that we had a squad worthy of progressing deep into the finals.

My level of confidence only grew on a Saturday afternoon in July. Our Round 19 clash with Canberra happened to be my 250th first-grade game. As a special surprise, the Cronulla board and management flew my dad down from Queensland to present me with my 250th first-grade jersey.

Snatching a 21–20 golden-point extra-time victory with a field goal from the boot of Valentine Holmes, I was a relieved man. Not only did we get the win, but I had also broken my milestone curse. In the past, I had almost no luck in milestone matches, losing my NRL debut match as well as my 100th and 200th first-grade games.

After our stirring and confidence-building win over the Raiders, as a playing group we began to fire. Leading into the 2015 finals series, we won six of our final eight matches. On a personal level,

I also secured a new one-year deal, guaranteeing me a spot in the 2016 roster at 34 years of age.

We finished sixth on the NRL ladder but, looking back, it was a case of a missed opportunity. We could've finished fourth if we had applied ourselves with the correct attitude. We only needed to beat Manly in our final home game of the season—Round 26 at Shark Park—to secure fourth spot and an invaluable second chance in the finals.

Sadly, Sharks fans will recall our one-off fluorescent yellow jerseys and our shock 14–12 loss—playing against a heavily depleted Sea Eagles side—in front of a big home crowd. It was a flat and uninspiring performance and one that I only began to understand the full impact of once the full-time siren had sounded and I was back inside the dressing rooms.

As a club, we'd just experienced eighteen months of turmoil underlined by the devastation of the ASADA scandal and the 2014 wooden spoon. So I would be lying if I said I didn't sense that, before playing Manly, there was a mood of satisfaction within the playing group thanks to the knowledge that, even with a loss to our Northern Beaches rivals, a semifinal berth was secured.

During that clash with Manly, I felt that as a group—for the first time in months—there was a hesitation to put our bodies on the line, knowing the semifinals were just around the corner. It was one game where, upon reflection, I felt disappointed that I had failed to live up to my motto of not just playing, but making a difference on the footy field. I sensed that the rest of the team felt like that, too. It was all on us.

Only we could recover and deliver success from sixth position and, thankfully, we responded in our opening semifinal against reigning premiers South Sydney, who had qualified for the finals series in seventh position. It was a memorable Sunday afternoon at Allianz Stadium as we ran away from a broken Bunnies outfit, 28–12. I enjoyed one of my better games of 2015 that day, producing one of the three line breaks against Souths that year.

Such was the authoritative style with which we pulled the Rabbitohs apart, the victory provided the playing group and coaching staff with a huge of dose of confidence ahead of a tricky elimination final against North Queensland. Aiding our buoyancy across the group was a strong winning strike rate against the Cowboys in Townsville. We certainly weren't frightened of the long trip north.

In an almost identical fashion to what I sensed ahead of Origin III, our preparation leading into our semifinal against North Queensland was flawless. Yet, just like the Blues, we were nothing short of terrible and embarrassing. And once again, I can't explain why. We'd just enjoyed a convincing win over the previous year's premiers, South Sydney, our training during the week leading into the match was spot-on and, yet, we were never even close to the Cowboys.

Playing club footy immediately after an Origin series defeat helps you deal with the disappointment of a series loss. But a loss like that in a semifinal—with your season declared over at a time when you were confident that 'this could be our year'—is crushing.

The Cowboys began the match well, and they never took their foot off our throats, hammering us 39–0 by full-time. Across the board, it was a shattering and completely uncharacteristic performance from us. As captain, the hardest thing in a match like that is that the scoreline says you're gone long before the full-time siren, but you need to try to motivate the boys to keep them going.

In that situation, all I could tell the boys was to focus on doing the simplest things right. Let's kick off correctly; let's not give away any penalties; let's complete the next five sets. But we couldn't even do that. We'd drop a ball, give away a penalty and kick out on the full. They'd make a break, and they would just keep scoring. It was one of the most embarrassing defeats I've ever been involved with.

It was an upsetting way to end the year that was supposed to be focused on restoring the Sharks' pride and character. And it was an ordinary way to farewell two huge contributors to our club, Jeff Robson and Michael Gordon, who were moving on at the end of 2015 to other clubs.

Inside the dressing rooms after the match, not a word was said for what felt like fifteen minutes. 'I know you're hurting, but that's good,' said our coach, Shane 'Flanno' Flanagan. 'Birdy [Jack Bird], you'll learn so much from this. Same with you, Val. We all will, and that's what's important. You've just got to make sure that whenever you get an opportunity again, you take it.'

They were wise words, given what 2016 would deliver.

31

Goodbye Demon

I began the 2016 season crying on Shane 'Flanno' Flanagan's shoulder. Seven months later, I was planting a big wet kiss on his cheek. I guess that's the power of sport.

Even at our lowest of lows, that one small wish for happiness, success and fulfilment in competition lures us back in. But, sitting inside a Townsville hotel room, close to midnight on a warm Saturday in March 2016, there was little hope.

Earlier that night, out on the field in our Round 1 match against the North Queensland Cowboys, I had heard a crack in my knee following what was a fairly rudimentary carry of the football with just sixteen minutes remaining in the contest. I felt instant pain, but nothing overtly sinister. It was more of a dull throb, which only revealed itself when I began to walk. With each step, I just couldn't put any firm downward pressure or force onto the ground.

I signalled to our trainers that I needed to leave the field. As my teammates surged forward in attack, I made my way off the field and up the tunnel. Sitting in the medical room, I was now in the hands of our medical staff. They immediately began a series of stability tests on my knee. In those first few minutes, when the process of swelling had not yet occurred and there were few muscle spasms, the members of the medical staff were confident of being able to deliver a positive diagnosis.

Both club physiotherapist Sam Madden and club doctor George Pitsis began to grapple with my knee joint, assessing it for a range of potential injuries, including the most feared: a torn anterior cruciate ligament. Placing my leg back down on the table, both Sam and George were of the belief that I had torn my ACL. This is how it ends, I thought, sitting on that medical table. Outside, the full-time siren sounded. The boys had been brave in defeat, losing to the 2015 premiers, 20–14.

As the rest of the team and coaching staff made their way back into the Cowboys' away-team dressing rooms, I asked our physical performance manager and head on-field trainer, Andrew Gray, to test my damaged knee. I also asked our other physiotherapist, Dan Lawson, for his opinion. Andrew and Dan both agreed with Sam and George—I had torn my ACL. I felt physically sick.

It wasn't until Flanno had delivered his post-match debrief that the players moved towards me to ask what was wrong. 'They think I've done my ACL,' I said. Our assistant coach, Steve Price, gave me a hug. Steve had torn his ACL during his playing days, so he could appreciate the enormity of the injury. I wasn't crying—I was just numb.

Back at our team hotel, the Doc called me into a spare room where he, Andrew, Dan and Sam also stood. 'We want to test it again,' the Doc said. So, once again, they jiggled and wiggled my knee. I lay there, hoping for a miracle. As they went about testing my knee, we had an open discussion about the options I had in order to come back from a torn ACL. Andrew was most vocal. 'You'll come back from this, Gal,' he said.

We quickly ruled out LARS surgery—where the ligament of a deceased human is used to reattach the cruciate ligament. 'LARS always fails. Whether it's day one or a year later, it will fail at some stage,' was the consensus. 'Do you want to do that? Or do you want to do it properly and you'll be out for the year?' they asked me.

As our medical team left me to ponder what this meant for my career, the Doc lagged behind. He turned to me and said, 'You know what, Gal? I'm just not 100 per cent convinced that it's torn. I'm 90 per cent sure, but not absolute. Let's just see what the scans show us when we get back to Sydney.' I agreed, but without any great optimism.

Flanno then told me to come to his room and, sitting there with him, I broke down. Shane Smith, our welfare officer, implored me to stay positive. 'After everything I've come back from, this was our year, this was our year,' I kept repeating, with tears streaming down my face. After an hour of beating myself up, I eventually retreated back to my room.

Wade Graham was my roommate and, as he snored away in the bed opposite me, I failed to sleep a single wink. With a heavy icepack strapped to my knee, I sat up in bed researching every way possible to come back from a torn ACL.

I waited until no later than 9 a.m. the next day—a Sunday morning—to phone a leading hip and knee specialist in Sydney, Professor Craig Waller. If there was anyone who had the knowledge and expertise to advise on how best to overcome a torn ACL, it was Craig. 'The other guys are right. LARS is your best option to get back, but it will fail at some stage,' Craig reiterated.

I flew back to Sydney with my teammates and from the airport drove directly to Miranda for scans on my knee. I then held my breath for the results. At about 8.30 p.m. on Sunday night,

the Doc—George Pitsis—called. 'You've suffered a torn poste-
rior ligament and meniscus tear,' he said. 'The ACL is intact.' You
could've knocked me over with a feather. To say that I was ecstatic
is an understatement.

'I knew it—remember I told you I wasn't 100 per cent convinced,' the Doc joked down the phone line. I couldn't believe the
24 hours I had just endured. From the conversation I had with
Flanno, where I was distraught, to now being out for a maximum of
six weeks, it was impossible to explain the relief. I only missed three
games in total, returning against the Wests Tigers in Round 5 and
scoring a try in our 34–26 win at Campbelltown Sports Stadium.

Incredibly, from the Sharks' entire magical 2016 season, I only
lost two matches that year. Of the twenty games in which I was
available to play, the only games I lost were our Round 1 match in
North Queensland and our Round 22 clash with Canberra.

Fairly certain that this would be my final chance to wear the
green and gold for Australia, my focus upon returning from
the knee injury was firmly fixed on proving to Test coach Mal
Meninga that I was worthy of selection for the ANZAC Test. The
2014 ANZAC Test had been the last time I had played for Australia,
so I knew I would need some luck to force my way back into
the side.

There had been plenty of media hype revolving around whether
Mal would pick me. At age 34 and after two years out of the
jersey, the critics were lining up to say my service for Australia was
over. Much, too, was made of a NSWRL dinner during which I
happened to be seated next to Mal. It was there that he said to me,
'I don't care about your age or what has happened in the past—I'm
going to pick the best team available.'

I said, 'That's good to know. All I can do is go out and play
my best, and that's what I'm going to do. Whether you pick me

or not, I'm not giving up on playing for Australia and the way I play.' And that was it—the conversation had lasted no more than 60 seconds.

My final match for the Sharks before the Test team was chosen was against the Brisbane Broncos at Shark Park. On a perfect Sunday afternoon in autumn, we beat the Broncos 30–28 for our seventh win of the season. And I can always tell my kids that I outsprinted Broncos star Anthony Milford, because in that game I managed to score a try by chasing down a neat Michael Ennis kick into the Brisbane in-goal.

In a perfect world, I would've enjoyed a drama-free build-up ahead of my return to the Test arena. But when has my life ever been perfect? During our win over Brisbane, the match officials had placed me on report for using my elbow on opposition forward Josh McGuire. Replays of the incident showed me dropping my arm into his throat as we wrestled on the ground. Thankfully, as Brett Kimmorley told Fox Sports, 'common sense prevailed', and the match-review committee failed to lay a charge. And with that, I was cleared to return to the green and gold. I entered camp with the Kangaroos, and would be coached by Mal for the first time.

The Test match was played at Hunter Stadium, the home of the Newcastle Knights. On our bus trip up the F3 freeway, I received a phone call from Infinity—a company that provides financial advice and assistance to their clients. I had met the Infinity team after they had generously offered to sponsor one of my fights. They were also the sponsors of the Parramatta Eels, but due to the salary cap scandal that had engulfed their season in 2016, Infinity was eager to sever ties. 'We're getting out of Parramatta, and we want to join the Sharks. How do we get involved?' I was asked down the phone line.

I hung up and then rang our head of sponsorship, Luke Edmonds, explaining that this was a real chance for the club to secure substantial support and financial backing. A week later, the Infinity group signed on as our back-of-jersey sponsor for the 2016 and 2017 seasons. I wanted to tell this story, because it indicates how quickly the wheel turns in rugby league. Three years earlier, companies and sponsors were running a mile from me. Now a major company was phoning to ask me for advice on how best to stitch up a deal with the club.

Once in camp with the Kangaroos, it wasn't long before Mal called a meeting. Invited were Cam Smith, Johnathan 'JT' Thurston, Darius Boyd, Cooper Cronk and Matt Scott. I was the only player from New South Wales in the room. It was impossible for me not to notice that.

I had never had any issues with the boys in that room, especially JT and Smithy. I had played 30 Tests with both of those boys, so I got on fine with them. But I suppose with ex-Maroons coach Mal there and a coaching staff that included Queenslanders Adrian Lam and Michael Hagan, there was a different feeling in the room for me.

Every single person in this room had come up with the game plans to beat New South Wales that I would've been on the other end of. Now I'd be plotting defeat with them. I could only chuckle to myself before pushing the odd feelings to the side. Because all I knew was that I wanted to play for Australia, and I wanted to win.

One of the first things Mal pointed out was that we haven't beaten New Zealand in four tests. I wasn't involved in those losses, and I was determined to help elevate Australia back to the position of number one in the world. With the way Mal spoke in that meeting, I can safely say that he is the best coach with regard to motivation that I have ever played under.

I knew after just one day of camp under Mal that if he had asked me to run through a brick wall, I would've. It's the way he talks—his delivery. With his demeanour, he doesn't rant or rave— he just talks. And what he says is not technical at all. It's about wanting to do things, and wanting to do them more than the opposition. It's about pride in your jersey, and pride in your own performance. I was completely in awe of the way he spoke.

Once he had finished the meeting, I sat down by myself and wondered if he was aware of how influential he is. Or did he have an aura just because he's Mal Meninga and that, as kids, we all knew who he was and how special he was as a player?

Being brutally honest, there was nothing he did the entire week that was one bit technical or structured. It was all man management from Mal. He wanted you to play for the jersey. It was about the team, but also your own performance and that of the man beside you.

As I said, under Mal I was ready to play from the first day of camp. But unfortunately, my knee wasn't as compliant. After each training session, even though my program was limited, my knee kept swelling. During the final session of the week—the captain's run—we warmed up at Hunter Stadium. Although it was only a light session, the hard playing-surface caused havoc with my knee. It swelled up like a balloon.

I iced it all night, and the next morning I said to the team doctor, Chris Ball, 'This is pretty bad.' He decided that he would need to drain the fluid from my knee, only a few hours before kick-off. This was something I had never done before, so obviously I was nervous about it impacting on my performance. I shouldn't have worried.

I was completely confident we would beat the Kiwis. The 2013 World Cup team was the best Australian side I had ever played with. And to Mal's credit, the 2016 ANZAC Test side featured the core of that 2013 group, so I knew that we would be able to perform well. In front of 27,724 supporters, we won the match 16–0. To be back and victorious in the green and gold was a great feeling. But to finish as man of the match was incredibly special.

As I've stated time and again throughout this book, the journey back into the Test arena was extremely challenging. So to be given the Charles Savory medal for the best player on the field was an extremely satisfying moment in my career. However, there was one element of that Test that I don't think will ever sit well with me.

During that ANZAC Test camp, Mal said in one of his speeches, 'You know what I'm like—we haven't won the last four Tests, so if you go out and win this match, I'll pick you all for the Four Nations tour at the end of the year. And if you win that, I'll pick you all again for the 2017 World Cup.'

I sat there and thought, 'It's highly unlikely I'm going to be around for the World Cup, but if we can get a win here, I'll have one last shot at playing for Australia in the Four Nations.' Well, we won the ANZAC Test and I was named man of the match— and that was all before I was able to then win the premiership with the Sharks. Yet, not only did Mal overlook me for the Four Nations tour, but only two players—Valentine Holmes and James Maloney—from our premiership-winning side were named to tour England at the end of 2016.

Maybe I was off and that man of the match award from the ANZAC Test really didn't hold much weight at all. Because ahead of the NSW squad being chosen for Origin I, a handful of commentators left me out of their predicted Blues team. There are always particular journalists who don't like you and therefore leave you out of their predicted line-ups. But I just couldn't understand how the current NSW captain could go from man of the match in the ANZAC Test—coupled with their club enjoying a record winning streak—to being replaced altogether. In the end, thankfully Laurie chose me to lead the Blues, for what was always going to be my final series in the sky-blue jersey of New South Wales.

In an all-too-familiar fashion, Queensland beat us on our home turf in Sydney, 6–4. I don't know what can be said. It was typical of Queensland. They only scored one try, and so did we. Yet somehow, we finished on the wrong side of the scoreboard.

Origin I of the 2016 series was the first game for New South Wales where I was used specifically as a front-rower, and as such I was substituted in order to rotate our big men. Being the captain, I felt deflated to come off the field for a rest. Every player will say the same thing—you want to be out there. And in previous Origins where I'd played as captain, if I hadn't played 80 minutes, I'd played 70 minutes plus.

Aaron Woods and I were on the bench a couple of times, and we both just wanted to get back out there. Perhaps, too, I wanted to give every minute possible on the field, as I knew it was going to be my last series.

Like on too many previous occasions, we were forced to save the series in Queensland at Suncorp Stadium. It was a massive obstacle, but one we were absolutely confident we could overcome. The history books would show that we couldn't do it, losing 26–16 to the Maroons, who celebrated their series success in front of more than 52,000 home fans.

After the loss, like clockwork, Phil 'Gus' Gould took aim at my leadership and the performance of my NSW teammates. Gus—and he wasn't the only one—declared that I should be omitted from the squad for Origin III. Not once did Laurie discuss leaving me out of his side. It was an example of how little impact the opinions of others really have on those within the squad who witness firsthand the effort, energy and commitment that a particular group of players invests in each other.

Much was made of Origin III being my farewell game and a chance for me to say goodbye to NSW fans. I would've been hurt if I wasn't picked, not because I wanted to say goodbye to Blues fans, but because I wanted to play for New South Wales.

I never received any phone calls or indication from Laurie or the coaching staff that I was going to be included for game three, until the day the team was read out. I received a phone call on the day to say that I was in, but my close mate, Greg Bird, had been overlooked, bringing to an end a great era of Origin mateship. I immediately phoned Birdy. That was a tough phone call to make. Naturally, Birdy was upset.

In a new-look Blues side, Laurie had one eye on winning the match and the other on the future. He selected my Sharks teammate, Jack Bird, plus Matt Moylan at five-eighth and James 'Teddy' Tedesco on debut at fullback. James Maloney, the regular five-eighth, was chosen to play halfback.

While everyone else wanted to talk about Origin III being my send-off party, I just wanted to win the game. The last try of the match is how I'll always remember Origin III. There were 80 seconds left in the game when, trailing 14–12, Matty Moylan put Blake Ferguson though a gap with a well-timed pass. As Fergo speared through out wide, he then passed to Teddy. Game over. That's what I thought as soon as Teddy accelerated down field. But no.

Remarkably, Maroons halfback Cooper Cronk cut down Teddy just inches from the tryline. With the seconds ticking away, we had to shift the ball to the opposite side of the field, where the Queensland defence was still desperately trying to retreat.

After Teddy's play-the-ball, Jimmy Maloney lofted a long cut-out pass. The ball bounced once before landing perfectly in my hands. But I thought, 'Just play what is in front of me'— similar to my thought process in the first-half when I managed to squeeze an off-load for a first-half try for teammate Tyson Frizell. So in that split second after collecting the bouncing ball, I passed left to our centre, Michael 'Jenko' Jennings.

Jenko is an athlete—all speed and power. Amazingly, instead of continuing to shift left, he cut hard off his left foot and began spearing back towards the posts. The Maroons' defensive line simply couldn't react to Jenko's superior footwork and desire. Jenko powered through the clutches of six Maroons defenders to score with just a few seconds remaining in the match. Who could ever forget Aaron Woods's leaping post-try celebration?

With victory secured, we separated from our huddle of high fives, and one of the boys said, 'Gal, go kick the goal.' I didn't have to be asked twice. This was a moment to savour. How many captains in their final Origin match can say that their last touch of the football for their state was to kick a goal after the final siren? Without much thought, I leaned in and converted my first goal since I was a boy playing for Wentworthville.

The 18–14 victory was bittersweet. While it was satisfying to win on home soil, albeit a dead rubber, in front of more than 61,000 loyal fans, it was hard to ignore the pain caused by losing the series. As we shook hands with the Queenslanders, the words Laurie had said earlier in the week sprang to mind. 'There's no way we are going to sit there and listen to them [Queensland] sing "Aye Aye Yippee Yippee Aye" [the Maroons victory song]—we're taking our captain on a lap of honour.'

So after Cam Smith accepted the trophy, I signalled to the boys that we should go and thank our fans. I was oblivious to the fact that Cam was speaking on stage. What a lot of people don't realise is that, down on the field, you can't hear much of what is being said by those speaking on stage.

Around you, there are radio journalists asking for interviews and TV producers pulling you over for a chat live on air. Some players are talking among themselves and, if you revisit the footage, even Cam's own Queensland teammates are giggling and laughing, oblivious to what he is saying. So when Cam lifted the trophy, I began to walk towards our fans.

I admit now that, if I had my time over, I would've ensured I was aware that Cam was still speaking. In no way was it ever intended to be a snub against Cam. I know how it looked; it's easy to be critical from an outsider's point of view and say that we snubbed him and walked away. But I made a point of speaking to Cam the next day. It was very similar to when he phoned me after the negative press the Queensland players involved in the Australian team received when they sang 'Aye Aye Yippee Yippee Aye' following a Test match win.

For some reason, there's a perception that Cam and I don't like each other. It's just not true. Even during the 2016 finals series and ahead of the 2017 season launch, journalists were continually writing that we don't like each other. I've never taken any notice of it because it has never been an issue for Cam or me. He actually raised that perception with me one day, saying, 'Mate, I think the journos care about it a lot more than we do.' Which is right.

I don't even know where it comes from. I understand the fact that we opposed each other for a long period of our careers as captains during Origin. But that's just Origin. What the same journalists chose to ignore was that we also played over 30 Test matches together, enjoying the greatest of highs, and we've never had so much as a bad word to say to each other. I don't even think we had a run-in on the field.

But after the backlash following Origin III, I thought it was important to call him. 'Look mate, it wasn't about turning our back on you and walking away from you when you were talking,' I said. 'It was about going to thank the fans and, I'll be honest with you, I wasn't going to sit there and listen to you guys sing "Aye Aye Yippee Yippee Aye".'

I continued by saying, 'Mate, I just don't have the energy for all this rubbish any more. It's such a relief it's over. I've played the villain in Origin for the past couple of years, and I'm done. And that's all I was thinking about. It wasn't directed at you. I just wanted to grab the boys and do one lap to thank the fans.' Cam was fine about it.

Back in the dressing rooms, we had a private moment with only members of the team allowed inside. Someone covered the Channel Nine camera, which was positioned on the wall of the room, so I knew I was about to receive some type of special treatment. Because everyone knows how much I hate beer, Robbie Farah called for silence in the room as he announced that I would now skol a full can of VB. But that wasn't all.

I have a devil tattoo on my backside. And at every NSW camp I was involved in, the boys would always call it the 'demon'. On a rare night of bonding, the saying was, 'When Gal goes out, the demon comes out.' So after a special night out 'bonding', when it was time to head back to the team hotel, Greg Bird would always say, 'Righto, it's time to send the demon home.' Collectively, they would all take turns smacking my backside as hard as they could.

And so, inside the ANZ Stadium dressing room, with the players and staff yelling and cheering, I moved towards the centre of a ring formed around me for Robbie, who had grabbed a belt to whip my backside as hard as he could. 'Let's send the demon home for the last time,' Robbie laughed. The following morning, I woke up with welts the size of tennis balls on my backside. It wasn't a series win, but it was a nice way to end my State of Origin career.

As I had said to Cameron, I was relieved that it was all over. Even in 2017, when I made a comeback for City in the final City–Country Origin match played in Mudgee, I had no burning desire to wear the sky-blue jersey again. I'd had enough of the sideshow that comes with Origin. Criticism from past NSW players and key Blues supporters, including Gus Gould, was disappointing.

Each of those past NSW Origin players and Gus—who had coached the Blues—know how challenging every Origin is mentally and physically, and the pressure that is involved. But the last two years of my Origin career, in 2015 and 2016, I lacked support from our own, which is not what Origin is about.

And so, when I walked out of ANZ Stadium for the final time as a Blue, I knew that I was done.

32

The Streak

Our premiership-winning streak began on 28 March 2016, and it wouldn't be until 24 July 2016 that we were halted. In all, we secured a club record of fifteen consecutive wins. Each victory was different. The majority were hard fought and challenging, while others were clinical and went exactly as planned.

Importantly, we were successful in those matches where, during every season, the result could go either way. An example of that was our two-point win in Round 9 over the Broncos. Critically, we also secured close victories over Canterbury in Round 13 (20–18), North Queensland in Round 14 (13–10) and New Zealand in Round 16 (19–18, in golden point). To me, they were the victories that instilled belief and confidence within our 2016 squad and an understanding, not only from within but also externally, that we boasted a serious football team.

Although our 62–0 thrashing of the Newcastle Knights in Round 10 at Hunter Stadium was our biggest winning margin of 2016—and the fourth biggest in the club's history—I disagree with many of our supporters that this proved we were premiership material. I actually felt sorry for the Newcastle players and fans that day. If I'm being truthful, I felt sorry for Newcastle that entire season. The 2016 Knights were the worst first-grade team I ever faced in my entire career.

I remember playing for Australia against minnow teams such as the United States, and the Knights were even worse than them. I only played about 30 minutes in our huge win over Newcastle, as my knee was still causing me grief. As soon as Valentine Holmes had scored his hat-trick of tries after 26 minutes, coach Shane 'Flanno' Flanagan ordered me from the field. From the sideline I could see that, although the opposition was vastly inferior, we showed little mercy.

As I said, I felt sorry for the Newcastle boys that day. After the game, I walked onto the field to shake hands, and it felt like I was grabbing the hands of kids. I didn't even know most of their names. It wasn't their fault.

I remember looking at Newcastle's Saifiti twins (Jacob and Daniel) in the forward pack. At just nineteen years of age, they were bearing the load against our experienced and ruthless forward pack. I hoped it wouldn't scar them. Losing becomes a habit, and I desperately hoped the repeated pummelling they were receiving wouldn't leave them questioning their motivation.

They were two boys who should've been blooded into the NRL alongside seasoned first-graders. In our team, they would've benefited immensely from playing four or five games with experienced players to assist their development. But at the Knights, they were front and centre. I give every player from that 2016 Knights squad huge credit, as they returned with a great attitude and improvement in their game in 2017.

Despite our huge win over Newcastle, I still didn't feel like we had achieved anything special. I had known from the pre-season that we had a quality squad, but I certainly didn't feel that in beating Newcastle by 60 points we had declared 'Look out, we're here'.

There were two other games that gave me a real sense that something special was brewing. The first was our win over Canterbury at ANZ Stadium on a Monday night in June. Against the Bulldogs, we trailed 18–14 with two minutes remaining. Ben Barba was instrumental in putting Ricky Leutele over for a try in the dying minutes, and then James Maloney kicked a sideline conversion for us to secure a memorable victory.

Our Round 17 win over Parramatta at Shark Park was similar, in that it allowed us to prove what we were capable of as a team and how we were learning lessons about competing until the eightieth minute. At one point, we were behind 18–0 on the scoreboard against the Eels, yet we fought hard to finish as 34–24 winners.

Those two games were a great barometer of where we were. It showed me that it didn't matter what the scoreboard looked like—we never gave up on each other. One of our team philosophies was that we competed on every play, didn't stop working and didn't stop scrambling, and we did just that. To come back from being 18–0 down against Parramatta, when they were full of confidence, yahooing and carrying on, I thought it was a really good sign for us.

Off the field, there was also a noticeable lift in professionalism. It had begun during the 2015 season. Within the club and among the playing group, there was a greater attention to detail with our prehab and rehab. The key was that everyone was buying in. It's so easy to take shortcuts—to skip doing rehab stretches, for example—if you really want to. But that wasn't happening. Everyone was 'all in'. The statistics show that, by the time we won the 2016 premiership, we had only used 24 players throughout the entire season.

With each victory, the media focus on our winning run intensified. How long will Cronulla keep going? Are they winning at the wrong time of the year? Internally, as a playing group, we were literally treating every week on its merit. That was the way we set up our pre-season.

In 2015, Flanno wanted to work in blocks of four or five matches, where we zeroed in and worked hard on achieving a certain number of wins over that block. As a strategy, I didn't entirely like it. I much preferred concentrating on one game at a time.

Winning becomes a habit, so using that momentum of success into the next week was quite easy. And our game plan was pretty simple, too. Defend hard, using the likes of Matt Prior, Andrew Fifita, Chris Heighington, Jayson Bukuya and me to rip into the opposition through the middle of the field, and complete the majority of our sets with the football. It was simple but effective. That's what we did through 'our streak' of 2016.

It was no coincidence that later in the season, when we began to lose a few games, our completion rate was way down by our 'streak' standards. Then during the semifinal play-offs, when we rediscovered our winning brand, our completion rates improved to sit just under 90 per cent.

It was up on the Gold Coast, against the Titans, that our fifteen-game winning streak came to an end—albeit in an 18–18 draw after golden-point extra time. I rate that match in the top five toughest games of the season, including the grand final. The Titans met us with aggression and were led wholeheartedly that night by Greg Bird. He was in everything. Leaving the Titans at the end of the 2016 season to play for the Catalans Dragons, Birdy's departure was glaring. The Titans struggled in the early period of the 2017 season, as they lacked his aggression and leadership.

As I said, it was an extremely physical game, and it wasn't a case of us being overly poor that night. The Titans were just very good. We had our chances to ice the game, highlighted by Jimmy Maloney's shot at field goal inside normal time, which hit the upright. But in perhaps a fair result, given the way the Titans scrapped away, we both finished with one point.

The following week, in our 30–14 Round 22 loss to Canberra, we missed the influence of our dummy half, Michael Ennis, who had pulled out ahead of the match due to injury. I, too, sat on the sidelines in our loss to the Raiders, because of a calf complaint. We were then soundly beaten 32–18 at Kogarah in Round 23 by our arch rivals, the Dragons.

Suddenly, we were staring down the barrel of three straight losses ahead of our Round 24 match against South Sydney at ANZ Stadium. I did everything possible to recover from the calf injury that had stymied my ability to get onto the field. But my calf just wasn't 100 per cent and, despite the boys going down to the Rabbitohs 12–6, I saw enough with regard to our attitude in defence to believe that we were edging back towards our old standards.

Of course, after three consecutive losses, the critics had us dead in the water. The overwhelming sentiment within the press was that this would be yet another false dawn for Sharks supporters, who would be forced to endure another season without an elusive premiership. However, I wasn't as concerned about our form, despite the critics declaring that we had the wobbles.

In the NRL, it's simply not feasible to be 'up' every single week. A team only needs to be 5 per cent down in attitude to be beaten. To play at a perfect level every single week is impossible. The first coach or athlete who is able to master the art of remaining on top of their game for 26 consecutive weeks is going to have a job forever, because it's physically and mentally impossible to ensure that seventeen players perform at 100 per cent every single week. You just can't do it. You never want to lose games, but I wasn't concerned by it, either.

To his credit, Flanno didn't change. Plenty of coaches would panic, focusing only on the past month, as opposed to what we could draw from the entire season. Our regular meetings among the leadership group didn't change, and the spine, which helped organise our game plans, weren't being placed under pressure by the coaching staff to do more or less.

I was able to return from my calf injury in time for our next match against the Sydney Roosters—the second-last match of the regular season and one that would see us return to the winner's circle. Scoring a try in our 37–12 victory at Shark Park, it was the perfect heart-starter for our final assignment of the year, against the Storm in Melbourne.

The last match of our season was a promoter's dream, as the winner would be declared the minor premiers—first on the competition ladder after the regular season. From memory, Fox Sports had a clock counting down the hours, minutes and seconds until the match from the beginning of the week. I was excited about the trip south. It was a great opportunity for the club. Melbourne had always proven to be our toughest road trip in the NRL. But this would be a nightmare trip for us, as evidenced by the fact that it wouldn't be until Round 6 of the 2017 season that we would secure our first victory at AAMI Park, after seven previous attempts.

The early battle for the minor premiership was typically tense. On a cold Saturday night at AAMI Park, we kicked out to a 2–0 lead through a penalty goal. And then, quite simply, that was as good as it got for us. The Storm powered away to a 26–2 lead before we were able to pinch a late try in the final minutes before full-time. Winning the match 26–6 and awarded the

J.J. Giltinan Shield for the minor premiership, the Storm celebrated in front of their home fans.

The full-time siren had just finished when I looked across AAMI Park at Mick Ennis. 'I hope we get through the finals and play them again,' I said to Mick.

'Me, too,' Mick said, with a glint in his eye.

I have since been asked, by those to whom I have mentioned this discussion between Mick and me, why it was that we both voiced our desire to play Melbourne in the finals, no less than 60 seconds after the final siren. To put it simply, it was because of Melbourne's attitude. They didn't respect us.

During their win, as they scored one of their tries, Storm centre Will Chambers ran past me and said, 'That really has to hurt, Gal.' I didn't say a word, but I parked his comment in the back of my mind for another day. It wasn't just Chambers. I finished that match with a sense that, after smacking us 26–6, Melbourne would take us for granted if we were ever to play them again.

The loss to Melbourne relegated us to third on the NRL ladder after the regular season, meaning that not only had we forgone the minor premiership, but also our first semifinal would be on the road. Under the NRL's top-eight finals system, as the third-placed side we were drawn to play Canberra, who had finished second. The Raiders had produced a tremendous season, so this would be far from an easy assignment.

I'm not certain if it was due to the journey home from Melbourne, but on the Tuesday before our Saturday clash with the Raiders I completed training feeling stiff and sore in my lower back. I first felt the soreness while in the gym, in the process of performing a bench pull. Later that night, I could hardly sleep.

The pain was immense. Anyone who has had back pain can appreciate how debilitating it can be. By Wednesday morning,

I couldn't move. Thursday arrived and, even though I had commenced a course of anti-inflammatory tablets, I felt exactly the same. The pain failed to subside.

By Friday, the day of our final captain's run, I was in absolute agony. My spine had literally twisted. I could hardly get into and out of my car. The only way I could get into the front seat was if Anne helped me. To get back out, I would have our physiotherapist meet me at the front gate of Shark Park.

I walked—if you could call it that—into training just over 24 hours before we were due to face the Raiders, groaning and moaning with every step. As our staff assisted me onto a bed inside our medical room, Mick Ennis stuck his head around the corner. He took one look at me and asked, 'Are you going to be right to play?'

'No,' I winced. That ashen look on Mick's face is a sight I'll never forget. He looked like he wanted to kill me, there and then. As soon as I told Mick that I was no chance of playing, he simply turned around without saying a single word and walked out of the room. I didn't see or speak to Mick again until after that memorable Raiders game. Mick was angry with me. But I thought, 'Stuff you, Mick—I'm lying here and I can't even move.'

It was at that point the Sharks' medical staff decided to send me to hospital. 'You're going to need a guided cortisone injection into the disc in your lower back,' they said. I climbed into the passenger seat of my car, and it was Mum who drove me to St George Hospital. I shuffled sideways through the front door of emergency. I must have been kidding myself, thinking no one had noticed me on the way in or out, because by the time I returned to the car, every news bulletin on the radio was declaring, 'Paul Gallen won't be in Canberra.'

The cortisone injection did little to relieve the pain. I would need a miracle to suit up against the Raiders. The agony was insane. The only thing I could do was lie on the lounge or in bed.

I was prescribed an anti-inflammatory called prednisone, which I could only consume after receiving clearance from ASADA. It's basically a cortisone injection in tablet form, but what prednisone can also do is break down your immune system. Unbeknown to me, this would have an impact on the biggest week of my life: grand-final week.

In total, the back injury left me floored for seven days. For that period, I couldn't get off the lounge. And that's exactly where I witnessed one of the greatest wins in the Cronulla club's history.

Emotionally, I was a mess on the day the boys were due to face the Raiders in front of one of the most vocal and passionate home crowds ever witnessed at a semifinal. To put into perspective the magnitude of how difficult travelling to Canberra was for our club, the Raiders were on a ten-game winning streak.

It's amazing how long a day seems when you're lying on your back, doing nothing. All I could do was wait for kick-off. From my lounge, I sent the team emotional messages via WhatsApp. I also spoke to Flanno. Despite the shuffle to our line-up caused by my injury—and the prospect of beating a Raiders side loaded with attacking weapons, in front of their home crowd—I still thought we could do it.

Canberra had always been a venue our club had enjoyed playing at, and I was supremely confident that our underrated pack could handle the Raiders' big men. However, I admit I was seriously concerned when Wade Graham was knocked unconscious following a typically strong carry from Raiders centre Joey Leilua, after just five minutes of the match. With Wade out of the game, young interchange forward Kurt 'Capes' Capewell was called into the action.

Maybe he was feeling overexuberant, because in the biggest game of his life, Capes shot out of our defensive line, which allowed Canberra hooker Josh Hodgson to cut through, juggle the footy and score beneath the posts. 'This poor bloke,' I thought, as I looked at Capes. 'This is his first semifinal, and this is how he's introduced.'

Well, Capes certainly made up for it, producing a remarkable 70-minute performance that he'll never forget. He had a blinder. From my lounge room, as I lay flat on my back, I was yelling at the boys on every play. I was literally screaming at the TV.

The Raiders jumped out to a 12–0 lead. And although the atmosphere was intense in Canberra, I remained upbeat, reminding myself that the lessons we had learned throughout the year (against the Bulldogs and Parramatta) had taught us how to come back from daunting deficits.

I cheered—and almost had a heart attack in the same moment—when Matt Prior powered through to score just before half-time. That was the best performance of Matty's career—he was absolutely crucial in helping to steer us to an inspiring 16–14 victory. When that full-time siren sounded, I couldn't stop crying. As vision of the boys hugging and celebrating was shown on the TV, I turned to Anne and said, 'I promise you, we're going to win the premiership. We just have to get there, we just have to get there.'

That night in my lounge room, as a person with a vested interest in the game, watching the boys beat the Raiders was one of only a few times during my career that I felt like a true fan. It was incredible. With tears in my eyes, I wrote, 'I love you boys' via a WhatsApp message to every player.

The victory can never be understated; it was a win that many believe was the catalyst for our premiership glory. Against all the odds and injuries, we displayed courage, spirit and class to deliver the winning result. Undeniably, the victory was made so much sweeter by the fact that, under the finals system, we automatically progressed to week three of the finals. Victory in week three would enable us to progress to the club's first grand final since the Super League decider in 1997.

On a personal note, the fact that the boys had been able to beat Canberra also allowed me another crucial week to overcome my back injury. Had we lost to Canberra, I would've almost certainly missed what would've been an elimination semifinal the following week. But with the week off, I knuckled down on my rehabilitation, which was focused on strengthening my lower abdominal muscles, and I began slow walking drills to ensure I would be ready to return for the preliminary final.

As the dominos fell, with North Queensland winning a gruelling 26–20 golden-point semifinal over Brisbane, our preliminary final would be against the Cowboys on a Friday night at Allianz Stadium in Sydney. On the Monday, just five days out from one of the biggest matches in the club's history, mentally I had convinced myself I would be ready to go.

Inside our high-performance centre at Shark Park stood a whiteboard. It was where training schedules were written, or key messages from Flanno about our next opponent were highlighted. You couldn't get into the gym without walking past the whiteboard. So, ahead of our preliminary final against the Cowboys, I decided to grab the pen. 'I want to play in a grand final,' I wrote.

Without being prompted, other players began writing their own hopes, goals and dreams for what they wanted. One player wrote what they were going to do to stop Cowboys wrecking ball Jason Taumalolo. Another player wrote what they were going to do on their left edge, while yet another wrote their intent for what they were going to do on their right edge. In a quiet moment, every player found a corner or space on the whiteboard to write his intentions. By the end of the week, the day before we were due to face the Cowboys, the entire whiteboard was full of mission statements.

I found them extremely powerful and meaningful. Oh, except for the one from my old smart-arse mate, James Maloney. Beneath where I had written 'I want to win a grand final', Jimmy had scrawled, 'I've already won one.' That was Jimmy—forever the class clown. But, it must be said, when it mattered—especially during our run towards the club's first premiership—Jimmy took the lead. In video sessions, instead of his usual wisecracks and interruptions to Flanno, Jimmy spoke with authority and made it clear what he wanted from us as a team.

As a playing group in that famous season, we never worried about the opposition; that was Flanno's job. There was a genuine calm among the group, due to our trust in each other—we all knew what we were doing and how we would commit to our role. Within the team, we had a saying: 'Do what we do well'. And that's exactly what we did.

Externally, within our community and fan base, after such a successful 2016 season with a team loaded with experience, class and youthful brilliance, there was a sense of destiny ahead of our preliminary final against the Cowboys. But within the playing group, I can't say we felt like that—we knew we had a battle on our hands. And really, what would we have achieved, if we were to bomb out against the Cowboys?

For me, that sense of taking nothing for granted was born out of having experienced defeat in three previous preliminary finals throughout my career. It was a point I made clear to the playing group prior to our clash with the Cowboys. 'In fifteen years, I've never advanced past this game,' I said. I had to make this point, because I wanted the younger players in our squad to realise how significant an opportunity this was. For guys such as Jack Bird and Valentine Holmes, I did not want them to take this for granted.

Our softly spoken prop, Sam Tagataese, had something to say, too. He had missed the past month of the season through injury, and after a decade of playing first grade—and now at the age of 29—he'd never played in a grand final. 'This could be my last chance,' he said.

Externally, our halfback Chad Townsend was the focus of attention due to the fact that Flanno had substituted him from the field late in the second half—and with the game still in the balance—against Canberra. I never considered Flanno's decision a major issue. Maybe I was too caught up in celebrating our win over the Raiders, but in my mind there was no way possible that Flanno was going to leave Chad out of the side to face the Cowboys.

Being replaced, especially as a halfback and playmaker, would've been undoubtedly shattering for Chad. I can understand him being disappointed. Flanno did what he thought was right, and it obviously worked at the time. But it was never an issue for me, to the point that I didn't even feel the need to ask Flanno if he was going to replace Chad at halfback against the Cowboys, because I just knew it wasn't a consideration.

Amid our preparation for the Cowboys, my focus on the match shifted as I went to say goodbye to a man I had always respected, Ron 'Mass' Massey. I've told the story of when I first met Mass many times. It was during an afternoon in 2009, at the request of my former coach, Ricky Stuart. I had experienced a few poor headlines due to my on-field antics at the time, and Ricky thought Mass would help 'open my eyes'.

The way Mass gave it to me in spades that day, calling me a 'f**king soft c**k', I thought the old man was going to punch the living daylights out of me. What he was telling me was that the toughest blokes are the ones who get hit, and then get back up.

We had stayed in contact ever since that day, but his ailing health soon slowed him down. However, I always made an effort, before a big game, to give Mass a call to say g'day. Such was the pleasure I took from Mass's company and how much I valued his advice that I wanted him to meet my son, Kody, before he passed away. Mass was in a terrible state when Kody and I visited him in hospital, and it was incredibly sad to see him like that. At his bedside, I introduced Mass to Kody. I told Mass how much I appreciated his guidance and what he had done for me throughout my life. 'You've done it all yourself,' Mass said. That meant so much.

Mass passed away four days before our clash with the Cowboys on the Friday night at Allianz Stadium. Fittingly, a minute's silence was held before our preliminary final. We also wore black armbands to remember one of the game's great tacticians and Supercoach Jack Gibson's right-hand man.

Mass lived in the Shire and was a former chief executive of the Sharks. There would've been nothing more that he would've loved than to see us lift that premiership trophy. As a hush fell over the crowd prior to kick-off against the Cowboys, I peered up at the big screen at Allianz Stadium, to see Mass's face staring back at the entire ground. It was special.

Of the 38,000-strong crowd at the game, 36,000 were Sharks supporters. I was slightly apprehensive about the one-sided support, because in 2008, for our preliminary final against Melbourne, it was a very similar scenario. On that night, we had failed to warm up out on the field prior to kick-off, and so when we ran out from the dressing rooms as a playing group, we were spooked by the noise and realisation of how many fans desperately wanted us to deliver for them.

No doubt, the parochial crowd impacted our psyche that night. A few of my teammates' faces were white when we ran out. We suffered from a serious case of stage fright against the Storm, losing 28–0. So, before playing the Cowboys in the preliminary final of 2016, I told the coaching staff it was imperative that we warm up on the field. Thankfully, they agreed. Being out there, soaking up the atmosphere and the noise, helped to break down the nerves when it finally came time to run out.

We hammered North Queensland from the opening whistle. Alongside Matt Prior and Andrew Fifita, I made it a personal mission to stop their forward pack at all costs. Prior to the preliminary final, hard-running Cowboys forward Jason Taumalolo had averaged 200 metres with the football. Against us that night, he managed eleven runs for 102 metres—the only Cowboys player to reach three figures in metres gained. By full-time, such was our dominance that we had six players who had run for over 100 metres.

Our tactics were that every time we had the ball, we would run directly at Taumalolo and Test prop Matt Scott. We wanted them to make as many tackles as possible in order to slowly sap their energy, so that when they did have the ball, they were too exhausted to run with purpose. By half-time, such was our dominance that the Cowboys had received just 36 per cent of the possession.

We led 14–0 at half-time and, although the Cowboys snatched a try three minutes after the break to close the gap to 14–6, we only had to maintain our discipline with the football to break any remaining spirit they may have had. Through tries to Luke Lewis and a double to Jimmy Maloney, we had the match won at 32–6 with just under fifteen minutes remaining.

Rarely in the NRL are you afforded the opportunity to think about the next week's match prior to the full-time siren. But that's what Flanno was able to do. Both Wade Graham and I earned an early mark in the last ten minutes.

The party atmosphere in the stands, as our loyal Sharks supporters soaked up the realisation that our proud club was at long last going to a grand final, was something truly special. But within our squad, when that full-time siren sounded, it wasn't a case of feeling shocked or disbelief that we were one win away from our lifelong goal. As far as I was concerned, I could believe that we were going to a grand final because we deserved it. We had worked extremely hard for everything we had achieved that season.

After the game, the dressing rooms were obviously filled with smiles and high fives. When it came time to speak, I simply spoke about enjoying the next seven days. But because I had never navigated through grand-final week before, I was also in unknown territory.

As a lower-grade coach and as an assistant coach, Flanno had previously been involved with Parramatta's and the Roosters' premiership campaigns, so he stood in front of us and spoke about how fast the week would go. 'There's a lot of commitments and expectations as far as media is concerned,' Flanno said. 'I'll do my best to ensure it is as pain-free as I can, but it's something that we've got to do and we're expected to do. So let's get on with what's required and not let it affect us.'

Luke Lewis, who had already secured a premiership ring with Penrith back in 2003, also spoke. Like Flanno, he emphasised how fast the week would fly by. 'But enjoy it,' he said. 'Don't get frustrated with what we've got to do. Soak it up.'

The thing is, when I look back now on that incredible time, I still feel like it wouldn't have mattered what anyone said—all seventeen players who were part of our grand-final squad were ready to be there that week. One of our team mantras was: 'It's our time'. And it was.

The perfect blend of experience and youth that we boasted in 2016 was spot-on. We had the older heads in me, Lewy, Heighno and Mick Ennis. We had the steady heads of Chad and Jimmy and the exuberance of Val and Jack, who didn't seem to care about anything that was being asked of him, despite his tender years.

Finally, one of the major factors we spoke about as a group was wanting it more than Melbourne. They may have had the world's best players, but you'll never be able to change my mind that, as a group, we wanted that premiership more than what they did. They had won their premierships. They had achieved rugby league's holy grail.

To repeat that desire over and over again, across seventeen players, is unbelievably difficult. And it is never more so than when you're playing a club, driven by the want of an entire community, which is chasing its first premiership in 50 years.

33

Premiers

On the Saturday morning after beating the Cowboys, I woke up happy but far from content. I made a conscious effort to stop myself being overcome by excitement. Why? Because now that we had finally reached the grand final, I wanted to win it. The thought of getting this far and losing was the perfect way to keep a lid on any excitement I felt.

Throughout grand-final week, I never looked further ahead than the next day. Our preparation wasn't about changing anything just because, all of a sudden, we were in the grand final. We stuck to the exact same system in our recovery, our team meetings, our training and captain's runs as what we had used for the entire season and what had gotten us to this point. I didn't feel the need to call any extra player meetings, or to speak to Wade, Mick Ennis and Jimmy, just because it was the grand final.

From home, I had watched Melbourne advance to the grand final by beating Canberra in the other preliminary final. I still feel like the Raiders were unlucky not to have won. In the end, the Storm won 14–12. To see Melbourne win and be confirmed as

Try time in my Test debut. We wore the traditional Kangaroos jersey at the Sydney Cricket Ground to celebrate 100 years of rugby league, in 2008. *NRL Photos*

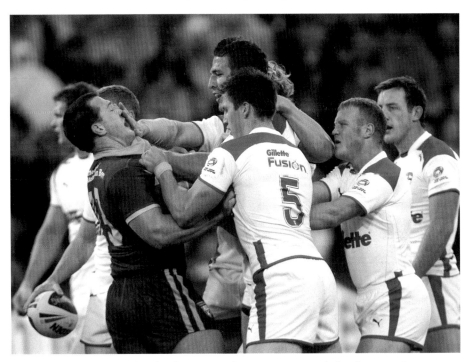

I loved playing in England. The atmosphere is great, and the fans just love their rugby league. This was a moment to cherish during another victory over England in October 2010. *NRL Photos*

A proud moment, holding the 2010 ANZAC Test trophy after beating
New Zealand at the opening of AAMI Park. *NRL Photos*

A great bunch of blokes, and 2012 Test coach Tim Sheens was one of the best
mentors I've had in the game. *NRL Photos*

Wearing the green and gold in the 2013 World Cup. *NRL Photos*

Winners are grinners. Me and Birdy after winning the 2013 World Cup at Old Trafford. *NRL Photos*

These photos remind me that the 2013 Kangaroos team was the best one I ever played with. It was loaded with so many talented players, and we played so well as a team. *NRL Photos*

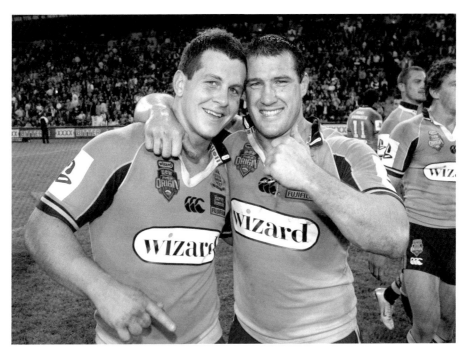

The Blues Bash Brothers. Origin III, 2007, was the first time Birdy and I played together for New South Wales. *NRL Photos*

Taking a hit-up for the Blues during the tough 2008 Origin series. *NRL Photos*

Overlooked for Origin I in 2010, I was sent to Brisbane to help save the series in game two. History shows it was an impossible task. *NRL Photos*

Heartache again. Johnathan Thurston consoles me after the Blues suffer a one-point loss in the 2012 Origin decider in Brisbane. *NRL Photos*

Congratulating Cam Smith for everything Queensland had achieved prior to the Blues' drought-breaking 2014 Origin series. *NRL Photos*

ANZ Stadium during the 2014 Origin series. I've said it many times: when it's sold out, this is the best ground in Australia. *NRL Photos*

Leading the charge towards victory during the 2014 Origin series. *NRL Photos*

Surrounded by
a sea of Maroon
during the 2014
Origin series.
NRL Photos

My mates from day one getting a little bit excited after I captained the Blues to
our Origin series win in 2014. *NRL Photos*

Embracing Blues coach Laurie Daley in 2014. You won't meet a finer man.
NRL Photos

That's my boy. Another special moment with Kody after our Origin series win in 2014. *NRL Photos*

I didn't support an NRL team when I was growing up. I supported New South Wales. So it was a dream come true to lift the Origin shield in 2014. *NRL Photos*

On the shoulders of Andrew Fifita and James Tamou for my last exit as a Blue in 2016. *NRL Photos*

I never expected to be back playing for City in the final City–Country Origin match in 2017, but I'm glad coach Brad Fittler called. A truly great experience. *NRL Photos*

Boxing debut. A photo to promote my first fight, against Hika Elliot in 2012. *Newspix*

Bye-bye, Hoppa, in 2019. I told you so. *NRL Photos*

A Ricky Stuart stitch-up. The coach of Parramatta told the media that I would run nude down the main street of Cronulla if the Eels beat us in 2013. It was a joke that we managed to turn into a $10,000 donation to the Men of League Foundation. *Newspix*

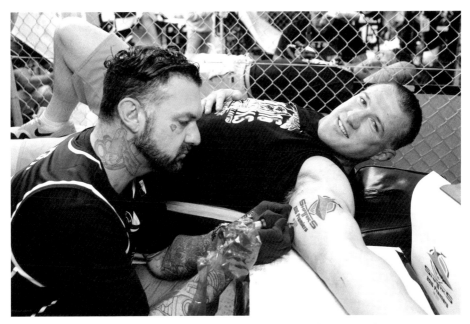

Inked forever. Getting a 2016 premiership tattoo just a few days after winning the title. *Newspix*

Family time at Australia Zoo in 2017.

Hello, Ruby! Our baby girl is born in February 2018.

My family is my pride and joy. Here we are, all together in Cronulla in 2017.

our grand-final opponents was a moment when, upon reflection, I felt slightly torn.

I suppose you've got to be careful what you wish for. Remember, Melbourne was the team I wanted revenge against for what they had done to us the last time we had played. But now with them as our grand-final opposition, I began to second-guess myself. 'Now we're here, maybe we'd have a better chance of winning the premiership if we were playing Canberra,' I remember thinking. But, as I've previously stated, after that match in Round 26, Melbourne was the team that we always wanted another crack at.

On the Monday of grand-final week, my troublesome back pain was still lingering. I continued with daily treatment, visiting Kay Macpherson, a Sutherland Shire osteopath, who I had used throughout my career. I had been receiving what I felt was referral pain from my back to my hip, so I thought a session with Kay would be timely.

I also had a little red mark on the point of my hip, leading Kay to ask if a spider had bitten me recently. I knew I hadn't been bitten by anything, but when I looked at where Kay was pointing there was clearly a rash starting to break out around my hip. 'If you haven't been bitten by anything, I don't want to speak out of school here, but I think you've got shingles,' Kay said.

Me being the panic merchant that I am, I began to sweat. 'What is shingles?' I asked. As I soon discovered, shingles is a viral disease that can appear in people who have poor immune function. It can lead to a painful skin rash with blisters on a particular area of the body.

The following night, Tuesday night, I went to bed and woke up with excruciating pain in my hip. Not wanting it to impact my training during grand-final week, I arrived at Shark Park and spoke to our physiotherapy team. 'That pain in my back is now in my hip,' I said. At this point, I didn't say anything about Kay's opinion that it was possibly a case of shingles.

'Let's just warm up for training and see how we go,' the medical staff suggested. And, sure enough, once I had warmed up it was fine. I had no issues. I almost forgot the pain was there during the day. But each night, the stinging pain would return to the point where I couldn't sleep.

By the Thursday of grand-final week, I had visited our team doctor, George Pitsis, and mentioned what Kay had said about shingles. At first, he didn't agree, but by Friday—when the rash had thickened and the pain remained—he conceded, 'Yes, it's almost certainly shingles.' Being just 72 hours out from the grand final, it was too late for me to commence a course of medication, largely due to the fact that we didn't know what side effects might occur. I could be at risk of diarrhoea, vomiting or dehydration, so the Doc said to just put up with the pain and ride it out.

After a week of ordinary sleep, I arrived at ANZ Stadium on Saturday for our final training session—the captain's run. Without wanting to take anything away from our preparation, it was such a boost of confidence for me that the final ball-work session of the 2016 season was no different to any of the previous captain's runs we'd performed that year. There was no sign of nerves, or of players going into their shell. From the point of view of both me and the players, there was a noticeable calm throughout the group the entire week.

Although I was experiencing discomfort in my hip because of the shingles, physically I felt ready, largely due to the way our high-performance manager, Andrew Gray, had designed our training during grand-final week. Andrew's training schedule was based on one thing: ensuring we were at our optimum in time for kick-off in the big one.

Even at the grand-final press conference on Thursday, a day that can prove draining for both grand final teams, the club had provided everything we would need, from drinks to keep us hydrated to massage balls for when we were sitting around, waiting. The entire week was perfectly orchestrated by the club's support staff.

Perhaps the only obvious difference during the captain's run was that some of our sponsors were sitting in the ANZ Stadium grandstand to watch us. Other than that, it was just another Saturday. As the session concluded, I managed to have a quiet moment of reflection.

I always loved the atmosphere at a grand final, the crowd and the hype before kick-off. During my career, especially in those final years at the Sharks, I'd send a text message to Flanno. 'I want to be there next year,' I would write. And, as I walked off the field from that final training session at ANZ Stadium, I knew that I would never have to write that text message again.

I woke at home on grand-final day to the excited screams of Charly and Kody as they ran through the house. It's funny, because I was more nervous about Kody doing what he had taken great delight in doing for a while now, which was to cheer for the opposition team, than I was about playing that weekend. I was desperate for him to avoid turning to me when I walked downstairs for breakfast and saying, 'Go Storm.' Thankfully, he didn't.

As a team, we were required to be at our Cronulla Sharks Academy fields at 4 p.m. to board the team bus bound for ANZ Stadium. I took my mind off the biggest game of my life by playing with the kids before sitting down for brunch at a Cronulla cafe. You might find it odd, given the hysteria that had gripped Cronulla and, indeed, the entire Sutherland Shire, that I would venture out and immerse myself in an atmosphere that could leave me feeling under pressure to deliver for so many supporters.

Remember, the club was chasing its first premiership in 50 years. Houses, cars, shop fronts, children, adults and grandparents were covered in black, white and blue. You couldn't stop at a traffic light without seeing a Sharks flag or sign hanging from a window. The entire community came together as one magnificent splash of blue, black and white.

However, that's one of the things I was always able to do throughout my career—on the day of a game, I could handle the pressure and not allow the expectations of others to get to me. I'm a big believer in 'if it's going to happen, it's going to happen', but I can also make it my choice to make it happen.

I returned home from the cafe at around 1 p.m., and to keep busy I had a swim in my pool. I then sat down for my game-day ritual meal of spaghetti bolognese before I had a shower and then a lie-down.

You can almost set your watch by my game-day emotions. It's around the time that I have a final shower when, for absolutely no reason, I become cranky and snappy, usually with Anne. That tension builds from the moment I begin to pack my kit bag at home to the time I get to the ground. That's when I can snap easily. Weirdly, once I get to the ground—be it Shark Park, Wollongong or Brookvale—I am okay.

It was always my poor family who had to put up with my short, sharp tongue. The good thing about Anne is that she is never afraid to fire back at me. A funny story Anne likes to recall is how, before one match during which I had a 'wow' of a game and had been subsequently named man of the match, we had had the biggest argument over absolutely nothing. We didn't speak again until I saw her after the game. The first thing she said to me with a smile was, 'See, I got you fired up to play well.'

Before most games, Anne would drop me at Shark Park and I'd say goodbye to the kids and head off to work. But as the time got close to 4 p.m. on grand-final day, I decided to drive myself to the Academy. Before I left home, the kids gave me their favourite send-off chant: 'Go Daddy Go'. I gave them a kiss and said goodbye.

On that five-minute drive from my house to where we were due to meet the team bus at the Academy, my anxious mind began to play a few tricks. I had two possible routes I could take to get to the Academy. But perhaps in an indication of how analytical—and paranoid—I was now becoming as each minute ticked closer to the game, I thought, 'If I go this way, we will win. But if I go the other way, we will lose.' Needless to say, I took what I felt was the 'winning' route.

I had now reached the time—a few hours before kick-off—when my head was scrambling all over the place. I didn't like the 4 p.m. time we were leaving. Being a Western Sydney boy, I knew that it would only take us 40 minutes to travel to ANZ Stadium, and that we were leaving the Shire much too early for what was scheduled to be a 7.24 p.m. kick-off. But instead of allowing that to irritate me, I reminded myself of a team motto that we had first spoken of in the dressing rooms after beating the Cowboys: 'Don't get flustered, just go with it'.

Sitting on the team bus, there was very little talk among the players. In fact, it was intensely quiet. We all found our silent space. For some of the boys, it was listening to music through headphones and relaxing. I like that still but tense calmness within a team, and on that grand-final day bus ride, that's exactly what it was. That quietness can often be mistaken for nerves. But I prefer to think of it as concentration. I prefer that focused quietness rather than my teammates joking and carrying on loudly.

Not everyone reads their coaches' tip sheet, which is basically a guide designed specifically for you by the coaching staff. On the sheet, the coaching staff points out the different strengths and weaknesses of the player you're about to oppose. I carried my tip sheet with me on the bus and had a quick glance at it before we arrived at ANZ Stadium.

Because we had played Melbourne only a month earlier, as a team we felt confident that we understood their style and what made them tick. Their big man, Jesse Bromwich, was a focus for us. He was the 2016 Dally M Prop of the Year and Melbourne's best forward when it came to gaining metres, so as a unit it was crucial that we stifled his power through the middle of the field and also nullified his ability to off-load the footy.

Another key for us—on which we had spent plenty of our time during our grand-final video sessions and out on the training paddock—was Melbourne's 'back five'. The Melbourne Storm fullback, wingers and two centres (Cameron Munster, Suliasi Vunivalu, Will Chambers, Cheyse Blair and Marika Koroibete) were outstanding in returning the football. Much of what the Storm was able to build on in attack commenced with the first or second carry from their 'back five'.

Flanno had identified that a large portion of Melbourne's overall metres began from their first or second carry of the footy. This was also particularly evident as their edge back-rowers, Tohu Harris and Kevin Proctor, weren't overly big in size. Instead of bashing the ball forward like most back-rowers, Harris and Proctor were used for their straight and hard line-running, making it imperative that we limit Melbourne's attacking opportunities inside our 20-metre zone.

We also had a plan to 'cage kick' their big wingers. 'Cage kick' was a tactic that would see Chad or Jimmy kick the football so it landed anywhere between Melbourne's 15-metre line and their goal line and, most importantly, towards the corners. This would allow our defensive line to tackle either Vunivalu or Koroibete close to their goal line at the exact moment they were catching the football, and in turn would stunt their greatest strength—their explosiveness as they ran with the ball.

Having arrived by bus at ANZ Stadium, we settled into the dressing rooms and began our own individual routines. Mick Ennis was always one player I found interesting to watch prior to a match. From the moment he changed into his playing strip until the moment he ran out onto the field, Mick would ask trainer Mark Noakes what the time was no less than 100 times. Every two minutes, Mick would turn to Noaksey and say, 'Mark, what's the time?'

Noaksey had no other choice but to answer Mick with a time that was to the minute. He could never say, 'Mick, it's almost 4.15 p.m.' He would have to say, 'Mick, it's 4.12 p.m.' And then when Mick asked again two minutes later, Noakesy would have to reply, 'It's 4.14 p.m., Mick.' As I said, everyone had their own routine, and that was Mick's.

One of my pet hates was walking onto the ground before a match. I don't know why, but I just never liked it. Once before an Origin match, I was made to walk out onto the ground for the coin toss. I was so annoyed.

I don't think the match officials and TV broadcasters have ever understood how each minute of a player's preparation is crucial. So, as you would imagine, for the 2016 grand final, I was extremely reluctant to walk onto the ground for the coin toss. Thankfully, it was decided that we would use a room adjacent to the home and away dressing rooms at ANZ Stadium.

Over the many years that we captained against each other, Melbourne's Cam Smith had always had the knack of winning the toss against me. And almost every time he won, he chose to kick off. I was desperate to kick off in the grand final. I wanted Melbourne to feel our defensive line intent from the very first tackle. We wanted to be physical with them from the outset.

So when it came to the grand-final coin toss, sure enough Cam won, like he always did. But the thing was, at the very moment the coin landed Cam's way, I unwittingly said, 'We'll run right to left.' With an almost confused look on his face, Cam looked up at me and so did the referee, Matt Cecchin.

'But Cameron won the toss—he decides if he wants to kick off or which direction he wants to run,' Cecchin said.

Straightaway I replied, 'But I know he always kicks off, so that's cool, we'll run right to left.'

To this day, I'm not sure if I somehow talked Cam out of kicking off, but just as quick he replied, 'No, we'll run left to right—they can kick off.'

I had to stop myself from laughing. In my mind I thought, 'No way, I've just talked him out of it.' It was the smallest of wins, but I took it. The fact that we could now rip into Melbourne in defence by kicking off was a victory in my eyes.

I returned to the dressing room to deliver my final message to the playing group. I kept it simple. As I've explained throughout this book, I was never one for Churchillian speeches. 'Every single one of you knows the exact job you need to do tonight,' I said. 'Let's do what we do best.'

As I emerged from the ANZ Stadium tunnel and ran out onto the field, I was bursting with joy. I felt lucky to be in this moment, not only to be in the grand final, but also to be the captain of a club and team that wanted so desperately to break their premiership drought. You only need to look at a replay of the grand final to notice that I'm smiling from the moment we're out on the field.

The sight of an entire 80,000-seat stadium filled with people wearing black, white and blue—barring maybe 1000 Storm supporters—was something to behold. I was overcome by pride in my teammates, the club, our loyal legion of supporters and myself.

To know what we had gone through during the previous five years, just to come out and be here on grand-final day, was staggering. There were times in my career when I thought it would never happen. I was just playing each year for the love of footy. There were games where I didn't think we'd have a chance of winning the match, let alone making a grand final.

From the opening tackle of the grand final, we did what we had promised. Four Cronulla jumpers launched into the Storm from their very first carry. However, perhaps because Mick Ennis knew that this was his last-ever match in the NRL—having announced his retirement mid-season—he let his arm fly just a little too high when Melbourne's Jordan McLean carried the ball forward on the second tackle. Penalised for his swinging arm, Mick yelled to me, 'Sorry skip.' Only a few minutes earlier in the dressing rooms we'd spoken about discipline and giving the Storm nothing. I wanted to be angry at him for giving away an early penalty, but truth be told I saw it as a message from Mick that, win or lose, he was going for broke.

We were able to pinch an early 2–0 lead in the eighth minute through a penalty goal after a high shot from Marika Koroibete left Chad Townsend flattened. Not many people know this, but out on the field that penalty triggered immediate flashbacks to a month earlier, when we had played Melbourne during Round 26 at AAMI Park. In that match, we took an early 2–0 lead from a penalty goal. But from that moment, we were never in the match.

So, in the grand final, I was torn about what to do when the opportunity presented itself. Deep down, I knew that at ANZ

Stadium, any points were like gold, especially in a grand final. Jimmy Maloney was saying, 'No, let's roll on.'

In my head was the Melbourne game, so I was listening to Jimmy and thinking, 'Yep, you're right, let's take the tap.' But it just didn't feel right. So I insisted, 'Let's take the two.' Thankfully it worked.

We enjoyed a strong ten-minute period of the first half that led to Luke Lewis being tackled only a blade of grass away from the tryline. Lewy's break was crucial, as we scored our first try from the next set of six tackles through a scrum-base trick play. It was Mick Ennis who called the play for a try that is forever etched in the Sharks' history.

With a scrum feed just 10 metres away from the Melbourne tryline, Mick turned to me and whispered into my ear, 'Big man down.' During the week before the grand final, we had spoken about using the play—which Ricky Stuart first introduced me to—because the Storm forwards had a tendency to break fast from a scrum.

Can you believe that I actually said, 'No, let's not do it now.' I said no because I was completely exhausted. It was only fourteen minutes into the grand final, but I was starting to fatigue—the shingles had drained my energy like I've never experienced in a game before.

Thankfully, Mick kept saying, 'Let's do it, let's do it.'

Reluctantly, I said, 'Yep, okay, let's do it.'

The goal of 'big man down' was to act like one of our big men, Andrew Fifita, was injured. But because Mick had only just told me, Andrew was now standing out to the left of the scrum, preparing to take the pass from the scrum for a rudimentary hit-up.

Not wanting to tip off the Storm about what we were going to do, I instead turned to Benny Barba, who was planning to pack into the lock position, and said, 'Go down as though you're injured.' Sure enough, Benny keeled over and started grabbing at his knee.

However, because our second-rower, Wade Graham, was on the opposite side of the field getting treatment, it was centre Jack Bird who was called into the scrum to pack down in the front row. Benny then had to pack down in the back row for Wade, and I had to lock the scrum. With so many players out of position, including no right centre because Jack had been called into the scrum, the 'big man down' trick shot that allowed us to create history should never have been successful.

I don't know how many of my teammates realised that the play had been called. The replay clearly shows Matt Prior spinning around from the scrum, not knowing who on earth had the football. And Chad, well he didn't know the play had been called because we banged heads as I shoved him to get the ball from the base of the scrum.

Storm five-eighth Blake Green sprinted towards where Jack Bird would normally be standing in the centres, seemingly oblivious to the fact that Jack had packed down in the scrum. With Green creating the gap, I simply had to pick up the football from the base of the scrum, draw in Cheyse Blair—who had packed down as the Melbourne lock and who only had eyes for me—and slip a pass to Benny.

We'd attempted the trick play twice before during the 2016 season. On the first occasion, I picked up the football but failed to pass it, leaving Flanno far from impressed. And on the second attempt, I passed the ball but Benny was smashed by the cover defender, who had read the play.

For the play to be successful, there are many moving parts that need to be in sync. On grand final day, despite the uncertainty about whether or not we could pull off the play, Benny received the time and space he needed to speed untouched towards the tryline. He planted the football down without a finger being laid on him.

We needed Jimmy to kick the goal. Pushing out to an 8–0 lead was vital. As Jimmy lined up the conversion, I turned to the boys and rammed home the point about how we weren't to change what we were doing. 'Let's keep doing what we do well,' I said. We had enjoyed an even share of the possession, but with Cam Smith on the opposition, I knew it wasn't going to be plain sailing for us. 'Momentum will swing; don't get shocked,' I told the boys.

If I was beginning to flatline before Benny's try, I was well and truly struggling soon after. At the seventeen-minute mark, our assistant coach and blue-shirt trainer, Steve Price, ran over to me. 'I'm gone Pricey,' I said through heaving lungs.

'Hang in there and get to the twenty-minute mark,' Pricey said.

I managed to grind away until the 25-minute mark. I knew I was completely stuffed when I made a tackle close to the sideline on Melbourne's fifth tackle, and I couldn't get up. I was petrified of missing a tackle or dropping a ball, so again I screamed to Pricey, 'I'm screwed.' He nodded and signalled to the bench for an interchange. It was the earliest I had left the field during a match, without being injured, for as long as I could remember.

I remained on the sideline until half-time. We led 8–0 at the break, but I was as nervous as hell. However, I refused to give any indication to the boys of how I was feeling. Perhaps the only person who picked up on my nerves when I was chatting to him at half-time was Pricey. 'I know eight isn't enough, mate—we need at least two more tries,' I said quietly to Pricey in the corner of our dressing rooms.

'Just relax mate, just do what we do,' Pricey said calmly. Looking back now, I believe the nerves were a sign of just how much I wanted to win. A premiership was the last trophy missing from my career. And, leading 8–0, the carrot was dangling there. Now, I just wanted it done.

Aware that I was nowhere near my physical best, Flanno walked beside me as we began to make our way out of the dressing rooms for the second half. 'I need you; I need you, Gal,' Flanno said. I knew what he meant. I had to finish the game.

Regaining my composure and energy after the break, I was back into the action about five minutes into the second half. Just minutes later, Storm forward Jesse Bromwich crossed for a try to strip our advantage back to two points. Bromwich's try was one we should never have conceded, largely because we had trained the entire week for that play. He beat three of our players with his size and power.

The try was of huge concern, because it was scored early in the second half with 30 minutes of the match remaining. From the try, Melbourne managed to swing the momentum of the match to their favour. But even then, we kept telling each other to stick with what we did well.

Personally, I felt my work rate increase in the second half. In every game I ever played, I always tried to 'empty the tank'. But in the grand final, I just didn't have that spring in my step. I was as flat as I've ever felt. The more the game wore on, the more worried I became. I didn't know how to conserve energy or catch my breath. I'd played when feeling sick before, but not for a long time. That's what I was most worried about.

I just kept saying to myself, don't miss a tackle, don't drop a ball and don't let anyone down. But sure enough, that's exactly what happened. I was involved in the defensive line that led to Will Chambers crossing in the 64th minute.

Collecting Storm bench forward Christian Welch around the waist as he carried the ball, I was unable to use my usual body weight to drag him to the ground. He wasn't pumping or charging with his legs, either, yet I was just hanging on. I poured all my body weight on him, but he still managed an off-load. I was fuming. From his off-load, Melbourne strung passes to our left, where Chambers was able to slice through our retreating defensive line and score. I threw my hands onto my head in disgust.

Cameron Smith's conversion saw the Storm lead for the first time in the match, 12–8. That hurt big time. Behind the tryline I knew what to say. But due to a combination of extreme disappointment in myself and the amount of air I was trying to suck into my lungs, it took me more than 30 seconds to pipe up. Trying to catch my breath, I told the boys, 'relax for a minute'.

As much as Jimmy Maloney's ill-timed humour and ability to annoy us at training each week was a pain in the backside, at that moment—standing on our tryline, with our premiership dream slipping through our fingers—he was incredible. It was an example of the experience and focus he showed in every video and training session during the 2016 finals series. He earned his money in those two weeks alone. As Smith lined up the conversion, Jimmy was the first to speak.

No one usually listens to Jimmy. I know I didn't half the time. But on this day, at this moment, he pulled us in together. 'If we thought we were going to have it all our own way, that we wouldn't have to fight for this, we were kidding ourselves,' Jimmy said. 'Forget what we've done; refocus on what we do best.' Jimmy's words Instantly struck a chord.

'Stick to our systems; don't change. We'll get an opportunity,' I said. Truth be told, you never really know if you'll get another chance. But you've got to have faith in what has proven successful for you in the past. And credit to each and every Shark, because that's exactly what we did.

We got back into the arm wrestle and said to the Storm, 'Righto, you want to go toe to toe—let's go.' Just four minutes after Chambers had crossed, big Andrew Fifita stepped up with one of the greatest tries ever scored in a grand final.

Awarded a penalty, we began a full set of six tackles just 15 metres away from Melbourne's tryline. As Mick Ennis looked to take a tap restart, he turned to us and called, 'Nine Tiger.' This was the name given to a play that was designed to set up Mick only a couple of metres out from the tryline. We got to that point of the field for Mick on the fourth tackle.

'Nine Tiger' allowed Mick to have the option of passing to me, as I charged forward after the play-the-ball, or he could send a hard-running Fifita directly at the posts. As Matt Prior rolled the ball 3 metres away from the tryline and just to the left of the uprights, Mick looked up at me with the eyes he always had when he was going to shovel the ball to me.

In my line of sight was small Storm utility Ben Hampton, so I thought, 'Yes, hit me Mick—I'll score here.' Little did I know that Mick had also given Fifita 'the eyes'. Mick wanted both Andrew and I to be charging as hard as we could.

No other player in the NRL could've scored the try that Andrew scored. The only way to describe it is freakish. It's incredible still to consider that at this point of the match, trailing 12–8 with twelve minutes remaining, Andrew found the energy, strength and power to crash past and over five Melbourne Storm defenders, contorting his huge frame around their legs, arms and bodies, before safely planting the football down beneath the posts with his right hand. Remarkable.

As the video referee was called for a final adjudication, I didn't know if Andrew had scored. The boys were going crazy, climbing all over Andrew in celebration. But, watching the replay, you can see the confusion on my face as I grab Andrew and ask, 'Did you score? Did you score?'

So many people have asked if—when that green try light was pressed and we pushed out to a 14–12 advantage—I knew at that point we'd won the grand final. I can absolutely assure you that in no way did I think we had done enough with ten minutes still remaining. And so again, I told the boys to 'just stick to what we do well'.

For nine minutes, we did exactly that. We were almost perfect until the final set of six tackles in the match, which handed Melbourne the ball and the opportunity to break our hearts. With 65 seconds remaining in the grand final, Chad drilled the football over the sideline. Melbourne would have six tackles to travel 85 metres.

Walking to that scrum, I was struck by the memory that was burned onto my brain of a match at AAMI Park several years earlier, where Melbourne had scored two tries in under two minutes to beat us. Before the scrum was packed, Ben Barba grabbed the ears of Birdy and Val. 'Don't shit yourself and leave your opposite number unmarked,' Benny said.

I've watched the last 60 seconds of the grand final, and everything that made us a champion side in 2016 was nowhere to be seen in that final play. It didn't matter how many times we spoke about 'sticking to what we do well' throughout the match—in that final frantic minute, it was a case of ignoring everything we had done so well.

For starters, our right-edge defence didn't move up. They hung back, allowing Melbourne to gain 30 metres in one carry of the football. So, after just three tackles, the Storm attack had already charged over the halfway line. Our left-edge defence was also timid, hanging back instead of holding our straight line. That's what nerves and fear do to you. Our boys were moving backwards in defence, which was the complete opposite to how we had trained, played and achieved all year as a defensive unit.

Physically, I was gone. I actually couldn't keep running. I wasn't the only one—everyone was gasping for air. It was as though the thirteen Sharks on the field in that dramatic final 60 seconds were on autopilot, willing to do everything possible to stop a Storm miracle.

The pass that saved us from a soul-destroying defeat was Cam Smith's pass to Ben Hampton, just 10 metres away from our tryline. Despite his champion qualities, Cam's pass was just off the mark for Hampton to catch. If Cam had passed to his teammate Tohu Harris with a short-pass, they would've come close to scoring the try they needed. But the pass to Hampton is what most fans remember. Had that pass met Hampton's chest, our scrambling defenders—including Birdy and Val, who had ignored what Benny had asked them both to do and had left their side—wouldn't have had the time to stop Melbourne from scoring. The pass forced Hampton to swing the ball back to their right before it found Marika Koroibete.

If you ask me when I knew we had won the 2016 grand final, it was then. Once the ball found Koroibete, I knew we had won the premiership. As powerful and quick as Marika can be, I knew our left centre, Ricky Leutele, was a solid defender. Ricky was never going to miss that tackle.

There's a story about that final agonising set of six tackles that failed to be shared amid all the hysteria and wild pandemonium of the win, and the reams of articles and 'drought-breaking' headlines.

I can tell you that, as a squad, we had trained over the course of the previous three months for that last 60 seconds. At training, we played a skills game where thirteen attackers would gather inside a 20-metre rectangle, with seven defenders standing opposite.

The aim of the drill was that the seven defenders had to keep scrambling non-stop for twenty tackles—stopping the attacking side for more than three consecutive sets of six tackles. It's a drill that tests you mentally and physically. The unfair number of defenders shows you that the attacking side always has the advantage. As a unit, that drill taught our defensive line how to trust the man next to you, while also giving us the conditioning to keep going under pressure.

In those amazing final few seconds of the 2016 NRL grand final, all that training came to the fore. That intensity and desire to never give up kicked in just at the moment we needed it most.

34

The Defence

What makes defending an NRL premiership so difficult? Prior to the start of our 2016 title defence, not a single NRL club had managed to win back-to-back titles since the 1993–94 Brisbane Broncos.

For more than two decades, some of the greatest players and coaches have failed to achieve the mighty task of consecutive titles—a fact that shows how tough the NRL competition is and how mammoth the job of winning a premiership can be.

Did this stop me from believing that we had the team to win the 2017 premiership? Not for a single moment. I absolutely mean that. I was certain that, with a little bit of luck, we could be back again on the first Sunday of October. No doubt, it would be a monumental assignment. But how is this different from any other season?

The one thing I struggled to comprehend at the beginning of 2017—and this mindset has never changed—is how an individual could have any less desire to achieve the greatest success in their chosen profession. This realisation, that not every player shares the absolute desire and willingness to defend a title, is something

I battled with terribly for at least a month after our swift elimination from the competition in week one of the 2017 NRL finals series at the hands of North Queensland.

On reflection, we had every excuse under the sun to fall short of going back to back in 2017. Yet outwardly, excuses were never broadcast by the team.

The 2017 season began with the most congested pre-season I have ever experienced. Before committing to the 26 weeks of an NRL season, as a team we had to navigate through the NRL Auckland Nines, NRL and Indigenous All Stars, a trial match against the Broncos in Brisbane and, of course, an exciting yet taxing trip to the United Kingdom for the World Club Challenge against Wigan. A media report at the time calculated that, by the time they had returned from the United Kingdom, Wade Graham and Jack Bird—who had played in the NRL and Indigenous All Stars in Newcastle—had travelled 20,000 kilometres.

As a team, we flew back to Sydney from the United Kingdom just nine days before we officially launched the NRL season against the Broncos at Shark Park on a Thursday night. All our training and pre-season preparation had gone to plan. I couldn't fault how the entire coaching staff had prepared us for the new season.

As individuals, we had spoken about marginal gains and looking for little areas to improve on from our 2016 games— and I definitely saw that in the gym and out on the training field. I wouldn't say our 2017 season fell apart in February, but we definitely struck hurdles that, in 2016, we were never forced to encounter.

On the same weekend that selected members of our squad were playing in the NRL Auckland Nines tournament, there were other players from our top-twenty squad trialling against the Broncos. Additionally, those players selected for the NRL Indigenous

All Stars match were saved from playing in the trial match. So, in those critical few weeks before Round 1, our top-twenty squad had been virtually split into thirds.

The fact that our most dominant half, game manager and shot caller, halfback Chad Townsend, had failed to train throughout the entire month of January due to a broken hand also complicated our preparation. Then, in the Brisbane trial match, our starting wingers Sosaia Feki (knee) and Valentine Holmes (hamstring) suffered significant injuries.

In the wake of Ben Barba's tumultuous departure, Val's injury was hugely detrimental to the potency of our side, given the vital role he would now play within the team at fullback. Val had trained the entire pre-season at fullback, but now coach Shane 'Flanno' Flanagan would be forced to scrap almost three months of training and attacking strategy, and he would have to find an able replacement. We had used 22 players to win the 2016 premiership, and it felt like we'd already used as many before Round 1. Flanno turned to Kiwi international Gerard Beale—a more than worthy replacement, but a completely different fullback to Val.

Our loss to Wigan in the World Club Challenge still eats at me. It's the only trophy in my entire career that I was never able to hold aloft. The trip itself was fantastic and a huge moment for the club, as it was our first trip to the United Kingdom to play for such a prestigious trophy. But Val and Feki's injuries forced Flanno into deputising rookie outside back Jesse Ramien in the centres and back-rower Kurt Capewell on the wing.

In typically testing north-of-England conditions—slippery under foot, wet and cold—Wigan played to their strengths, beating us 22–6. In the aftermath, Sharks fans made a lot of the refereeing performance. And sure, if a few calls had gone our way, it could've been a different story—but we simply weren't good enough on the day.

This wasn't the same Sharks side that won the premiership. There was no Barba, Holmes or Feki. No Mick Ennis, either. At times in the match, we played like a team that had never before been in the heat of battle together. The retirement of Mick and our inability to cover his loss was always going to be a question mark over 2017. However, one of the true highlights to emerge from the defeat to Wigan was the debut performance of our twenty-year-old hooker, Jayden 'Brails' Brailey.

I rate that match against Wigan as one of the most physical and intense matches that I have ever played in. Yet here was Brails, in his first match in the NRL, holding his own and tackling his heart out in the middle of the field against seasoned English forwards, almost as though he'd been playing first grade for the past five years. That performance from Brails did so much for our team's confidence and belief that we had more than a capable replacement for Mick.

Before tackling the Broncos in Round 1, we celebrated the Sharks' 50th anniversary as a rugby league club with a 'Black, White and Blue Ball' gala dinner at Darling Harbour. It was a night I'll long remember. In the room that night were so many special people who had poured their heart and soul into our great club. There were past coaches and officials, administrators, wives and girlfriends—all of whom, over 50 years, gave so much of their lives to this proud franchise. There were plenty of tears as players past and present celebrated the history of the Sharks.

Obviously, the buzz from our premiership success remained as strong as ever in the room that night. But the purpose of the evening was to recognise the contribution of the greatest players to have ever pulled on the Sharks jersey. The night culminated with the announcement of the 'Team of the Half Century'. Rugby league's most brilliant and uncompromising players—including Andrew Ettingshausen, Mat Rogers, Gavin Miller, David Peachey, Steve Rogers, Greg Pierce and Cliff Watson, to name only a few—were selected in this amazing team. I was visibly emotional as I was chosen in the lock position and as captain of the '50-year Sharks'. What a truly wonderful honour. We celebrated as a club that night—one last party before we set ourselves up for a huge season ahead.

Clunky. That's the simplest word to describe the way we played and, ultimately, how we navigated through 2017. Our home record was embarrassing, winning just five games from twelve matches for our loyal members and fans. However, at least we presented those same fans who gave up their weekends and travelled with us on the road something to cheer for, because as a unit we were doing enough away from home to keep our noses in the win column.

By Round 13, we had won nine of twelve matches, to be sitting second in the competition. So there was no denying that we had the confidence and position on the ladder to be a threat. However, while we were winning games, we were ultimately winning through our class and toughness rather than any polish or authority.

There were many contributing factors to the inconsistent style with which we were playing and then, when it mattered most, why we finished the regular season outside the top four and in fifth position. By inconsistent, I'm not only talking about on the field.

Off the paddock, I just had a sense that several players—if only a few—were distracted by or focused on things other than what should've been the only aim, which was the success of the Sharks. The first distraction was when our chairman, Damian Keogh, stood down unexpectedly and in difficult circumstances.

Then there was our strike centre, Jack Bird, who was about to be engrossed in a contract negotiation phase ahead of the 2017 season. With every month that Jack was consumed by deciding where his future might lie, I felt that the speculation, headlines and focus just got worse for both him and the team. It also felt like there was endless debate in the media over James Maloney's contract—despite the fact that he was contracted until the end of 2018.

Damian stepping down, Jack's and Jimmy's contract debates . . . these were all things that weren't happening the year before. I suppose, once the season was over, that is what aggravated me the most. Because the thing about footy is that it all comes down to actions. That's, ultimately, what it's all about.

I have been in Jack's and Jimmy's shoes before. I've attracted the headlines, and people have hated me—in some cases, I encouraged it. But even my most ardent detractors would know this: whatever I have said or done throughout my career, I have always backed it up on the football field with the way I played the game.

Analyse my games, and even my most scathing of critics would concede that there was never a significant margin between my best game and my worst game. I have no doubt that's why I was able to consistently play representative football and participate with a level of consistency for my club. If you poured over my performances during my 300 games, there's not a great deal of difference between them.

Absolutely, there were some games I failed in. I made a wrong call, a dumb play or produced a silly pass. I know that. But it's your ability to play consistently over a long period that reflects an attitude and willingness to leave nothing in the tank. I look back at 2017 and things just felt different.

The club did have plenty to be proud of in 2017. The entire board, administration and coaching staff were superb in recognising the special feat of three players achieving the rare 300-game milestone. All three of us—Chris 'Heighno' Heighington, Luke 'Lewy' Lewis and me—experienced different styles of recognition.

Heighno was first to achieve the feat in March. Anyone who knows anything about footy knows that Heighno is a terrific bloke. He signed with the club in 2013, when Flanno felt that not only did we need quality footballers, but we also needed a few characters. Heighno was signed alongside fellow ex-Wests Tigers players Beau Ryan and Bryce Gibbs. It worked a treat, with Heighno fitting in famously at the Sharks. He finished his career with two premiership rings, having already won his first in 2005 with the Tigers. Every week, Heighno and I would sit in Cronulla Mall having a coffee, having a laugh and sharing war stories.

All three 300-game presentations were different. On the eve of Heighno's 300th game, against Newcastle in Round 5, the club organised a surprise presentation for him and his friends and family after our final training session. Andrew Ettingshausen presented Heighno with his 300-game jersey. I know Heighno was absolutely appreciative of the club's recognition.

Next to join the 300-club was Lewy, in July against South Sydney. Lewy received a rousing reception at his presentation in front of his closest family. There was a video tribute from across the game, while close mate Mick Ennis delivered an emotional speech. Lewy, typical of the style of bloke he is, said simply, 'I'm so appreciative of all this, but truly boys—I would give it all back to beat Souths tomorrow night.' We did that for him, winning 26–12.

As I watched Heighno's and Lewy's presentations, in the back of my mind I knew that I had my own 300-game milestone just around the corner. The boys know I'm a bit different, so they understood that I wasn't being disrespectful when I told the club I really didn't want any of the fanfare that Heighno and Lewy had experienced.

I can be funny like that. Everyone would think that I enjoy the spotlight, but to be honest I never really embraced milestones throughout my career. I've always felt that, once your footy career finishes, this is when you can sit back and be proud of your contribution. I guess, in a nutshell, I was always too busy looking forward or chasing the next goal.

The other thing I've realised is that, once you retire, you're probably only going to have a few people who are going to stick by you long after you've played your last game. So that's why I wanted to share my 300-game moment with someone who was going to be with me forever: my son, Kody. As it turned out, Flanno secretly organised a little more than that, with a mid-week dinner in Cronulla with friends and family and then a surprise visit to our Brisbane hotel the night before our away game against the Broncos by my former Test coach, Mal Meninga.

On the morning of my 300th game against the Broncos, the club flew Anne and my kids up from Sydney. My dad—who now lives in Queensland—was already inside the dressing rooms when it was time for me to be presented with my jersey.

Kody, who was six at the time, had spent the entire week writing a speech that he planned to read to me in front of the entire team and coaching staff. Cheekily, what he had written down was, 'I love my dad . . . because he's scored 61 tries in his career, but I've scored 71 playing under 6s.' However, as he walked over, I could tell he was nervous. Kody is a shy boy at the best of times, and I could see that he had that nervous look in his eyes as he stood up in front of the room full of players and coaches.

He approached me, then handed me the jersey and gave me a hug. I sensed that he wanted to get out the words he had written down, but he started shaking and simply said, 'I love my dad.' It was incredibly special to share that with him.

With emotion filling the room, it was time to suit up and run out onto the field. We needn't have bothered—we got absolutely played off the park. We were horrendous. We had a shocker. Everyone did.

Until then, Round 23, I had been fortunate enough to produce just two errors the whole year—yet in this most special 300th game, I came up with three errors in that one match. It's difficult to say if the performance was a result of complacency or a feeling that we would win just because it was a special day.

I certainly didn't prepare any differently (throughout my entire career, my preparation did not change from game to game). Ahead of my 300th game against the Broncos, I prepared with the same attitude I had carried from day one: to be the best player on the field, no matter who or where we were playing. It meant little on the night. As a group we moved on from that loss, but without a doubt the memory I forever hold dear whenever I reflect on my 300th game is Kody presenting my jumper to me—not the woeful performance we delivered.

The State of Origin period would prove to be our Achilles heel. As 2017 was the first year I was no longer eligible for selection for New South Wales, this undoubtedly rejuvenated me through the slog of a long season. For the first time, I was devoid of the hype and pressure of Origin and instead could devote every ounce of energy to the club. However, there was one final chapter to be written in my representative career.

A phone call halfway through April triggered my comeback for City in the last-ever City–Country Origin clash, which was to be played in Mudgee. Steeped in history and long regarded as a stepping stone towards NSW Origin selection, the fixture had lost its lustre over the last decade for a number of reasons, not the least of which was that the best players in New South Wales were rarely chosen; they were, instead, preserved from injury by both the NSW Origin coach and, understandably, their clubs.

However, when City Origin coach Brad 'Freddy' Fittler asked if I would be interested in playing one last game for City, I gave it serious consideration, chatting to Anne before taking up Freddy's generous offer. I'm so glad I did. The last match I had played for City—playing from the interchange bench under Tim Sheens in 2006—was my only previous game in the blue and gold jersey. That performance led to my eventual selection for the Blues.

This time around, my selection was obviously under much different circumstances. However, I made the decision to treat my selection with great respect and to ensure that the younger boys in the City side gained an understanding of what playing in this last City–Country clash meant. Freddy also made me captain, which was satisfying because it allowed me to work in a leadership role and also alongside Freddy himself.

Anyone who knows rugby league would've heard a story or two about Freddy, his quirkiness and his laconic nature. But a more caring, passionate and deeply invested coach in his players you could never meet. After a week in camp with Freddy, which included many interesting moments—such as a mandatory ten minutes of meditation before we disembarked from the team bus each day before training, and the banning of all mobile phones—I have nothing but respect and admiration for his positive outlook on life. His infectious character allows players to play their best football.

From the moment I was chosen for City as captain, I wanted to lead the boys to victory. Predictably, much of the press before the match was shaped around my selection for City developing into a trial for a potential comeback for New South Wales. Publicly, I said that I 'wouldn't ever rule anything out', but privately, I was never going to return to Origin. As I've alluded, my stress-free and sole focus on the Sharks was undeniably aiding my performances and, mentally, I had moved on from returning to the Origin furnace.

Beating Country 20–10, the City boys did everyone proud with their performance in what will forever be marked down in history as the final clash between the two teams. It was a week of hard work and fun, highlighted by the boys taking great delight in passing me the footy to convert a goal from the final try of the match.

The last thing I wanted to do was play poorly in my final match for City, so clearly I was delighted to receive the coaches' award after running for a game-high 190 metres. I thanked Freddy for inviting me to play, chuffed to this day that I was able to play under him ahead of his appointment as head coach for the Blues in 2018.

I felt that the break from club footy would rejuvenate our squad at Cronulla while also providing a soft introduction to how we needed to balance our focus and preparation between club and rep footy, ahead of the upcoming Origin period. However, unlike in 2016, when we hardly skipped a beat through the gruelling Origin period, the same couldn't be said in 2017.

As it was in 2016, the Sharks had five players selected for Origin, including Wade Graham, James Maloney, Jack Bird, Andrew Fifita and Valentine Holmes, who represented the Maroons for the first time. But this time around, Origin took its toll on us as a team. From Round 12 to Round 20, we failed to win back-to-back games.

I know—and I, too, have felt the hangover—it took Wade at least a month to get going again after Origin. Andrew also struggled to maintain his rich form following the Blues' gut-wrenching series loss. The emotional and physical investment required to play Origin is one thing, but the skill to then continue to maintain that level once you return to your club is something that takes time as a player to truly master.

The loss against the Broncos in my 300th game in Round 23 hindered our pursuit of a top-four finish. And while we responded with a strong 26–16 win in Townsville in Round 24, our top-four chances were scuppered when we were beaten 16–14 by the Roosters at home in Round 25. We rounded out the season with a comfortable win over Newcastle—ensuring that we finished fifth on the ladder and would play an elimination final against eighth-placed North Queensland at Allianz Stadium.

I must say, there was certainly no sense of doom from within our team despite our failure to secure a top-four finish. As a group, we all agreed that by finishing fifth we had actually secured the better side of the draw, with the opportunity of avoiding Melbourne—which I considered the benchmark—until the grand final.

I remember talking to Flanno in the week of the elimination final with the Cowboys, and I had the feeling that, no matter how ugly it was and no matter how we did it, this first week was simply about survival. We just had to get through this game, and then it would all open up for us. It never happened.

Our performance against the Cowboys, on a warm spring Sunday afternoon at Allianz Stadium—with everything to play for—summed up our entire season: clunky. In patches, we played like the short-priced favourites which we were to beat the Cowboys. But when it mattered, we attempted to splutter our way to victory and we lacked the focus and clinical polish to hold off the eventual grand finalists. Michael Morgan ended our season with a go-ahead field goal in extra time.

Like our entire season, there were moments in the game that hurt us and that we didn't handle well. Jimmy Maloney, who unbeknown to him was playing his final game for the Sharks, was sin-binned for a professional foul close to half-time. The Cowboys kicked a goal and scored a try in Jimmy's absence—but as a group we should've been better equipped to handle it.

Externally, the loss was overtaken by Flanno's post-match retort about the standard of refereeing. Flanno was slugged with a $30,000 breach notice by the NRL for his comments. He would later concede that he regretted the way he handled the moment and that his words reflected the mood that filled our shattered dressing room.

As we sat in silence, several players started to speak openly about how disappointed they were with the refereeing performance. And I agree, there were some calls—and you'll never be able to change my view of this—that were wrong. However, I was more gutted with the outcome.

Sure, at the time I felt we received some calls that I didn't think were correct, but sometimes that's just the way it goes. They go with you—and they go against you. For me, the bottom line is that we should've been better at closing out the game. That's what left me so angry.

After we had thanked our teammates who would no longer be with us in 2018, I couldn't get home quick enough. Traditionally, the call is made to drown our sorrows together. But I was so furious with the way our season had petered out, I couldn't think of anything worse than sitting at a pub—so I went home.

Sitting in my lounge room alone at 1 a.m. wasn't the plan. That's the thing about 'no second chances' in finals footy—one minute you're telling yourself, 'If we win today, I know we can get to the grand final.' And the next minute, you're sitting alone thinking, 'I shouldn't be here.'

It took a whole two weeks for my anger to subside. For a full fortnight, I had the shits, upset and disappointed with our season. Primarily that anger stemmed from knowing what we had achieved the year before. There is no greater feeling in the game than winning a premiership, and I so desperately wanted to taste that again.

Within a week of our loss to the Cowboys, every player was summoned to an individual season-review meeting with Flanno and the coaching staff. This is a meeting that every club holds at the conclusion of every season with every player. It's very similar to meeting with the principal. Every player is given a meeting time, and the review takes almost twenty minutes per player. It's an opportunity to look back at how a player performed, what worked and what didn't.

In my meeting, I was handed a statistical run-down of my season and a physical assessment of my body. Pleasingly, despite having just completed my seventeenth season at age 36, I recorded my lowest fat percentage, highest muscle mass and fastest speeds in three years. Overall, I had finished the 2017 season in the top 1 per cent of our fittest players at the club. I also played the most games (25) I had ever played for the club in one season since 2005.

There are many reasons why I was able to stay on the field in 2017. I knew my body and managed my training load while simultaneously striving to achieve greater results than the year before. I was free from the physical toll of State of Origin and, of course, I had few injuries and maintained a dedicated rehabilitation plan.

Individually, I was pleased with my 2017 season. However, there was still a sense of great awe and pride when I was chosen as the Dally M Lock of the Year for the third time in my career, after finishing equal fourth for the overall Dally M Player of the Year at the annual awards night.

Having also received the Player's Player award and Player of the Year award—for a fifth time in my career—at the Sharks' presentation night, many people suggested that I should hang up the boots there and then. But I was contracted to the Sharks for the 2018 season.

I didn't just want to play—I craved what I wanted in 2017. I guess that's what has always made me different. I wanted to lead my club to another premiership. And again, I was of the firm opinion that we could do it in 2018.

35

One More Year

On a Wednesday night in May 2018, I sat down with a pen and a piece of paper to make the hardest decision of my entire life. My call on whether to retire from the game I love in 2018 or go on for one more year in 2019 was very much a process of elimination.

I began writing a list, beginning with the year 2001. Next to my first season of NRL, I wrote: 'First-grade debut'. Below that, I wrote for 2002: 'Played in Grand Final qualifier'; for 2003: 'Regular starting player every week in first grade'; for 2004: 'On the verge of representative selection'; and for 2005: 'Played every game that season at an average of 80.1 minutes (extra time included)'. The list continued through until 2018.

Beside each season that I had played, I wrote a highlight or greatest achievement. The list included my first Sharks Player of the Year award in 2007, my Test debut for Australia in 2008 and my back-to-back Harry Sunderland Medals in 2010 and 2011. I noted my Dally M Lock of the Year award and the World Cup win in 2013, leading New South Wales to victory in the 2014 Origin series and, of course, the 2016 premiership.

'Leading the Sharks back to the finals after the ASADA nightmare' is what I jotted down alongside the year 2015. For 2017, I scribbled: 'Dally M Lock of the Year'. And I finished with '2018 . . . ??'.

The idea to create a written highlights reel of my career was important. It assisted me in understanding and determining whether I could achieve and deliver one more purposeful season in 2019. Unequivocally, it needed to include the same level of quality that I believe I had managed to largely maintain for the majority of my career. 'I can be good again, but can I be great?' I wrote.

I had begun the 2018 pre-season with great intent, driven to repeat the efforts of 2017 that had seen me win the Dally M Lock of the Year award at 36 years of age. But just when I thought I was physically ready for the season ahead, I suffered a calf injury three weeks before our Round 1 clash against North Queensland.

I was doing some extra conditioning after training, and I felt my calf tighten when I was 20 metres from the end of the running drill. I underwent a routine MRI scan, which showed that I had suffered a grade-one calf strain. It meant that I would miss the club's pre-season trial matches, and I would be racing the clock to be fully healed in time to tackle the Cowboys, in what would be Johnathan Thurston's 300th NRL game. I busted my backside in rehabilitation to overcome the calf issue and, thankfully, I made it onto the field for our narrow 20–14 defeat.

The process of preparing for the first three matches of the 2018 season was absolute hell. Compounding my ability to overcome my calf issue was a foot injury—plantar fasciitis—that had come about simply through wear and tear on my body.

Questions flooded my mind. Could I do this for another season? Am I done? But as the season rolled on, my love of the game lured me back in.

I wasn't too worried about missing a training session if I had to. I'd experienced periods previously in my career where I'd hardly trained, and I ended up playing some of my better games. I knew that once I got out onto the field, I'd be fine.

The greatest challenge for an athlete going through an injury battle is dealing with the mental stress. To have to sit at home and ice the injury for hours upon hours, to spend more time in the physiotherapy room than out on the training paddock, is mentally draining. On your day off, when you've got other things you want to do, you're constantly treating your body woes. It becomes a 24/7 mission to overcome your injuries so that you can get back onto the field.

I'm fortunate and thankful that my focus on preparation off the field ultimately aided my cause. By Round 4 of the season, I had begun to feel like my normal self again. Playing against arch rivals Melbourne, amid the backdrop of an NRL-instructed refereeing crackdown, we hung tough as a team to win 14–4 at home. The drama-charged match included a ridiculous 33 penalties, and fans will forever remember the game as the one where my old mate Cameron Smith was sent to the sin-bin for the first time in his career.

Beating Melbourne made it two wins on the trot, after we had successfully rolled the Eels one week earlier. Those wins gave the footy team the belief and confidence that we might just be able to go deep into the finals in 2018. Yet as soon as you're on a high in the NRL, you come crashing back down.

We dropped our next games against the Roosters and neighbouring rivals St George Illawarra. The latter, in Wollongong, was a nightmare in more ways than one. Not only did we lose 40–20 to the Dragons, but our dressing room also resembled a casualty ward as Wade Graham (hamstring), Luke Lewis (knee), Andrew Fifita (knee) and myself (knee) failed to finish the game.

As soon as I felt my knee collapse just thirteen minutes into the match, I knew I'd suffered damage. MRI scans the following day showed that I had a grade-two medial ligament tear, with the ligament partially popping away from the bone. I would spend the next four weeks on the sidelines, returning in Round 11 against the Bulldogs.

I had not been this nervous before a match for several years. Although I had passed the necessary training tests to illustrate a return of stability in my knee, I just wasn't sure how it would cope under the pressure, the strain and the lifting and twisting of an NRL match. Thankfully, we beat the Bulldogs, and I finished the match without any issues.

Amid the daily grind of overcoming injuries, preparing well and helping lead the club to victory, I sat down with Anne and asked, 'What I should do? Do you think I should make 2018 my last year?'

Not once did Anne tell me to retire. She told me that when I couldn't maintain my standards, that's when I'll know that I can't go on.

My calf, foot and knee problems—and a pectoral injury that I had suffered during the pre-season but had kept secret—restricted my greatest area of focus and pride throughout my entire career: my strength. Mentally, I just didn't want to risk any further injuries by pushing and lifting to the heights that I had previously reached in the weights room.

During 2018, because of the pain in my knee and a groin strain that had also flared up, I couldn't squat the weights I wanted. In 2017, I had squatted 210 kilograms. But now I could barely hold 150 kilograms.

My range of movement was also a quarter of what it once was. This was because I didn't want to push myself as hard as before, just in case I did more damage.

Nevertheless, I assured myself of one thing—I was strong enough, and I didn't need to get stronger. My efforts in the weights room were merely to create purpose in my training, to satisfy the need I have to constantly challenge myself.

On game days, I was still excited, ready and willing to be the best player on the field. After every match, I eagerly reviewed the data gathered on my performance. It usually showed that I had played as well as—if not better than—my teammates and opposition, some of whom were more than ten years my junior. This further clouded the agonising dilemma of whether I should continue playing into a nineteenth NRL season.

My decision was also impacted by an offer in June 2018 from English Super League club Wigan. Then my former coach at the Sharks, Steve Price—who was now head coach of Warrington— wanted to sign me to a 2019 stint in the United Kingdom.

I had always planned on playing one season in England at the end of my NRL career. There was something special about both the footy and the fans in the United Kingdom, and I wanted to experience them firsthand as a player. However, I knocked back Steve's offer for a number of reasons.

First of all, Steve needed an answer during the middle of the 2018 season, and I just wasn't willing at that time to say, 'Right, that's it, I'm retiring from the NRL and going to play in England next year.' There was also the huge impact on Anne as well as on the kids' schooling. And I was mindful of my transition into post-retirement life; several employment options outside of football were dependent on me remaining in Sydney. But deep down, the idea of playing for another club was what stopped me.

I've achieved many wonderful accolades and shared the greatest memories that rugby league has to offer with my state and country teammates. But without a doubt, my proudest claim is that I've stayed at the one club—the Cronulla-Sutherland Sharks—for my entire career, despite being lured to leave the club and play elsewhere.

During the ten-year period when I believe I was at the height of my career—from 2006 to 2016—I could've left at least twice for more money. And then in 2017, the Newcastle Knights football manager Darren Mooney offered me $750,000 for the 2018 season. It was the biggest contract offer of my entire career. Who would've blamed me for going?

But I stayed at the Sharks for a contract worth half of what the Knights had proposed. For a bloke who is well known for loving his money—which I do—to say 'no' to the Knights' offer was not as difficult as it sounds.

I'm the Sharks' first premiership-winning captain. That's something money can't buy. And you could never put a value on the comradeship developed during those tough times when the club was being run on the smell of an oily rag.

I'm a fan of the game, so I know that the only thing supporters understand is results on the field. But every Sharks fan can look back on the period between 2011 and 2013 and proudly say that Gal and Shane 'Flanno' Flanagan did everything they could to turn the Cronulla Sharks into a successful footy club.

To be brutally honest, back in 2011 we were hopeless. And I mean in every facet—financially, on the footy field and in our ability to recruit quality players. The entire club was being run on the NRL's $4.3 million salary-cap grant. How were we supposed to compete? But we stuck it out.

Flanno managed to keep me going. He was the coach, the welfare manager, the part-time CEO and the recruitment officer. I tried to help him with the latter job. Brick by brick, we got there— and the Sharks have been a consistent finals team ever since.

In retirement, I desperately want to see this club be like the Roosters and the Melbourne Storm—competing every year for the premiership. I'd be shattered if, as a club, the Sharks ever went back to where we were in 2011. This amazing club, which gave me my start, is in my blood and forever in my heart. It must strive to be great—not just good.

This is the same motto of desire that I have carried with me every day from the moment I played my first NRL game in 2001—to be great, not just good. And it's the motto I used to make the toughest decision of my career. Be great, not just good.

I looked at everything I was doing and compared myself to my teammates. In 2018, Andrew Fifita was one of the best forwards in the game. We had recruited Aaron Woods, a Test forward, and we also had Matt Prior, who had been selected for the NSW Origin team. According to the coaching staff, my performances showed that I was matching it with my teammates, who were setting the bar higher and higher each week—and in some cases I was edging them out.

Ultimately, the only reason I was contemplating retirement was because of my age. With that in mind, I had several discussions with Flanno. He had no concerns about my ability to deliver on-field contributions, but his biggest issue was related to training. He knew how hard I liked to train, as I've always believed that the harder you train, the better you play. Unfortunately—after almost twenty pre-seasons of NRL, coupled with my many nagging injuries—that level had undeniably decreased.

I knew that if I were to push ahead into 2019, I would need to reassess my output and gradually take a back seat to my teammates. If that meant less time on the field, then so be it. I was more than happy to bring the next wave of Sharks forwards through to the NRL. With six weeks remaining in the 2018 season, we made a decision as a club to move forward on a new one-year contract for the 2019 season.

If I had to identify one match in particular that helped me make the decision, it would have to be our Round 22, 17–14 win in Melbourne over the Storm. I played over 70 minutes that day and made more metres than any other forward from either team—against a side that is not only one of the toughest to play at their home ground, but would go on to make the 2018 grand final. After that match, I knew I could still do it.

Sure, there were going to be times in the future when I wouldn't play to that level. But my performance against the benchmark of the league showed me that if I needed to step up and deliver, I could. The decision to continue playing enabled me to move on mentally, ending the daily tug-of-war in my mind and allowing me to set sail for the finals with the Sharks.

On the field, we were beginning to find our groove. With a month of footy to play in the regular season, we were hovering around fifth spot—yet within touching distance of first place. But one game in 2018 cost us the minor premiership—the 33–32 loss to Manly in Round 21 at Shark Park. With the lure of solidifying a top-four position, we blew it when Manly's Daly Cherry-Evans slotted in a match-winning extra-time field goal for the struggling Sea Eagles.

Defensively, the tries we leaked that day were ordinary. Manly have been somewhat of a bogey side for Cronulla over the past ten years, but to score 32 points against them and yet still be beaten was terribly disappointing.

The key was not to beat ourselves up over the loss. As a group, we instead zeroed in on the positives. These included the increasingly strong combination of our halves, Matt Moylan and Chad Townsend, and the weekly rise and rise of Valentine Holmes at fullback.

Valentine's transition from wing to fullback in 2017 had begun in steady fashion, but by midway through the 2018 season, he had found a rhythm and understanding of his role—something he had failed to consistently show before in the number-one jumper. Injuries to the only other contender for the fullback position, Josh Dugan, gave Valentine confidence. He knew that the job was his for as long as he wanted to keep it.

Our run to the finals was strong. We won our last four games of the regular season, including Round 23's match against the Cowboys (Johnathan Thurston's final game at Shark Park). We thrashed the Knights in Round 24, with Kyle Flanagan making his NRL debut in the halves, before our final-round danger game against Canterbury at ANZ Stadium.

I say danger game, because the struggling Bulldogs only had pride to play for. For us, it was about ensuring that we took confidence into week one of the finals while also navigating through the match unscathed. We won 30–18, and it was a highly professional victory by the boys. It cemented us in fourth position on the ladder, gifting us a valuable second chance in the finals.

We faced minor premiers the Sydney Roosters in week one of the finals at Allianz Stadium. It remains one of the best games I've played in. I still recall thinking after the match that if you were a fan of the NRL, you couldn't ask for much more than that. It was fast. It was physical. It was end to end, and there was nothing in it on the scoreboard. But we lost. And what hurt most about the loss were the tries that we bombed during the match.

The first one was by Ricky Leutele, who could've scored himself in the first half. But instead he threw a pass that sailed behind wing partner Sosaia Feki. But the big miss came in the final ten minutes of the match, when we were trailing 18–12. Luke Lewis was denied a four-pointer by Roosters centre Latrell Mitchell's try-saving tackle of the year. Had Mitchell not forced the ball free from Lewy's grasp, after he had chased and regathered a Chad Townsend kick, we would've locked up the game at 18 all.

In the end, it was a turning point in the game that the Roosters capitalised on, taking control of the match to advance to a preliminary final. It left us gutted and also battered; we had already lost co-captain Wade Graham to a season-ending knee injury in the first half.

When I look back, I realise that this was the game that cost us a second grand-final appearance in two years. Had we won that game, we would have earned the second week off, which would have given my injured teammates more time to recover. The advantage of this week off can't be understated. It's massive.

As it was, we didn't have time to wallow. There were just six days before our elimination final against Penrith. The Panthers are a side that we have always matched up well with and a side that has never really given us any great fear. Despite all the pre-match hype and debate in the media over which team, Cronulla or Penrith, had fared better in the swap of five-eighths Matt Moylan and James Maloney, we had already beaten Penrith twice during the 2018 season.

Any paper talk or debate was buried within twenty minutes of our must-win clash with Penrith, as we raced to a superb 18–0 lead. And while we gave our fans a fright as we hung on for a 21–20 win, I felt that we had shown how clinical and professional we could be as a unit.

Victory took us to a preliminary final against our arch rivals, the Storm, in Melbourne. Just two years after the Sharks' greatest success, we were 80 minutes away from another grand final.

However, the grand-final qualifier against Melbourne would be a match that I would take no part in.

In my first hit-up of the second half against Penrith, my shoulder had jammed awkwardly as I impacted with Penrith forward James Tamou. Everything in my left arm had immediately shut down; when I tried to lift my arm over my head, it dropped limply to my side. From the moment the injury happened, I knew my finals series was over. I had suffered exactly the same injury in 2007 against Papua New Guinea.

Given the enormity of the Penrith match, I had desperately tried to play on through the pain, but I just had no fight or drive in the two or three following hit-ups that I took. I lasted eight minutes after the injury before signalling to the trainer that I needed to come from the field. Scans taken later that night showed that I had damaged my AC joint and had torn a stabilising ligament off the bone.

Although the injury was painful, the nagging soreness wasn't the main problem. The biggest issue was that I couldn't lift my arm. I did everything I medically could to improve my chances of tackling Melbourne. I received three cortisone injections over three days, and while there was marginal improvement, I knew within myself that I was a long shot to play against the Storm— and also to play in the grand final, should we make it.

Beating Melbourne is hard enough with a full-strength team. But we were now without Josh Dugan (shoulder), Wade Graham (knee) and me (shoulder). Also injured playing against Penrith, Luke Lewis had a calf complaint. And while Lewy would play and lead us as captain in the final game of his career against Melbourne, he was far from 100 per cent. Melbourne could smell blood in the water, and they went in for the kill. They beat us 22–6 to end our year.

If you want to win an NRL premiership, there are two things you simply can't do without: a dose of luck, and seventeen of your best players being fit and healthy. In the 2018 preliminary final against Melbourne, we were brave and courageous—but healthy, we were not. On top of the sorry casualty ward on the sideline, Jayson Bukuya tore his medial ligament during the first half, and powerful winger Sosaia Feki was taken from the field, also in the first half, after injuring his shoulder.

I was incredibly proud of the team's effort that night. We never stopped fighting. And had a couple of refereeing calls gone our way, the match could've changed quite easily.

One of the biggest calls of the night centred on Storm star Billy Slater. He was penalised for a shoulder charge on Feki, who was attempting to cross for a try in the left-hand corner of the field. The incident became the biggest talking point of the entire 2018 grand-final build-up.

I said it at the time, so this will come as no great surprise: Billy delivered a copybook yet illegal shoulder charge on Feki. I remain stunned that the incident created such a polarising slew of opinions. To me, it was blatantly obvious and undeniably clear that Billy had used his shoulder to charge in an illegal fashion and blunt Feki's efforts. But many people believed that Billy didn't deserve to miss a grand final and what would also be the last game of his entire NRL career.

I love Billy Slater as a player, and he's a terrific fella away from footy. So I was happy that, in the end, he received the chance to finish his career in a grand final, by being exonerated by the NRL judiciary. But in my opinion, the NRL judiciary's decision to find Billy not guilty of a shoulder charge was wrong.

Plenty of experts and commentators suggested that the on-field referee should've awarded Feki and the Sharks a penalty try—not just a penalty, as was the case—for Slater's act, which according to the on-field referee was one of foul play, hence the penalty. I also think it should've been a penalty try. And I say this knowing full well that while a penalty try would've changed the scoreboard, I can't be sure we would've gone on to beat Melbourne. I don't know if we would've been able to seal the deal due to the injuries we were dealing with that night. We were busted and broken when it mattered most.

It was obviously a disappointing end to our year. But the fact that we were 80 minutes from a grand final just two years after winning a premiership said so much about the strength of our club. On reflection, I'm certain our fans would agree that it was a huge effort in 2018, especially considering that we began the year with a brand-new halves combination in Matt Moylan and Chad Townsend.

What was sad for the group was saying goodbye to some of the club's most influential characters at the end of 2018. Luke Lewis's stunning career at Cronulla Sharks had come to an end, as had that of Ricky Leutele, a superb footballer who had arrived at the club when he was sixteen. Also moving on were Jesse Ramien, James Segeyaro and Edrick Lee.

As a player, you love to share a few special moments in the dressing room with the guys after their final match. It's a great opportunity to reflect and say thank you to the people who, ultimately, you have spent as much time with as your own family. But it seems almost impossible to get that chance, with the line-up of sponsors, board members, family and media commitments required after the final game of the season.

Had I known at the time that it was his last game in Cronulla colours, I would've liked to have shared a more memorable farewell with Valentine Holmes. Eight weeks after our season was over, I was watching my son play Oztag on a Monday afternoon in November when I received a call from a sports reporter asking if I could provide a quote for a story related to Val's decision to quit the Sharks and join the NFL. I was dumbfounded. I hung up and rang Flanno. He also had no idea about the news that was soon to break.

Sure enough, the next day the club confirmed that Val was off to the NFL. I'm not going to lie—the way Val handled his departure from the club annoyed me. I had no problem at all with Val wanting to pursue a new challenge, but rugby league is a team sport. And if you're going to make a decision that will impact the team going forward, make sure it's handled in the correct manner.

Not one of Val's teammates knew of his decision to quit the club. Not the club captains nor the head coach. One of the most disappointing things about the decision was that Val had committed to the Sharks until the end of 2019. He was under contract for at least a further twelve months.

Of course, the club had made no secret of their desire to extend Val's life at the club beyond 2019. They had been talking to him about a new deal since the pre-season of 2018. It was almost a third of the way through the 2018 season before Val told the club that he wouldn't be making a decision about a new deal until the end of the season.

When we arrived at the end of the season, Val still hadn't indicated whether or not he was accepting the Sharks' offer. Meanwhile, other NRL clubs were buying and swapping some of the biggest names in the game. The Cowboys purchased Ben Barba, who would've returned to the Sharks had Val made his call earlier than November. On top of that, the Sharks lost a potential star in Jesse Ramien to Newcastle. He could've been enticed to stay had the club known that the $1 million set aside for Val was available for other players. It was simply through good luck, not good management, that we were later able to snare Shaun Johnson from the Warriors.

The timing of Val's decision to chase his dream in the NFL is what frustrated me most—for the club, the fans and us as a playing group. At the time, I made a public statement that was born out of my frustration and a desire to protect our club and our team. I said that Val should be banned from the NRL for life.

I concede that I went too far. However, I won't back down from my belief that if players are under contract and they want to leave the code, there should be a roadblock stopping them from coming back to the game.

In the end, Val's management played the cards they needed to play, and they fell well for him. But I also know that the full story of how Val's management obtained the release from his contract has never been told publicly.

I phoned Val the day before he left for the United States, just to clear the air. The last thing I wanted was any bad blood between us, because we had shared too much together on the field. I reiterated that my statement wasn't about whether or not I supported him chasing his dream. I would never wish him to fail. If anyone had the ability to make it in the NFL, Val did—his power and speed would see to that. But I just didn't like the way his departure was handled.

On the phone, Val said, 'No worries, Gal. I understand.'

Val's exit from the club wasn't the only off-season bombshell. The Sharks' self-report to the NRL about a salary cap irregularity was revealed in August of the 2018 season. And just five months later, Flanno would resign— but this had nothing to do with the original investigation. It was a stunning, shattering and emotional time for many at the club, and yet another wave of unwanted turmoil.

The players knew little about the NRL's investigation into alleged salary cap breaches when the story first appeared on the front page of *The Daily Telegraph*. However, once the season was over, the players were interviewed by the NRL Integrity Unit.

My interview went for 40 minutes, and half of that time was taken up by the NRL explaining how I could have my contract ripped up if I didn't answer their questions. I answered the questions asked of me as honestly as I could.

How Flanno became embroiled in the investigation came as a major shock to everyone at the club. The NRL had confiscated the club's software programs, computer server and emails during the investigation. Allegedly, the NRL uncovered emails showing that Flanno had communicated with the club during his 2014 suspension.

Having been at the club in 2014 as a player and a captain, I can safely say that whatever communication Flanno had with the club had no impact whatsoever on the 2014 season or the playing group at the time. Yet just one week before Christmas 2018, the NRL announced that Flanno was suspended effective immediately. It was a devastating blow for the club as well as for Flanno and his family.

Personally, I was shattered for him. I sent him text messages and tried to call him, but with his world in a spin, it would be weeks before he responded.

The club had no alternative but to react quickly. CEO Barry Russell asked the senior playing group to attend a meeting at the club, where he explained that assistant coaches John Morris and Jim Dymock would be taking charge on an interim basis, until we returned from our two-week Christmas break.

The entire drama left me upset for my mentor and concerned for my playing group, which was now without the one constant we had had for the past seven years. I felt it was imperative that we showed stability and unity as a club.

After the meeting, I phoned Barry to ask if I could sit with him at the press conference to be staged the following day, 19 December. I suggested that our senior players—Matt Prior, Andrew Fifita, Chad Townsend, Josh Dugan and Aaron Woods—should also be in attendance. Co-captain Wade Graham was on a family holiday in Canada, but was in daily contact with the group.

For me, it was a line-in-the-sand moment. Yes—we were down and out. Our coach had been stood down, and we were also without major corporate support or a major jersey sponsor. But at the press conference, I described the Sharks as the most resilient brand in Australian sport. And I mean that. This club has lurched from one drama to the next, but it remains unbroken.

As much as I respect Flanno and the bond we have, I knew that outside our four walls, the opposition would be salivating over our perceived demise. Not one ounce of sympathy would be shown towards us during the 2019 season, particularly from Newcastle, our Round 1 opponents. So my focus turned to helping ensure our preparation was at its optimum for the start of 2019, my last season as an NRL footballer.

36
Heart and Soul

I'm a 38-year-old man who can't throw a tennis ball more than 20 metres. That's been the case for a few years now. It's funny—although I can't toss a little ball, I can throw a punch in the boxing ring. I guess it has to do with the slightly different shoulder movement required for both actions, and the fact that my right shoulder is sore 24 hours a day. It's probably partly due to the two elbow surgeries and two shoulder arthroscopies I had during my career. I was also supposed to have a shoulder reconstruction when I was nineteen, but I never did.

How my body will feel—how easily I will be able to run, walk and swim—in retirement is something that is impossible to predict. Retirement won't come easy for me, as I have played this great game since I was boy. But I'm confident that I've got the tools to work it out. And I'm confident that my selfish commitment to preparing my body each week before games will also help me in the long run. I'll expand on that point in a moment.

There's an old saying that rugby league players simply 'know when you know' that it is time to hang up the boots. For some

341

players, it's injury that ends their careers; for others, it's form. Other players find that it's simply a financial decision—knowing a career outside football can provide greater security.

For me, I knew I had made the right call to retire during training for the 2019 pre-season. I had just completed my annual dip into the boxing ring, which allowed me to step away from footy and focus on boxing only.

As I've mentioned already in this book, the training regime for boxing is completely different to that for footy. I always found that I was supremely fit after six weeks of preparation for a fight. But there is always a trade-off when you're trying to be your best in two completely different sports.

On the one hand, you're fit and fast as a result of the torturous boxing sessions. But on the other hand, your physical strength has decreased and is below what is required for an NRL player. You don't need to lift big weights when you're boxing, and I also wasn't doing the contact or wrestling sessions that my teammates were doing at training.

After knocking out John Hopoate in a fight at the Hordern Pavilion on a Friday night in February, I returned to training with the Sharks the following Monday. The session included a defensive drill that saw me trying to tackle the best young forwards at Cronulla, including Jack Williams and Braden Hamlin-Uele.

As they barrelled towards me, I said to myself, 'Oh geez, leave me out of this.' I wouldn't say that they breezed past me, but the impact of the collisions and the strength of these young bulls . . . I could feel every inch of every tackle.

Due to the boxing training, I only weighed 101 kilograms, and my body fat was as low as it's ever been, at 13 per cent. And so I was feeling everything. I thought, 'I don't know how much longer I can do this'.

A rib injury in Round 3 actually had a silver lining. While I was disappointed to miss the next two rounds, the injury allowed me to get to work in the gym and strengthen various areas of my body. I returned to the field a fortnight later at 104 kilograms and, as a result, found consistency in my form and preparation.

I can talk to you about preparation for days. I believe it's the one ingredient that separates me from my rivals. But it doesn't just relate to rugby league. Preparation can also separate any person from others in their field. It will give you the best chance for success.

Everywhere I go, I take a lunch box with me. I've got an apple, a banana and a box of nuts in it. For the past fifteen years, I have not left home without it. Anne packs it every day for me—yes, I know how lucky I am—and places it next to my keys so it's ready when I walk out the door.

Early on in my career, I would try to eat every two hours. That's why I always have food with me. It's about always being diligent with regard to what I eat and how I prepare. I rarely eat takeaway food throughout the week. Maccas, KFC, pizza—they are a treat once a month.

The same goes for drinking alcohol. I've got no issues with a few drinks and a pizza after a game, but never during the week of a game. The only time this might change is if I had longer than a seven-day gap between my last and next game. But otherwise, never. Ever.

That's something I try to drum into the younger players. I know that some blokes do have a beer, but I just don't think it's the right thing to do. Sacrifice separates great first-grade players from regular first-grade players.

I've missed my own mother's wedding. I've missed my best mate's two weddings—I've promised him that I won't miss his third. I've missed friends' birthdays, engagements, christenings—you

name it. I've even missed Kody's junior footy training and games—
and I'm the coach.

Why? Because I'm diligent about my preparation.

If we were playing on a Saturday and there was a wedding on
the Friday night, I wouldn't go. I just couldn't do it. I know a lot
of other guys would, but I'm selfish. You've got to be selfish to
prepare yourself for the game of rugby league.

However, in a lot of ways, it's not selfish—because if you do go
to the wedding, you're letting down your teammates. The question
ends up being 'who are you being selfish for?' It's selfish to one set
of people and not to the other.

Preparation is picking up your kids from school and taking
them along while you attend a recovery session or gym session
that isn't part of your weekly schedule. If we had Friday, Saturday
and Sunday off, I'd still go to the gym on Saturday. I wouldn't be
there to lift weights and get stronger, but because my shoulder is
so sore. I have no choice but to keep up the strength in my rotator
cuff. If it wasn't the gym, I'd have a sauna or ride an exercise bike
for five minutes.

I've spent my entire career thinking about the next week, and
how I can get to the start line on game day as best I can. I've always
believed that if it can't hurt you, it can only help you. This is why
I had a special ritual.

Not many people know this, or have ever noticed it—which
is incredible, given that everything I have ever done during my
career has been analysed—but as I emerged from the tunnel of
every game and ran out onto the field, I had a process of using my
fingers to touch certain areas of my body. I would tap my head,
cheeks, chin and shoulder. Find a replay of any game over the past
ten years, and you'll find me entering the field of play dabbing at
those parts of my body.

Mum is deeply passionate about spiritual healing and in particular reiki, a form of alternative healing. She says that the ritual I was committed to performing as I ran onto the field helped to balance my body. I have no idea how or why. But even if it helped me half a per cent, it was important. That's how close it is between success and failure in the NRL.

What will I miss most? Without a doubt, it is competing. When you become a senior player, sometimes other players become a bit wary of you. They don't want to chip you or muck around with you at training because they almost feel scared. But I've always made myself approachable. This is why the boys would freely give it to me on the training field with a joke or jibe—they knew that I would always bite back because I'm so competitive.

Matt Moylan was relentless. He'd say stuff to me that he knew wasn't true, just to get a rise out of me—which happened without fail. I'll miss that.

I'll also miss competing in the gym. During every session in the gym, I would compete with my partner to try to lift more weights.

I'll miss the dressing room after a training session. It sounds weird, but it's so much fun being in a room full of blokes, talking about blokey things, after you've just belted each other on the training field. I'm not overly sentimental, so I won't take a dressing-room memento or anything like that—I'll just take the memories.

Having said that, I did have one moment of sentiment during the 2019 Magic Weekend in Brisbane. I was sitting in our hotel, playing cards with Scott 'Sorro' Sorensen, Kyle Flanagan, Bronson Xerri and Blayke Brailey. I remember looking at the faces in the circle and thinking that this was pretty cool.

I'm 38 and, except for Sorro, the rest of the guys are twenty or twenty-one years of age. Here we were, mucking around and playing cards in the middle of the day before our game that night. As I was sitting there, I was thinking that these are the guys my little boy will look up to for the next ten years, and I'll get to say that I played with them. They may—or may not—have been thinking that it was pretty cool to play cards with me. But it was probably a bigger buzz for me.

I'll be interested to see if I continue my little traditions in retirement, such as eating spaghetti bolognese the night before every game. Maybe in the future, I'll feel the need to eat spaghetti the night before an important meeting or particular commitment that I want to nail the next day.

Anne will no longer have to go to Bunnings at the start of every season to buy ten rolls of green and yellow electrical tape, which I wrapped around my bootlaces every game from my junior days until my very last match. Or maybe she will, because now Kody—without me even asking him to—has started wearing tape on his bootlaces.

I'd be lying if I said that I was excited about life after football. Even though I feel like I've got the tools to handle the transition, I know there will be ups and downs.

Over the past decade, I've built strong relationships with senior leaders in the corporate sector, and I've spoken to them about how to deal with the lack of competitiveness in retirement. Each one of them has said, 'Trust me, life is very competitive.'

Since 2014, I've consciously prepared for life after footy by working for three different companies in the field of business development. For the final two seasons of my career, I earned more money away from football than I did on the field.

What I've learned is that rugby league players can open many more doors to opportunity than anyone else can. I don't care what anyone says—I've seen it with my own eyes. But being a rugby league player doesn't guarantee work or that you will bring in business for the company that you work for.

Some players undersell themselves, and some don't want to stretch themselves because they're happy in the bubble. I wouldn't describe the latter as lazy, but they get comfortable and refuse to concede that their career is ever going to end. But when they do get to the end, they sit there and say, 'What's going on—why aren't I earning $200,000 a year?'

There's a perception that rugby league players are dumb—but I'm not saying that. However, players have to realise that this isn't going to last forever, and that they must be willing to think outside the square. I remember driving myself to my first-grade debut. The car I drove, the weather, the whole thing. Now here I am, retiring in 2019 . . . life goes by in a flash. The sooner players realise that this won't be their only job, the easier their transition to retirement will be.

When I was a boy growing up in Western Sydney, I would never have predicted the career I've enjoyed. I would never have considered the people I have met, the friends I have made—who will remain friends for as long as I live—or the countries I have travelled to.

I would never have believed that I would share the same field as the greatest players of any era, or the same dressing room as the greatest of coaches.

I would never have envisaged my role as a father to the beautiful family that I've been blessed with. I would never have believed that I would be incredibly fortunate enough to have a loving wife who is forever by my side.

I would never have predicted that the game of rugby league could inflict such depressing lows or excruciating physical pain and emotional torment.

I would never have believed that an army of fans inside 100,000-seat stadiums and across the Shire would embrace me as their own, while others took delight in my demise.

I would've shaken my head at the impossible notion of playing more NRL games for Cronulla than any other player in the club's history. Or that on a night which brought grown men and women to tears, I would hold high the Sharks' first premiership trophy in 2016.

And, most certainly, I would've shaken my head at the prospect of captaining my state and representing my country. But that's the secret to all of this.

It doesn't matter who you are—your upbringing, your size, the infinite setbacks—or that your goal appears to be nothing more than a dream. Give your heart and soul, and you'll stand proud when your story ends.

37

Between the Ropes

My fascination with the sport of boxing started at the age of fourteen, when I began dropping in to a gym in Merrylands. Never could I have envisioned that, by the age of 38, I would have fought in nine professional fights—and that I would remain unbeaten.

For me, boxing began as something simple: another form of training for footy. And that's all it was—a way to increase my fitness, while also learning how to throw a nice uppercut. It would be more than fifteen years before I climbed between the ropes for a legitimate fight.

My first forays into the ring were through two amateur bouts for charity. I was invited to be part of the Fight For Life charity boxing night in New Zealand. It was 2012—I was 31—and my first tentative step into the ring as an amateur was to fight New Zealand All Blacks rugby union forward Hika Elliot.

After beating Hika in a unanimous decision, I was invited back to New Zealand to participate in the Fight For Life card twelve months later, in December 2013, to fight another All Blacks forward, Liam Messam. Again, I won the fight.

There's a funny story that I like to tell about what occurred prior to my bout with Hika. Fellow NRL players Greg Bird and Willie Mason were also invited to fight on the Fight For Life card, and on the morning of our fights we were eating breakfast at our Auckland hotel with the Mad Butcher. As most rugby league fans will know, he is a famous New Zealand Warriors supporter. But he is also one of the most generous men when it comes to supporting charities and promoting rugby league in New Zealand that I've ever been associated with.

Despite having never stepped inside a boxing ring before, I had a gut feeling that I would be able to handle what Hika threw at me. As we chatted over breakfast, Birdy turned to the Mad Butcher and asked, 'Are you having a bet tonight?'

The Mad Butcher replied in his thick Kiwi accent, 'No, the odds for you three boys are way too short.' He must have misread the odds that the bookies had set for me. I was paying $4 to beat Hika.

'Mate, you've got that wrong because I'm $4, which is good odds in a two-horse race,' I smiled.

'Yeah, but you're fighting Hika,' the Mad Butcher said, suggesting I had no chance.

'I'll beat him,' I said simply. History will show that I beat Hika convincingly.

I was obviously pleased to collect my first victory inside the ring, but surprisingly I wasn't the only one who was happy. As the fight referee raised my hand in triumph, it was impossible to ignore the cheering and screaming head of a middle-aged man standing in the crowd. It was the Mad Butcher. He didn't have to say a word to me—I knew that he had backed 'Paul Gallen to beat Hika Elliot' at the price of $4.

PRO FIGHT 1: 19/2/2014 VS HERMAN ENE-PURCELL—HORDERN PAVILION, MOORE PARK

Two weeks before my first professional fight, I was extremely nervous about getting knocked out. And nervous about losing.

This was different to anything I had experienced before as an amateur against Hika and Liam in the Fight For Life charity bouts. Over in New Zealand, I was the mug—the footy star flown to Auckland so that boxing fans could witness my lights being punched out. I was the one everyone wanted to see lose. That never bothered me.

But my first professional fight would be here in Australia, in front of friends and family. It would also be on TV, and the whole country could watch it if they wanted to. I knew that defeat in front of that audience would hurt. I had signed off on a contract to fight Herman Ene-Purcell, a budding young 116-kilogram heavyweight from Toowoomba, who would develop into a knockout puncher with twenty fights under his belt by the end of 2017.

What flipped that entire sense of doubt and uncertainty on its head was the belief that I had in my training, to which I had applied myself with the same dedication that I had used throughout my entire footy career. It gave me confidence to know that I had prepared with an intensity that I was certain my opposition wouldn't have.

Three days before the fight, I was convinced that I would win my first pro fight. Five minutes before I was called to enter the ring, I felt a comfortable ease and composure within myself. As I stepped into the ring, it hit me. 'This is real now—my first pro fight.'

I caught a glimpse of Herman from the corner of my eye, and from that moment we failed to take our eyes off each other. He was staring at me, and there was no way I was going to turn away. The staring competition was all the evidence I needed to know that he was serious. I also knew that if Herman was going to beat me, he would have to knock me out. And that worried me.

As far as fitness levels were concerned, I knew I had him covered. More than a decade of NRL conditioning would give anyone that type of belief. But in the first round, Herman caught me with a left, dropping me into the ropes for the first time in my fledgling boxing career.

As I stumbled backwards, I knew what was happening—I was on the way down. I got to my knee as quickly as I could. I then found my feet and began pacing back and forth, telling myself, 'You're all right; you're all right.' I looked over to my corner, where my trainer, Mark Gambin, was standing. He appeared dumb-founded. His jaw had fallen with me to the canvas. His face was white, and that only worsened the sick feeling in my stomach.

The bell for the first round sounded, and I walked towards Mark and my corner. In my head was the message that my team had repeated over and over again in the lead-up to the fight. 'You've got to win the first round.'

I stepped back into the fight for the second round, and immediately I got in close to Herman and got busy. Every time I hit him in the stomach, I could feel the air sucking out of his lungs.

Pulling away from me, Herman goaded me by holding his hands down. I remembered Mark had said that, if he carried on like that, don't try to knock him out with one punch. Just keep punching him.

I hit him with a body shot, and the combination of him once again gasping and his eyes rolling back towards his corner was the green light. I went for him. I landed a clean hit to his head.

In my head, I was saying, 'Be violent, be violent.' I wanted to knock him out. But after seeing that I had done enough damage, the referee stopped the fight in the second round.

In my first pro-fight victory, I was both delighted and relieved. But really, it was just like footy. I had performed like I had trained, and immediately my attitude was 'right, who do I fight next?'

PRO FIGHT 2: 3/12/2014 VS ANTHONY WATTS—HORDERN PAVILION, MOORE PARK

My second professional fight lasted just 88 seconds. I'm glad it only lasted that long. Because three days before my fight with former Cronulla teammate Anthony Watts, I was lying in hospital. Amid the drama of being permitted to return to footy training after serving my three-month ASADA ban, I picked up a golden-staph infection in my groin on just my second day back with the Sharks.

I had agreed to fight Watts on the undercard of Daniel Geale and Jarrod Fletcher's bout at the Hordern Pavilion. I had also switched trainers in the lead-up to my bout with Watts, joining Geale's experienced corner man Graham Shaw.

On the Friday before my Wednesday fight with Watts, I was given a general anaesthetic and underwent surgery to kill off the infection at Kareena Private Hospital in Caringbah. I was discharged just 72 hours before the bout. It was as bad a preparation as you could ask for before a fight. Thankfully, it didn't matter.

My fight with Watts was anticlimactic, to say the least. In the first round, Watts dislocated his shoulder, forcing referee Mick Heafey to call off the fight. It was an empty victory.

Although it was a win, I'm glad the fight ended quickly as I wasn't even close to being physically ready. Such was the lack of energy and strength I felt as a result of the infection, it would be two weeks before I was able to resume full training.

PRO FIGHT 3: 31/1/2015 VS RANDALL RAYMENT—ALLPHONES ARENA, OLYMPIC PARK

After two reasonably easy victories to commence my boxing record, I was invited onto the undercard of a Channel Nine Fight Night in January 2015. Sonny Bill Williams was the headline act, and the fact that I was on the same card only exacerbated interest in the possibility that, one day soon, Sonny and I would face off.

Sonny is a promoter's dream, so the entire fight card would be shown on free-to-air TV. I recognised that my fight with Randall Rayment was an opportunity to show the boxing world that I was more than just a footy player with gloves on. There was also another reason I needed to take this fight seriously—as it was my third professional fight, it represented a step up in opposition. It would be my toughest and most challenging fight so far.

The advantage that Randall had over me was ring experience due to a lengthy Mixed Martial Arts (MMA) record. He was tough, could take punches and he also had a distinct height advantage.

But under the valuable and increasing tutelage of Graham Shaw, I attempted to fight Randall with patience and persistence. During the bout, it came as no surprise that, because of Randall's MMA background, he was intent on hugging and holding me whenever we stood nose to nose.

Randall tagged me at the end of the second round and once in the third, but ultimately I was proud of how I responded on both occasions, replying with uppercuts and body shots. The judges were obviously impressed with the way I fought, deciding that I had scored a unanimous four-round points win over Randall.

During an interview immediately after the fight, I was asked the obvious question related to taking on Sonny. 'I just want to get back to footy and put my heart and soul into footy,' I said. 'It's my last year on contract. I don't know what's going to happen there.

Come the end of the year, I'll look at it [boxing], but my main goal is just to get back to footy at the moment.'

PRO FIGHT 4: 3/11/2015 VS BODENE THOMPSON—SKYCITY CONVENTION CENTRE, AUCKLAND

By now, I had come to learn how incredibly frustrating and time-sapping the fight game could be. After three pro fights, I had reached a point where I wanted to challenge myself by taking on better fighters. I didn't want to be fighting for the sake of an easy pay cheque. I wasn't worried about my ranking—I wasn't attempting to become the next world champion—I just wanted a challenge.

I enjoyed boxing because I found it to be the best way to keep motivated outside of pre-season footy training. I was also wise to the fact that, in boxing, people either wanted to see me win or have my head knocked off. Financially, that was appealing to a promoter.

The phone calls from promoters were constant. I had boxing promoters from all along the east coast of Australia wanting me to be part of their fight night. But because of the money being offered—and this is what is so harsh for the many talented boxers in Australia—the offers were virtually unacceptable. I'm talking about offers of around a couple of hundred bucks a round. I was being offered fights against guys I had never heard of. Time and again, I would politely knock back the offers from promoters.

In the wake of the 2015 NRL season, I received a phone call from a promoter asking if I would fight former Wests Tigers and Warriors forward Bodene Thompson. Undeniably, it was an attractive offer. However, I also saw this fight as an avenue to progress as a fighter, against someone I always recognised as being a tough competitor on the footy field.

To be fair to Bodene, I completely underestimated how tough an opponent he would be. Even though I was aware that he boxed with a southpaw style, not once did I prepare by sparring against a southpaw at training. Graham and I were under the false impression that Bodene would be a typical footy player, whose tactics would be to simply walk forward and try to hit me with bombs. I failed at what I had always prided myself on: putting in the work. And it showed.

Bodene launched at me in the first round, smothering me with a wave of punches. I managed to hang tough and absorb his flurry before regaining the advantage through my conditioning and ring smarts. The fight needed to go the four-round distance. Although I won every round, Bodene was an awkward fight and he surprised me.

To this day, I believe Bodene was someone who could've pursued boxing further if he had wanted to.

PRO FIGHT 5: 29/1/2016 VS HERMAN ENE-PURCELL—RUMOURS INTERNATIONAL CONVENTION CENTRE, TOOWOOMBA

I began 2016—the most exhilarating year of my footy career— inside an arena that I still rate as one of the most hostile environments I have ever experienced as an athlete. Convinced that I was lucky to have beaten him in my first pro fight, Herman had been chasing a rematch with me ever since. And, during that time, he had built up a decent bank of eleven pro fights.

I eventually agreed to the rematch, which was held in Herman's home town of Toowoomba, inside the Rumours International Convention Centre. Despite the fight being held in Queensland, where I was largely despised, I was absolutely stunned by how welcoming the people were upon my arrival in Toowoomba. That was, until I got to the Convention Centre.

The event was sold out, with almost 2000 people packed into the hot and hostile function room. Walking into that room, I was reminded of an old-school boxing venue where the ring is close to the paying public, and the boxers can hear everyone spit abuse and heckle. Such was the atmosphere within the room—which I loved—that it bordered on spilling out of control.

I had requested a six-round fight, but aware of my favourable conditioning, Herman's team wanted nothing of the sort. We ended up settling on a five-round contest.

I regard this fight as the best one I've ever fought. Everything that Herman threw at me, I could see happening. I honestly felt like a boxer, not a footballer, for the first time. If he was throwing slow punches, I was throwing fast punches. Herman hardly laid a punch on me.

The referee stopped the fight in the fourth round after Herman's corner threw in the towel. I was awarded the victory by TKO. It was just my fifth fight. And each of those fights had been won despite a limited preparation of no more than a month's worth of training. That's what excited Graham and my team the most—with more ring experience, I could continue to develop as a fighter.

PRO FIGHT 6: 9/12/2016 VS JUNIOR PAULO—HORDERN PAVILION, MOORE PARK

Despite the view of many people from within the sport of boxing that I could pursue a career, my pessimistic personal view of the fight game hadn't altered. The opportunities to challenge myself, by taking on better fighters without tarnishing my development, were few and far between.

'The only way you're going to make money is to fight blokes with profiles,' a well-known promoter told me. And so, with that, I took on Canberra forward Junior Paulo as the main event on a footy fight night, following our premiership success at Cronulla.

As such, I was using the fight with Junior as a kind of sparring session—albeit a paid fight instead of a routine spar.

There was a delicate nature attached to my fight with Junior, as just two weeks later I would be bankrolling and promoting my own fight night at Shark Park. Junior was suddenly a dangerous fighter because if he were able to knock me out, I would be required to spend a mandatory month out of the sport. My sole priority was to avoid getting knocked out—and that's a risky approach to any fight.

I'll say one thing about footy players: they're as tough as nails. And so, after agreeing to three two-minute rounds, I knew I was never going to be able to knock out Junior that quickly. In hindsight, it's probably why this was seen as a much tighter battle than my other fights—the crowd expected me to make short work of Junior.

The hugely pro-Junior crowd rode every punch he threw. To his credit, he managed to jag me a couple of times. Ultimately, the victory was a unanimous decision in my favour.

Junior wasted no time stating that he wanted a rematch. He clearly felt he'd handled himself well. I was more than happy to accept the offer.

PRO FIGHT 7: 23/12/2016 VS RYAN CARR-KETU—SHARK PARK, WOOLOOWARE

I've faced some challenging tasks in my time, but the stress and anxiety I felt before hosting my first fight as a co-promoter were like nothing else. In the wake of our historic premiership win at Cronulla, I decided to host my own fight night at Shark Park just two days before Christmas.

I'd had the idea for a number of years and, given the excitement within the Sutherland Shire community in 2016, the time was right to turn the dream into a reality. So, along with promoter and former boxer Ryan Waters, we took responsibility for organising the ticketing, the venue, the security, the sale of corporate boxes, sponsorship, promotion of the event, the catering, the fighters on the undercard and even the boxing ring itself. The outlay amounted to $30,000.

The difficult nature of being the co-promoter was that I also had to prepare for a fight. It was a fight that I was desperate not to lose in front of my home fans.

Ryan Carr-Ketu played his role well in promoting the fight, going public with a rant about me being the 'Head Bogan' of Cronulla. I'd be lying if I said the barbs didn't fire me up even more.

I can safely say that Ryan—who had a height and reach advantage over me—hit me harder than I've ever felt before, especially in the first round. For the first time in my boxing career, I was worried. I could feel his punches. They were heavy and boasted force.

There were 2500 spectators seated around the ring and in the grandstands of Shark Park. Cognisant of how heavy Ryan was punching, at the end of the first round I just sat in the corner and told myself, 'I can't lose here.' I couldn't comprehend losing a fight that I had organised.

Somehow, despite Ryan continuing to step forward, I managed to weather the storm. I had regained control of the fight by the back-end of the second round, before knocking him out 43 seconds into the fourth round. The win capped off the perfect 2016.

PRO FIGHT 8: 10/11/2017 VS PUNA RASAUBALE—CRONULLA SUTHERLAND LEAGUES CLUB, CRONULLA

Immediately after I beat Ryan, Puna Rasaubale began calling me out. Puna was a former lower grader at the Sharks and Roosters and also a former Commonwealth Games boxing representative from Fiji.

Back in 2005, when we were both lower graders at Cronulla, we would spar each other as a form of extra fitness. I also sparred Puna in the lead-up to my fight with Bodene Thompson. On more than one occasion, Puna got the better of me in sparring. He was tough, had a good amateur record and boasted valuable ring experience.

Ryan Waters was hosting another footy fight night, and he invited me to co-promote with him again. This time the event would be held inside the Cronulla Sutherland Leagues Club, not in the open air of Shark Park. But the logistical work was just as hard.

The stress I felt prior to taking on Ryan Carr-Ketu returned and perhaps more so, due to the fact that I wasn't really interested in boxing anymore. Organising a fight night is draining and a day-to-day grind within itself. But when you're the drawcard—the main act—you have to ensure that you put in the work at training as well. I didn't do that—and so I knew it was going to be a hard night.

As I expected, Puna was willing throughout and landed punches, but my sharper jab and superior conditioning got the job done with a six-round unanimous decision. Stepping between the ropes and out of the ring that night, I thought that it could be my final fight.

However, unbeknown to anyone, I had actually met with Sonny Bill Williams' manager in March 2017 and agreed on the financial terms of a contract that would see me fight Sonny in January 2018. The fight that Sonny always said he was willing to take on was going to be held on the Gold Coast, in New Zealand or in Sydney. Personally, I didn't care where it was held, as it was the fight I always wanted.

History now shows that the fight never happened.

PRO FIGHT 9: 8/2/2019 VS JOHN HOPOATE—HORDERN PAVILION, MOORE PARK

The opportunity to fight former Test player and Australian boxing champion John 'Hoppa' Hopoate had been offered to me a couple of times over the previous two years. I had sparred with Hoppa several times, either before one of his fights or as a way of training solidly before one of my bouts, but I wasn't ready to take him on in a proper boxing match when those invitations came.

However, prior to Christmas 2018, there was a renewed attempt to bring us together in the ring. And while the mainstream media were beginning to spruik a possible 'Battle of Footy' fight, it seemed that a deal couldn't be reached. That's when I decided to pick up the phone to Hoppa. 'Is this true? Do you want to fight me?' I asked.

Hoppa explained that it was nothing personal—we were mates, but this was business—so I told him that I was happy to agree to a fight. He then told me, 'I just don't want to stand in your way of progressing as a boxer.'

I treated that as an early jab from Hoppa, as if he was saying that he had my measure. 'Stuff you,' I thought. 'I'm going to beat you.'

In his mind, Hoppa probably felt that he would beat me, which would then impact any potential future fights that I may or may not want to chase. And in fairness, when we had previously sparred, it was clear that he was more experienced than me and that I was just getting started in my dalliance with boxing. But I didn't think he was that dominant when we sparred— perhaps he thought differently. So when he made that comment, I thought, 'Let's do this.'

There hadn't been any previous animosity between us. I like Hoppa; I know he's got a polarising reputation, but I also know he's a devoted family man. However, what riled me up was Hoppa's decision to make public something that was only intended to be private banter.

Over the Christmas break, Andrew Fifita chatted to members of his Tonga team via the messaging application WhatsApp. Hoppa was part of the WhatsApp group. After a couple of drinks, Andrew filmed a video of himself saying, 'He's coming for ya'—meaning that I was coming after Hoppa. What disappointed me was that Hoppa then lifted the video from the private group and posted it onto his social media channels so that the wider public could see it.

I decided to out Hoppa publicly. 'WhatsApp groups are designed for teams or groups of people where there's an element of trust that you don't share what's put on there,' I responded on my own Instagram account. 'Andrew Fifita posted a video on a private WhatsApp group, and Hoppa has ripped that off and posted it on social media. I think it's pretty ordinary myself.

'I just want to remind you, Hoppa, and everyone else, that you chased this fight. You're the one who called me a coward; you're the one who said, "sign the contract" and that I'll never fight again. Well I've signed it, mate, and I'll be there. I promise you right now you're not going to handle what's coming.

'I'm really looking forward to the night and I'm training hard and I hope you are as well, buddy. Because like I said, this will be your last fight, you won't fight again after this because I will knock you out, champ.'

As a rule—and we've seen far more damaging and graphic videos emerge because of people doing this—I still believe it was an ordinary thing to do.

I had prepared well despite the Sharks' pre-season schedule, and I knew that all I had to do once I was standing toe-to-toe with Hoppa was to get through the first round. Hoppa had refused a request for three-minute rounds, so I realised that his stamina wasn't great and that he was aiming to knock me out in the first two-minute round.

I admit that I was concerned about him doing something dirty, like a low blow—and he did crowd me and push me against the ropes for as long as he could in that first round. But an opportunity came in the second round. I managed to work Hoppa into the corner midway through that round, laying into him with a flurry of punches that caused him to fall face-first onto the canvas.

I was obviously elated that I had won the fight, and it enabled me to take my boxing record to 9–0 (5KO). But when Hoppa couldn't get up off the canvas almost a minute after I had delivered my final punch, I was legitimately worried. I went over to Hoppa to make sure that he was okay. Thankfully, he slowly found his feet.

There had been a tense build-up to the fight, and I know a lot of words were said, but I was glad that Hoppa was all right. He came into my dressing room after the fight, and we thanked each other.

The fight was held on a Friday night, and I went back to footy training the following Monday. I didn't know if that would be the last time I would ever step into a boxing ring.

38

Best of the Best

I was fortunate to be able to play at the elite level of rugby league for a long time. Because of this, it's difficult for me to comprehend the unbelievable array of superstars and champions of the game whom I was lucky enough to play alongside and against.

As I've written previously, when I was a young boy I never held a desire to mimic any of the former greats, and I didn't look up to the best rugby league players of my childhood. But I now know what it means to the kids of today, who see their favourite players as idols and inspirations. Because I was fortunate enough to stand alongside them.

I could pen page after page on what makes so many of the great players I've played with unique. I could quite easily form a list of 100 players who, for varying reasons, left me captivated by their ability, their motivation and their mindset, and why they ultimately helped me become a better player—and person.

Of course, the 2016 premiership side will always be at the forefront of my thoughts whenever I'm asked about the most talented team I've played with.

Individually, Andrew Fifita and Matt Prior were our steel up front while our fullback Ben Barba produced things on the footy field that season that I don't think the great Billy Slater could've done.

Then there's Greg Bird, Jarryd Hayne, Greg Inglis, Danny Buderus, Luke Lewis and Brett and Josh Morris who would headline the list of quality individuals who, as opposition, always ensured you were set for a tough day at the office, but as team-mates you cherished running out onto the field with. However, there are seven players—all with completely different skill sets, and all varying in levels of toughness and ability—whom I hold in the highest regard.

JASON 'STEVO' STEVENS

I was lucky enough to play with Stevo for the first five years of my first-grade career at Cronulla. From the moment that I was able to share the footy field with Stevo during my NRL debut season in 2001 until his final season before he retired at the end of 2005, he remained one of the best forwards I ever played with.

Stevo was a big man with a huge heart. I often watched on in awe as he churned through 80 minutes on several occasions, making over 10 metres with each carry of the footy. He would be driving his legs as hard in the first minute as he would be in the last minute.

Deservedly, Stevo played State of Origin for New South Wales and represented Australia. He was tough and ruthless on the field, he boasted a superb off-load and, gee, he was a dirty player, too. When I say dirty, I mean that if it wasn't Stevo's knee lunging into the defensive line, he was using his elbows to sting the opposition as he surged forward. The number of players I saw him run over the top of, leaving them rattled in his wake, was like nothing I had ever seen before.

While I'll always hold Petero Civoniceva in the highest regard when it comes to front-rowers, I think the fact that I played with Stevo and got to know him so well on and off the field has left me convinced that he was the best front-rower I ever played with.

BRETT 'NODDY' KIMMORLEY

Noddy was the ultimate competitor and, in that category, the best I ever played with. When the time came when I was able to play alongside Johnathan 'JT' Thurston, it was Noddy whom JT reminded me of most.

For a small man, Noddy held no fear. He would be left battered and bruised every week after placing his body on the line every time. And every time, he would bounce back up, kick down field and be the first one to meet the fullback head-on.

Just like JT, Noddy could control a football team. He was equal to JT in that regard. Noddy was like a second coach out on the footy field, knowing exactly where each attacking set would end as he herded our forward pack down the park.

I'll always remember that Noddy had a tendency to be extremely talkative before and after the game, but that was probably just his way of letting his nervous energy out.

There weren't too many games that I didn't walk off the field at full-time amazed at one particular kick, tackle, pass or run that Noddy had produced. He would put his head where you wouldn't want it to be, and that's all you can ask from a player of his size.

JOHNATHAN 'JT' THURSTON

JT is the best halfback I ever played with. He could do freakish things on the field—the most incredibly skilful things—but the reason I hold him in the highest regard is because of his ability to compete for the entire 80 minutes. On every play, and in every second of every match, he was there competing.

Like Noddy, JT always puts his body on the line. Sure, he has his misses, simply due to the sheer power-to-weight ratio of his opposition, but he was never afraid to bounce back up and go again. And nine times out of ten, he would then beat up his opposition where it hurt most, on the scoreboard.

JT is never half-hearted in anything. I promise you this—New South Wales would've won more State of Origin matches if he hadn't been playing for Queensland.

CAMERON SMITH

Cameron is the best player I ever played with or against. It is the way he controls the game that I firmly believe makes him stand out above all the rest. Cameron plays like a conductor of an orchestra; he is a ringmaster, dictating and determining where his teammates move on the field, while simultaneously controlling what the opposition does to combat his next play. He is always one step ahead.

Cam never says a great deal on the field, but when he does, people listen. He speaks with his actions. He controls training sessions and matches through the speed at which he is able to stream his forwards through the middle of the ruck. He sets the tempo for his team's entire attack.

The way he tackles—he knows how to bend the rules. Cam gets away with more wrestling and niggling than any other player I have ever played with. I guess that's what makes him so brilliant. When you are on his side, it is great. But when you aren't, it is utterly frustrating. There is no way of beating him, because Cam knows he can get away with it, which is a credit to his class.

There were Origin or club matches where I would be playing against him, and he would stand at dummy half completely calm and collected, while his opposition were stressed, baffled and had no idea which way the ball was about to swing. He always looks like he's going one way, but he actually goes the other.

Cam is an artist, and a tough one at that. He has the body shape of an accountant, but without doubt he is as tough as anyone I ever played with.

DARREN 'LOCKY' LOCKYER

On tours with the Kangaroos, I never stepped inside Locky's hotel room, but you just know it would've been immaculate. Locky wasn't only one of the greatest players I've ever played with, he was also the best dressed. His shirts were always neatly pressed, and his locker was precise and tidy. And I guess, in some ways, this reflected who Locky was as a player. Just perfect.

When you stood beside Darren Lockyer, you knew everything was going to be okay. He was calm under pressure, reliable in defence and a leader in every facet of the game.

One of Locky's greatest attributes was the faith he placed in his teammates. In the 2011 ANZAC Test on the Gold Coast, Locky turned to me during an attacking set and said, 'Support me on my outside, and I'll give you the ball.' My role in that match was to play through the middle, not out on the edge, where Locky wanted me to run. But clearly, he had already envisioned what the next play would look like.

I followed his instructions and, sure enough, Locky passed me the footy, gifting me a three-on-two situation, leaving me to merely throw a cut-out ball to our winger, Jharal Yow Yeh, who touched down for a try. Plenty of halves wouldn't have had the confidence to single me out as their support runner.

As immaculate as he was off the field, Locky was equally meticulous at training. After a long field session, when the rest of the team had made their way to the showers, he would remain outside, kicking ball after ball to different parts of the field: bombs, long kicks and grubber kick after grubber kick.

I firmly believe Cooper Cronk adopted his professional approach to training from having watched Darren. That's Locky's greatest legacy.

BILLY SLATER

Billy was similar to JT and Noddy in his level of competitiveness. Like Thurston and Kimmorley, Billy turned up on every play, every second of every match. Billy was one player who trained his backside off. He is widely regarded as one of the game's greatest fullbacks ever, and I put that down to the countless hours he spent perfecting his game after hours on the training paddock.

At the end of every training session, Billy was the last one to leave. He's kicking balls, catching bombs and practising plays with Cameron Smith. With the amount of times you see him score a try from the plays he has practised at training, it is no wonder he was so special.

But for me, Billy's best asset was his defence. He's renowned as one of the game's greatest try-scoring fullbacks, but Billy was also fearless in defence. Watch a replay of a try being scored against Melbourne, Queensland or Australia, and sure enough you'll see Billy hurling every inch of his body at the attacking player. At the Sharks, I would return from a Test series with Australia and spend as much time as I could talking to our fullbacks about Billy's focus on defence.

A former track-work jockey, he played above his weight in every match he played in. Where other fullbacks give up if they know they can't stop an opposition try from being scored, Billy would be virtually jumping on the opposition's back.

I vividly recall Billy holding up NSW forward Anthony Watmough during an Origin match. Watmough would've scored that try nine times out ten. But Billy stopped him, stretching every part of his body to protect his tryline. I still don't know how he did it.

DAVID 'PEACH' PEACHEY

Who doesn't love Peach? He was the most naturally gifted player that I ever played with at the Sharks.

As far as training goes, Peach wasn't exactly the hardest trainer. Unlike Locky or Billy, Peach was never one to commit to extra practice after training. But wow—he could make magic happen. Some people are just natural-born athletes, and Peach was certainly that.

Against Penrith one day, on my way to sticking my head into a scrum, Peach called out and said, 'Gal, stand outside me and run with me.' Peach was standing in the five-eighth position, and he wanted me to stand at centre.

I shot back, 'Why, what are we doing?'

In typical laconic Peach fashion, he said, 'I don't know, just playing footy.' So instead of packing down in the scrum I went and stood outside Peach. Sure enough, he put me over for a try.

So damaging was Peach to the opposition defence, Ricky Stuart even named a defensive structure after the Sharks' champion fullback. Peach loved to float across field with the footy, waiting for just one player to break the chain in the defensive line ever so slightly, before 'whoosh'—he would slide through and race away.

Peach had the ability to drag people out of that line and go straight through. Some of the breaks he made and tries he scored were freakish. So at training, long after Peach had retired,

Ricky renamed our defensive structure the 'Peachey defence'. We were to form a wall where, no matter what, nobody was to break the line.

It said a lot about how brilliant Peach was in creating something out of nothing.

Acknowledgements

I have the opportunity to individually thank people in this book. At the risk of missing someone, I'll be as brief as I can.

Over the past twenty years, I have been lucky enough to meet so many amazing, caring and generous people who have affected my life in ways they'll never know. I've also seen the other side of people, those who can be fake and judgemental. But without all this I wouldn't be who I am today.

I want to thank Dave Riccio for his efforts in writing this book. It has been years in the making. I value your hard work, professionalism and friendship, and thank you for being a good sounding board for me whenever I called you.

I want to thank Mum and Dad, who did everything they could to get me where I am today. I'd like to thank all my brothers and sisters. I love you all. My extended family, especially Suey and Lance—thank you.

My wife is the most amazing, loving, caring, beautiful person inside and out I have ever met. We both know I'm not perfect, but I will always do my best to love you and provide for you.

ACKNOWLEDGEMENTS

The four most special people in my life are my four beautiful children. They are the reason I do anything I do. My only goal in life now is to provide for them.

My three beautiful girls make me smile every day. Charly, when you were born I smiled like never before. It was the most amazing experience I have ever had. Seeing you for the first time was when my life really changed for the better. Macy, my cheeky little princess, you make me laugh every day. Ruby, my baby, I could watch you for hours. You change every day, and I can't wait to see you grow up.

Kody, my man, you make me proud of you every day. You're the greatest little kid I could ever imagine. All I will ever ask of you is to always try your best at anything you do.

Special thanks go to my mates. I talk to you on a regular basis, and you know who you are. You've kept me grounded and motivated at the same time.

The game of rugby league has certainly given me my highest highs and lowest lows. It has been extremely challenging, but also extremely enjoyable. When I say 'thank you' to the game of rugby league, I am saying thank you to past and present players. The game doesn't exist without you.

And to all the fans who have either loved or loathed me, thank you.

I'd like to thank Grant Trouville and Matt Long of the NRL for generously giving their time to provide photographs for use in this book.

Finally, to the Cronulla Sharks: I've dedicated twenty years of my life to the club, and talk about ups and downs! You've been a part of them all. I promised myself I would deliver the club its first premiership. I'd be driving along in my car or sitting home alone and I would promise myself I'd fulfil that vow. I'll be honest—there were times when I thought it just wouldn't happen with what we had, or that I'd probably be on the coaching staff but not a player when it happened, but I always promised myself I'd be there in some form when we got our first premiership. And in 2016 it finally happened, and with a group of players I'll never forget, plus Shane Flanagan. We did it. Up, up Cronulla.

This is me, and this is my story. I really hope you enjoyed the book.

INDEX

INDEX

INDEX

INDEX